Praise for *What If It's True?*

"What if it's true for you? Answering the most important question of life is often a journey people are afraid to take because they don't think they have the right tools or the right guide. This book is both. It is a tool the Holy Spirit will use to bring freedom to the soul, and it is a guide to hold your hand as He leads you into the places you need to go. Inside these pages, you will find the compassion of Jesus, the Father heart of God, and the endearing call of the Holy Spirit. Each chapter is a journey in and of itself, each prayer a healing balm to the wounded or wandering heart. If, indeed, God's Word is true, then it is true for you—and Charles Martin has painted a picture of the hope this world desperately needs."

—RYAN BRITT, EXECUTIVE MINISTRIES PASTOR, THE CHURCH OF ELEVEN22

"I'm so glad my friend Charles Martin has written this book! It's a book like none other I've read. He shares some of the deepest truths of the gospel, rooted solidly in Scripture, through an honest and hopeful glimpse into his personal life and faith. You can hear his voice, heart, conviction, passion, and creativity on every page. Sometimes you read a book, and sometimes a book reads you. Sometimes you work your way through a book, and sometimes a book works on you. In the best possible way, this book definitely does the latter. Charles's authenticity, boldness, and humility in these pages causes me to want to grow in my faith in and affections for Jesus."

—ADAM FLYNT, PASTOR OF MULTIPLICATION, THE CHURCH OF ELEVEN22

"If you ever wanted an honest glimpse into the heart and mind of this gifted author, then look no further. Or, far better yet, if you have ever longed for a greater understanding of your own heart, and of God's heart for you, then this book is a must-read. Every chapter places an incandescent spotlight on the only One who can provide the answers and freedom each of us were created to crave."

— JONATHAN CHRISTIAN, DISCIPLESHIP PASTOR, THE CHURCH OF ELEVEN22

T0054453

"We are encouraged by the apostle Paul to let the word of Christ dwell in us *richly*. In this book, Charles Martin leads us to where deep biblical understanding and the redeemed imagination meet to help us accomplish just that. In *What If It's True?*, Charles helps us experience the living and active Word of God in a way that only a gifted novelist can. My relationship with Jesus is better for having read it."

—MICHAEL OLSON, DIRECTOR OF WORSHIP
GATHERINGS, THE CHURCH OF ELEVEN22

"*What If It's True?* paints a strikingly vivid picture of what it must have been like to personally experience the unfolding of God's redemptive plan for the sins of all mankind. Purposefully written, undoubtedly prayed over, and Holy Spirit empowered, Martin's latest prose left me in tears with my soul yearning for a deeper relationship with our risen Lord."

—KELLY ADCOX, FACILITIES DIRECTOR, THE CHURCH OF ELEVEN22

"When Charles Martin gave me his new book *What If It's True?* to read, my first thought was that it would be a cross between *More Than a Carpenter* and *The Case for Christ*. It isn't. It's so much more! Martin's beautiful depictions of familiar stories from Scripture bring so much life to those stories that it almost felt like I was reading fiction. Far from it. The richness that Martin's creativity provides only deepens—if that's possible—the tangible love and grace of our wonderful Savior. Martin's transparency about his own life and need for that grace and loving-kindness is disarming and inviting. This is a book I will give to everyone I know."

—LEE ANN RUMMEL, CHAIR OF THE BOARD, CHRISTIAN HEALING MINISTRIES

Note from Charles: The guys below are the guys
I "do life" with in our small group.

"The Lord has used these words—by the power of His Spirit—to set me free from generational sin, curse, and bondage. Through them, Jesus has cared for me as Father and brought dramatic and deep change in me, in my heart, and in my identity in Him. This book is a roadmap for the trenches we have walked, the warfare we have encountered, and the victory Jesus has bought. It has brought lasting life change here and on to eternity with Jesus."

—HANK BRINK

"When I first heard the gospel preached, I said to myself, "If this is true, it changes everything." It is true, and it did change everything. My brother in Christ Charles Martin has battled with me through some of the hardest moments of my life. This book is a refreshing and anointed reminder that the gospel is true and does change everything."

—RICK CROWLEY

"What If It's True? offers a clarity to the truth of the gospel unlike anything I've experienced. Charles Martin's detail of the Word of God combined with his ability to put you in the midst of a setting provides a unique understanding of the real healing and freedom Jesus made available to us on this side of the cross."

—GREG FARAH

"These chapters are the intersection of Charles's heart for proclaiming the truth of Christ's sacrificial rescue mission and his inspired gift for telling the story in a way that makes it real, simple, applicable, and entertaining. This book is not just something to read. Other than Scripture itself, this is as close to "being there" and walking through the events and implications of the cross and tomb as one can get. It convinces us that none of our "stuff"—no matter how messy—is beyond His reach."

—JOHNNY SARBER

"What If It's True? is an incredible life examination for every believer. If you read this and allow the Holy Spirit access to work in your heart, you will be transformed! I especially believe every men's group should walk through this spiritually impactful literary journey and see what God can do in each person."

—MIKE HOHMAN

"This book speaks directly to the heart, specifically to the places that need it most. Charles has taken the biblical stories I've heard hundreds of times and given them new life. His gift of storytelling mixed with the Word is powerful. This book should be in the hands of everyone, including believers and the soon-to-be believers. The chapter on blessings and curses, 'Choose This Day,' is a game-changer for all God's people."

—JASON WATSON

"The lessons in *What If It's True?* bypass your mind and heart and strike directly at your soul. Charles Martin's teaching provides a gut check for your faith while showing you the path to strengthen it. Drink from the cup of this book and ignite your covenant with Jesus."

—BRIAN COOK

"These are the words I need to hear. Over and over. Tears accompanied most of them, but the freedom they provide is life-changing. I'm indebted to Charles for so faithfully walking me through God's Word. *What If It's True?* has pierced my heart and placed me face-to-face with Jesus."

—JON LIVINGSTON

"Charles Martin took me on an intimate, behind-the-scenes guided tour of the life and death of Jesus Christ. His uniquely descriptive stops along the way allowed me to feel I was personally seeing, feeling, hearing, smelling, and experiencing each moment. Martin's willingness to be personal, raw, vulnerable, and honest in his words guided me into self-examination, where I glanced in a mirror the reflection of my heart. And his prayers at the end of each chapter poured into me and carried out of me the kind of emotion, passion, intimacy, and unconditional love only choosing a relationship with Christ allows. This book forced the removal of my neat, easy, comfortable view of the story of Jesus and demanded I face the raw, emotional, and uncomfortable truth of Jesus's life, further deepening my love and appreciation for Him and His sacrifice of love."

—JOE VEGERANO

What If It's True?

What If It's True?

A Storyteller's Journey with Jesus

CHARLES MARTIN

W PUBLISHING GROUP

AN IMPRINT OF THOMAS NELSON

Published in Nashville, Tennessee, by W Publishing, an imprint of Thomas Nelson.

Author is represented by The Christopher Ferebee Agency, www.christopherferebee.com.

Thomas Nelson titles may be purchased in bulk for educational, business, fund-raising, or sales promotional use. For information, please e-mail SpecialMarkets@ThomasNelson.com.

Unless otherwise noted, Scripture quotations are taken from the New King James Version®. © 1982 by Thomas Nelson. Used by permission. All rights reserved.

Scripture quotations marked KJV are from the King James Version. Public domain.

Scripture quotations marked NASB are from New American Standard Bible®. Copyright © 1960, 1962, 1963, 1968, 1971, 1972, 1973, 1975, 1977, 1995 by The Lockman Foundation. Used by permission. (www.Lockman.org)

Scripture quotations marked RSV are from Revised Standard Version of the Bible. Copyright 1946, 1952, and 1971 National Council of the Churches of Christ in the United States of America. Used by permission. All rights reserved.

ISBN 978-0-7852-2148-7 (eBook)
ISBN 978-0-7852-2146-3 (TP)

Library of Congress Control Number: 2018958172
ISBN 978-0-7852-2132-6 (HC)

20 21 22 23 24   LSC   10 9 8 7 6 5 4 3 2 1

For Charlie, John T., and Rives

Contents

Introduction. . . . .*xiii*

Chapter 1: The Word Becomes Flesh—And Dwells Among Us. 1

Chapter 2: We're All Bleeders 17

Chapter 3: The Chorus of the Unashamed. 30

Chapter 4: What Are You Taking to the Grave? 40

Chapter 5: Talk to the Hand—JCILOA. .60

Chapter 6: What's That You're Carrying?. 78

Chapter 7: The Toughest Thing You and I Will Ever Do 107

Chapter 8: Choose This Day 133

Chapter 9: You Will Be Hated by All 162

Chapter 10: No Gone Is Too Far Gone 196

Chapter 11: The Deepest Wound of the Human Soul. 205

Chapter 12: The Peg on Which Everything Hangs. 225

Chapter 13: Will You Bear His Name? 254

CONTENTS

Epilogue. 268

Author's Note. 270

Appendix A: The Word Became Flesh 271

Appendix B: Blessing and Curse Scriptures 281

Notes 287

About the Author 293

Introduction

WHAT IF?

He is stumbling now. A trail of blood marks His serpentine path on the narrow street out of the city. The wood is heavy but that's not what's crushing Him. Three-inch thorns are pressing into His skull. Much of the flesh has been removed from His back, neck, and sides. The local rulers want to make an example of Him. A public deterrent. A public execution on a well-traveled road just outside of town. They also want to shame Him, and they have. He's completely naked.

By 9 a.m. He's outside the gate. On the outskirts. Out where they burn the trash. Somebody from the crowd spits on Him. Another plucks out a handful of His beard and reminds Him of all the ridiculous things He said leading up to this moment. A third suggests that if He really is who He says He is, then He should be able to do something about it. All talk. No action.

A group of fishermen watch from a distance. Pained faces. Breaking hearts. The road rises, and the bleeding carpenter stumbles to His knees. He tries to stand, falls again, and one of the soldiers comments how this could take all day. The soldier eyes a North African man in the crowd, points a sharp sword at the heavy wood and commands, "Carry that."

Simon steps onto the road, kneels, and black hands lift a bloody cross. Face to face with the condemned, he's never seen anyone so marred. So grotesque. The two whisper words no one can hear as they slowly trudge forward.

Behind them the town is readying for a feast. The place is packed. A few hundred yards away in the temple, the high priest is preparing the sacrifice. Sharpening his knife on a stone. The morning incense wafts heavenward. Fresh showbread has replaced yesterday's display. Simon carries the wood until the soldier tells him to drop it. When he does, soldiers slam the condemned Man onto the wood and stretch wide His arms. Two men hold His hand in place, one swings a hammer. The nail pierces His wrist, separating the bones. His screams echo off the enormous rocks that make up the city walls.

Out of respect for His nakedness, the women have gathered at a distance. His mother is inconsolable. A second woman stands nearby. Nobody really knows her name. All we know is that for the last twelve years, she has bled constantly. Making her an outcast. Defiled. Unable to enter the temple. She spent her life savings on a cure with no relief. Then she met the condemned. Clung to the "wings" of His shirt. Now she doesn't bleed anymore.

The soldiers drive skinny spikes through the Man's other hand and both feet; they lift the wood. Like Moses lifting the serpent in the wilderness. Gravity tears the flesh as they unceremoniously drop it into a hole. A sign above Him, written in Greek, Latin, and Hebrew, reads, "KING OF THE JEWS." He is flanked by two common and dying men.

The crowd is larger than usual for a morning execution. A fact not unnoticed by the soldiers. A beggar named Bartimaeus watches through tears. Having heard of the trial and the invented charges, he walked the road up from Jericho. Some twenty miles through the night. The two met a few years back at the city gate. Bartimaeus had been begging because he was blind. Then he met the Man. Told Him, "I want to see." Ever since, Bartimaeus has had perfect vision—but now he doesn't like what he sees.

Nicodemus is here, as is a man named Lazarus who stands quietly with his sisters. He's rather well known north of here. His story is of some renown because he died and had been decaying four days when the criminal called him out of the cave. Even he has a tough time believing his own story. A local boy, a former paralytic whose friends had lowered him through the roof of a crowded house where the criminal was staying, paces nervously nearby. A centurion stands quietly off to one side. Respectful. He's not with this garrison. A man under authority, he's come to pay his respects. Standing in the shadows, an angry fisherman waits impatiently. One hand on the hilt of his sword. As the hours pass, the other fishermen grow more vocal. Barabbas is here too. He is a murderer. Released just this morning from a death sentence. He stands in the shadows, in utter disbelief.

Fights break out in the crowd. The soldiers grow nervous. Reinforcements are summoned and sent.

Last week, the criminal claimed that zeal for His Father's house consumed Him. Now He's consumed by torment. Painted in His own blood. It trails down His body and drips into the dirt where the earth silently swallows the crimson stain. Above, up on the crosses, the three condemned men have a conversation. Something about paradise. One believes. One does not. Clustered on the road nearby, the soldiers play a game. Wagering for the Man's clothes. Over the next few hours, the Man suspended on the middle cross pushes up with His legs, pulls with His arms, and tries to fill His lungs with air. Each breath harder than the last because His lungs are filling. He grows weaker.

It's not long now.

Many in the crowd are weeping. They've torn their clothes. Mourning the leader of a failed rebellion. Last week the entire town was ready to install the Man as ruler. Shouting. Waving palm branches. Throwing down their clothes. Praising the one to take on Rome. Even the rocks cried out. But the Man made outrageous claims. Didn't back them up. A flash in the pan. Now, He's a nobody. Shamed. Rejected. Bruised. Crushed. Little more than a common, nameless criminal. A grain of wheat falling to the earth. The song of drunkards.[1]

For the last three hours, an eerie darkness has spread across the earth.

His mother approaches, hanging onto the arm of one of the fisherman.

The dying man speaks to both. She buries her face in the other man's shoulder. Her knees buckle and he holds her. She is shredded. They retreat, and the Man is thirsty. A soldier dips a sponge in something sour and holds it to the Man's mouth, but He refuses. A scribe, a learned man, watches the hanging Man refuse the sponge and thinks to himself, *Could it be . . . ?* as the words of a psalm echo in his mind, "For my thirst they gave me vinegar to drink."[2]

With considerable effort, the Man lifts His chin off His chest and scans the crowd.

His breathing grows more shallow. He is drowning. Summoning His last ounce of energy, the Man pushes up one last time and screams heavenward. A shadow falls across Him, shrouding Him in darkness. Even God has forsaken Him.

In the temple, the high priest slices the throat of the lamb and catches the warm blood in a basin. Through an incense cloud, he walks into the Holy of Holies carrying the blood and paints the mercy seat. The bells on his shirt jingle as he walks. The rope tied to his ankle trails behind him and disappears beyond the curtain.

On the road outside the gate, the condemned Man exhales, dies, and gives up His spirit.

Below, the earth quakes. Above, the sky falls pitch dark. A light in the heavens has been turned off.

No. *The* light.

The crowd huddles in hushed silence. Lightning flashes and spiderwebs across the sky. The air turns cold. Nearby, a soldier shakes his head, whispering something about the Son of God.

The two men on either side are dragging it out. To speed things along, soldiers swing heavy bars and break their legs. No longer able to push up, the condemned drown quickly.

With little more to see, the soldiers disperse the crowd. The criminal hangs alone. Dead. Eyes still open. The life that had been there moments ago is gone.

Blood still drips off the toes of His left foot. The words of Moses echo:

"For the life of the flesh is in the blood, and I have given it to you upon the altar to make atonement for your souls."[3]

The lifeless Man hangs at an odd angle, and His bones seem out of joint. Off to one side, His mother won't leave. She is screaming at the top of her lungs. Abruptly, a soldier shoves a spear into the chest cavity of the dead Man, and water and blood spill out from the hole. The splashing sound echoes. The earth trembles and shakes with angry violence. The stones of the temple are rocked. The curtain tears in two. The sky thunders and lightning flashes. The sign above His head reads, "King of the Jews."

What If It's True?

Years ago, I opened my Bible and began wrestling with this question: What if every single word of this story is absolutely true and I can trust it? What if Jesus really is who He says He is? What if the King of the universe is speaking directly to me through the words of His book? What if what He says is more true than my circumstances? Than what my eyes see and my ears hear?

And if His Word is true, how do I respond? Something in me should change, but what? How? Because if this story is true, then the King of all kings, the infinite God who spoke the Milky Way and me into existence—because He loves me deeply—stepped off His throne and embarked on a rescue mission to save and deliver a self-centered slave like me.

What kind of king does that?

What if the death and resurrection of Jesus the Christ is the singular most important event in the history of mankind, and what if one drop of His blood is the most powerful thing in this universe or any other? What if dead and crucified Jesus came back to life by the power of the Holy Spirit and He is alive today? Right now. What if, having conquered the enemy, He empowers us to do what He did? Anointing us with defense against evil. Against addiction. Against sickness. Against generational sin and curse. Against the hardness of our own hearts. What if His singular desire is for us to know the love with which the Father loved Him before the foundation of the world?

Are you kidding me?

Our enemy, using every tactic and weapon at his disposal, has attacked this gospel. These words. The greatest war in the history of history and beyond has been waged against this very word. *The* Word. It's been watered down, abused, adulterated, manipulated, and changed. With so much stacked against it and us, we have trouble believing it means today what it was meant to mean today. Many of us, either consciously or not, just have trouble believing that the shed blood of a Man named Jesus two thousand years ago has anything to do with us here today.

As a result, we live in the crossfire and we're not sure what to believe.

But—what if?

What if His story is true?

What if this Jesus, the One who walked out of the tomb shining like the sun, holding the keys of death and hades, is alive—in you? In me? I write fiction for a living, and that's either the craziest thing I've ever heard or it's the most important word ever spoken.

Let me give you an example: Jesus talked more about the kingdom of heaven than anything else. In Matthew 13, He compared it to a dragnet which was cast into the sea where it gathered some of every kind. When full, it was dragged to shore where the good was gathered into vessels but the bad was thrown away. Jesus was speaking of a future event in history which is really going to happen.

Jesus continued to explain that at the end of the age, the angels will come, separate the wicked from the just, and cast the wicked into the furnace of fire where there will be wailing and people screaming at the top of their lungs. Of this event, Paul told the church in Corinth, "For we must all appear before the judgment seat of Christ, that each one may receive the things done in the body, according to what he has done, whether good or bad" (2 Cor. 5:10). But look at what he said next: "Knowing, therefore, the terror of the Lord, we persuade men" (2 Cor. 5:11).

Make no mistake about it—Jesus said some things which struck His listeners as just plain crazy. Maybe none better than this: "Most assuredly, I say to you, unless you eat the flesh of the Son of Man and drink His blood, you have no life in you. Whoever eats My flesh and drinks My blood has eternal life, and I will raise him up at the last day. For My flesh is food indeed, and My blood is drink indeed. He who eats My flesh and drinks My blood abides in Me, and I in him" (John 6:53–56).

Imagine being in the crowd when He said this—which incidentally, occurred just after He walked on water. If I found myself following a guy who could walk on water and yet talked about my cannibalizing Him and washing it down with a pint of His blood, I'd be scratching my head and reevaluating my decision-making paradigm.

If you look closely at the scripture above, you'll find this: "Therefore many of His disciples, when they heard this, said, 'This is a hard saying; who can understand it?' . . . From that time many of His disciples went back and walked with Him no more" (John 6:60, 66). Even His disciples found it tough to believe, and they were standing in His presence!

If Jesus is who He says He is, and He did what Scripture records Him as having done and is doing, then His life and His words, by their very nature, demand a response. And no response is still very much a response. We cannot look with cavalier indifference and/or resignation at the life and words of Jesus of Nazareth.

You and I have a problem, and the appearance of a baby boy in a nameless stable in Bethlehem is our first clue that the problem is out of our control—that after a few thousand years of pleading with us to return to Him, He has come to us. To save us from ourselves.

The problem—the reason the King of kings stepped off His throne and came here—is my sin. Your sin. And our utter and complete inability to do anything about it. Our knowledge and understanding of this predicament have been watered down by time and a clever enemy, but in God's economy, for reasons I don't and can't understand, sin requires a payment.

Sin requires blood.

I can't explain why. It just is. Somewhere in here, I came to grips with the beautiful, tender, magnificent, barbaric, soul-shattering, eternal, unequivocal reality that the birth, life, and death of this innocent boy and magnificent Man are simply my King's first step from throne to trough to cross to tomb to hell to God's right hand.

As a result, I am blood bought. Blood washed. And blood redeemed. And you are too.

What kind of king does this? The weight of the answer pierces me because I know me. I am not worthy.

Why Write This Book?

A few years ago, when I first pitched the idea of this book to Christy and my agent, Chris, they asked, "What's the takeaway?" And in the two or three years since, every time I've presented this book to anyone, they've asked the same question. If I'm honest, I'm still struggling with that answer. Not because I don't know it, but because it doesn't fit well in a sound bite. There's a lot here, but if you press me I can give it in one word: "Freedom." Freedom from the stuff that wants our heads on a platter.

If you are down, broken, brokenhearted, shattered, bleeding from the inside out, staring at a lifetime of bad decisions and now the bars of worse consequences, ashamed, struggling with getting out of bed and facing today (or facing the next minute), thinking more about checking out than digging in, angry (no—pissed), shaking your fist at God, screaming at the heavens, staring at your hands knowing what they've done and wondering how God could ever love you, unable to breathe from the weight of the wound in your chest, mopping up the pus spilling out of your heart because you trusted someone, sitting with your head in your hands watching the slideshow of all the faces you betrayed who no longer trust you and wondering where to start, searching the horizon for any sight of your prodigal but they aren't even in this time zone, waking up a long way from home wondering how to get back and unable and unsure how to face the mushroom cloud you left behind, covered up in soul-wrecking grief and spirit-breaking sorrow, unable to see daylight for the blanket of darkness, unable to get off the unmerry-go-round and stop the cycle of medicating your pain with pills or drink or sex or money or anything other than the tender and magnificent love of Jesus—I'd give you this book.

Admittedly, some of the things I'm writing about require a little imagination. I'm taking license with stuff we just can't know and can't prove. I have no idea if the woman with the issue of blood, the centurion, Bartimaeus, and others were present at Jesus' crucifixion. I certainly can't prove it. But if I were them, and Jesus had done to me and in me what He did to them and in them, I'd have been there. I've tried to think like that. I'm also well aware of the warning in Revelation 22:18 to anyone who adds anything to this book and the plagues he will suffer. With trembling fingers, I've attempted to write within those boundaries, painting scenes while not speaking blasphemy.

Having said that, Jesus still speaks. Today. To you and me. I talk to Him all the time. Can I tell you that I hear Him like you're hearing me now through this book? Of course not. But whether through His Word, the council of many, an impression in my spirit, or an audible, still small voice, I do hear Him. (Although, I will admit the audible voice is not a common thing.)

In this book, you will read a lot about my conversations with Jesus. For the record, I am not claiming new revelation. If you sense that in these pages, you should close this book. God's Word is perfect, inerrant, inspired, and completely true. Everything we need is in there. But, there are places in this book where I will talk about how His revelation is new to me. I will talk more about this in a later chapter, but I am sharing that newness with you in the same way C. S. Lewis shares it with us in the *Screwtape Letters* or *Mere Christianity.**

I don't question whether the God of the universe is still speaking. He is. I want to know what He's saying. So, there are times in these pages

---

* And no, I'm not setting myself up as the next Lewis. I'm simply using him as an example. St. Bernard of Clairvaux said we are dwarves perched atop the shoulders of giants—and Lewis is a giant.

when I'll share some idea of what He's saying—to me. If I were you, I'd check me. How? Well, spread these pages out next to God's Word and check for yourself. Secondly, there's counsel in the wisdom of many. I'd encourage you to seek that counsel. Lastly, ask Jesus about it. "Jesus, is this true?" Then use the same process to check what you might hear as the answer. I grew up in a church where folks claimed to have heard Jesus. Truth was, some had. Some had not. And it wasn't always immediately clear who had and who had not. So, I've seen this abused. I pray I don't fall into that camp.

Today, as a man who has walked with Jesus as Lord and Savior and King for over forty-five years, my problem is not with folks claiming they hear the voice of God—we can usually check that. My problem is with folks who claim to know Him and yet don't hear from Him. Who claim He doesn't speak to us the way He did when He was here. My question for them is this: If Jesus is not speaking to you, then do you know Him? And if so, how?

If you want to hear Jesus, I believe He will speak to you. He tells us to seek Him while He can be found. To come to Him like little children. To call on Him. Further, you don't have to be some different or improved version of yourself to hear Him. The question is, are you listening? My hope and prayer for you as we walk through these pages is that you learn to hear Him. Just as Samuel, Elijah, the apostles, and Paul did. I would love nothing more than to walk you up to the feet of Jesus and for you to close this book, take His hand, and hear His voice.

Also, I am not writing this as a theological exercise. I have no formal training in theology. As much as I know my own heart, my goal is freedom. Period. Both yours and mine. Given that, this is not really a book you just read. I hope you read it, but once the words have entered your eyes and taken a few laps around your brain, I hope they migrate down into your heart and that you "do" these words.

There is stuff here to be done.

Some of this is messy and uncomfortable. Some of it was uncomfortable to write. But, for the last ten plus years, I've walked with a group of men (and as a couple, Christy and I have walked with various women) through difficult places in their lives. And they've walked with me. What I discovered is that just filling a pew on Sunday morning did absolutely nothing to bring freedom. I'm not knocking church. We should all be in one. I thank God for His bride. But the traditions of our churches and our theological systems are often impotent to kill the stuff that's killing us.* So I am, and have been, simply looking at people in prison and chains of their (and my) own making, and I'm wondering how to get them (and me) free.

Guided by the idea that's there's got to be more, I began asking the question, "Lord, where is the power of Your gospel? Where is the You that I read about in the Gospels and Acts? Where is that life? That freedom? That power of that kingdom? Where is that love?" We all, each of us, are just broken children of God, and what you will read in these pages is the record of that journey to freedom. Of our walk from broken to not broken. To whole. To new.

One of the things I have realized is that when Jesus was talking to the scribes and Pharisees, when He continually called them "hypocrites," He was talking directly to me. To you. There's no getting around it. We are them. When He told them they "cleanse the outside of the cup and dish, but inside they are full of extortion and self-indulgence" (Matt. 23:25), He was talking to and about us. Most of the time, if left to myself, I am that man.

What follows in these pages are the things we did and prayed that the Lord used to cleanse the inside of our cups and dishes. The inside of us. The Cross—the blood of Jesus—works *for* us, *in* us, and *through* us. This is a book primarily about how it works *for* and *in* us. Right now I've got an outline of the book that will show how it works *through* us. But first walk, then run.

At the end of each of chapter, I've written a prayer. Something I've prayed myself and put down on paper. I'm inviting you to join me in those prayers. In praying, I'm inviting Jesus into His rightful place. To be the

---

* Jesus talked about this very thing in Mark 7:1–16.

King He is. Don't rush through these pages. Don't hurry to the next chapter. Linger here. Read them slowly. These prayers are some of the most important words you and I will read through together.

The following is my prayer for you.

Lord Jesus, I give You these words. If they are true, multiply them. If not, erase them. For the last twenty years, I've written fiction. Now I'm writing about You. Telling Your story. And telling my story with You. I know You look to the one who is contrite and trembles at Your word. I pray that when You see me penning these pages, You find me contrite and trembling. I pray that You also find me fist pumping, mic dropping, and dancing. And in the end, I pray You are increased and I am decreased. I pray that like Psalm 45 my pen is the tongue of a ready writer and that I make Your great name known to the nations.

Jesus, because of You, I am blood bought, blood washed, and blood redeemed. That thought shatters me. So touch my lips, my fingers, and these words with a burning coal. Forgive me in advance if I say anything in error. Use these words to break chains, fling wide prison doors, heal the brokenhearted, release the captives, give beauty for ashes, anoint with the oil of joy, and wash away mourning. Wrap your children in a robe of praise and deliver them and me from any spirit of despair so that we might grow up as oaks of righteousness, ministers of our God, and priests in Your kingdom.

Jesus, without Your spirit of revelation, these are just black marks on a page. Please reveal to us, through the inspiration of Your Holy Spirit, what all this means. Walk us through the door and into Your presence. We invite You to come and be released in and through us to show us what You mean and who You are. You've told us that Your Spirit is the Spirit of truth, the Helper. Please speak truth to us and help us.

I've always loved Paul's admonition to the church in Ephesus, so let me end with that: I pray "that the God of our Lord Jesus Christ, the Father of glory, may give to you the spirit of wisdom and revelation in the knowledge of Him, the eyes of your understanding being enlightened;

*that you may know what is the hope of His calling, what are the riches
of the glory of His inheritance in the saints, and what is the exceeding
greatness of His power toward us who believe, according to the working
of His mighty power which He worked in Christ when He raised Him
from the dead and seated Him at His right hand in the heavenly places,
far above all principality and power and might and dominion, and every
name that is named, not only in this age but also in that which is to
come. And He put all things under His feet, and gave Him to be head over
all things to the church, which is His body, the fullness of Him who fills
all in all" (Eph. 1:17–23).*

    In Jesus' Name, amen.

One last thought before we get started: let me encourage you to make this book a working document. The words I've written here may shake some stuff loose in you. They did in me. So, make a record of the shaking. Write in the margins. Write the date. Where you are when you read it. At the end of chapters. Everywhere there is white blank space. Don't just read this. Read this and wrestle it out. Start your own conversation with the Lord. Circle. Underline. Dog-ear. Highlight. Read with a pen in one hand and a Bible in the other.

Some of this has been tough for me to write. But if you walk into a deeper place with Jesus, with deeper understanding, deeper revelation, deeper intimacy, and deeper love, then I'd gladly write it again. So, let me encourage you to start a dialogue with Him. Really. Like on that white space just below this paragraph. He—Jesus, whose name is above every other name and at whose name every knee will bow—desires to have a lifelong conversation with you. Actually, He wants an eternal conversation, but we'll get to that. So, cover these pages in those words. That conversation. Create a written record of your own process and the words you speak to Him and He speaks to you. I think you'll be amazed at the conversation that rises to the surface.

CHAPTER 1

The Word Becomes Flesh—
And Dwells Among Us

The night is cool and turning cooler. The air smells of wood smoke, lamp oil, and manure. Quirinius is governing Syria. Caesar Augustus has issued a decree: "Register the world! Take a census."[1] Under the dominating hand of Rome, men and their families scurry to their ancestral homes to register. Jerusalem is overflowing. Bethlehem is packed.

It is dark. Past the evening meal. A young man leads a young girl riding a donkey up a small trail into Bethlehem. He is pensive. Every few seconds, he glances over his shoulder.

The rumors have preceded them. As have the whispers. She's pregnant but not with his child, and to complicate matters, they're not married. It's a scandal. According to Jewish law, he should put her out and she should be stoned.

The innkeeper has had a long day. He watches warily. The tired young man asks, "Sir, do you have a room?"*

The innkeeper shakes his head. "Full up."

The young man strains his voice. "You know of . . . anywhere?"

The innkeeper leans on his broom handle. Half-annoyed. His patience is thin. "Try down there. But you're wasting your time."

---

* I have written Joseph as a young man here. It's quite possible he was an older man at this time. How old? I don't know. The events at the crucifixion suggest Joseph was already dead.

The girl winces. The contractions have started. The stain on her dress suggests her water broke. The innkeeper's wife eyes the barn and whispers, "We can make room."

Hours later, the couple returns. The young girl is sweating. Doubled over. The young man is frantic. The innkeeper is in bed. Upon hearing the knock, he rises reluctantly and unlocks the door. "Son, I told you . . ."

"Please sir . . . ." He points to the young woman. "She's bleeding."

The innkeeper's wife appears over his shoulder. She says nothing, which says plenty. The innkeeper trims his wick and, for the first time, looks into the young man's eyes. The innkeeper gently grabs the reins of the donkey and leads the young woman to the barn where he spreads fresh hay to make a bed. His wife appears with a towel and some rags. She brushes the two men out and helps the girl.

The innkeeper and the young man stand at the door of the stable—little more than a cave carved into the rock wall. The animals seem amused at the ruckus. The innkeeper lights his pipe. The young man shuffles nervously.

Behind them, the screams begin.

The innkeeper speaks first. "You the two everyone is talking about?"

The young man doesn't take his eyes off the cave. "Yes sir."

Another puff. Another cloud. "What happened?"

The young man is not quick to answer. "You wouldn't believe me if I told you."

The innkeeper laughs, "I don't know. I was young once. She's a pretty girl."

Another scream echoes out of the barn.

"Is the baby yours?"

The young man rubs his hands together. Calloused, muscled. They are the hands of a stonemason.* "No, he's not. I mean, he will be but . . . I'm not the, well. . . ."

---

* It is my opinion that Joseph, and hence Jesus, probably worked more with stone than wood, although I'm sure they worked with both, which is why I here use the word stonemason. I think the problem for us probably arises out of earlier translators who used the word carpenter. I will use both interchangeably.

The innkeeper chuckles. "You sure it's a he?"

The young man nods. "Pretty sure."

"You intend to marry?"

The young man glances over his shoulder. "Soon as she heals up."

Another scream and the innkeeper changes the subject. "You here to register?"

The young man nods.

"What family?"

"House of David."

The innkeeper raises an eyebrow. "Good family."

The screams have risen to a fever pitch. The young girl is out of her mind. The innkeeper's wife calls from the stall. Her voice trembles. "Honey, I need some hot water."

The innkeeper disappears and leaves the young man alone. He stands repeating the same phrase over and over and over. *"Hear, O Israel: the* LORD *our God, the* LORD *is one! Hear, O Israel. . . ."*[2]

Above a star has risen. Abnormally bright.

Made Flesh

Elsewhere, in the throne room of heaven . . .

They are arranged in laser-perfect rows. Ten thousand in a row and tens of thousands of rows. Trailing out farther than any eye can see. They are radiant and barefooted. Every shade of skin color dressed in a sea of brilliant white robes. Decked in glistening gold. Chiseled, elegant features. Blond, auburn, ebony hair. The floor upon which they are dancing is reflective. Shiny. Not a speck. Not a smudge. They stand somewhere above ten feet tall. Many have hair to their waists. Some pulled back in a ponytail. Their wings stretch another ten feet into the air, the tips are almost touching. They are frozen in time, holding the same choreographed pose each was holding when the music stopped. Along with everyone else, they are waiting for the music to begin again and send them into the next movement. Right now, they are catching their breath and waiting for orders. Heads bowed, beads of sweat drip onto the mirrored floor.

The air carries with it the fading echo of a drumbeat and the receding sound of the concert of a million feet dancing and tapping to perfection. It's a powerful, penetrating rhythm felt in the depths. Several miles in the distance, there is a bright light. Brighter than the sun. It is the most piercing and penetrating light in the history of light. The breeze created by the angels' wings brings with it the smell of mint, rosemary, lavender, lemon, and eucalyptus. This place is an architectural wonder. Planes could fly in here. A thousand planes. A river flows through the middle. A roof above. In the distance, fiery stones.

This is the banquet hall of all banquet halls.

Rising on the air is a chorus of voices. They come from higher up. Thundering. Declaring. Proclaiming. Pitch perfect. While each is distinct, they layer over each other. The melody forms and rises. They are reading from an ancient text. The acoustics are perfect and unamplified.

The first voice speaks of how He will be born of a woman. Another states that He will come from the line of Abraham. Another, the tribe of Judah. The House of David. Born of a virgin. Will sit on the throne of David. An eternal throne. Emmanuel. Born in Bethlehem. Worshiped by wise men. Presented with gifts. Called out of Egypt. Called a Nazarene.

The voices continue—He will be zealous for His father. Filled with God's Spirit. Heal many. Deal gently with Gentiles. Rejected by His own. Speak in parables. Enter triumphantly into Jerusalem. Praised by little children. A cornerstone. Perform miracles—which some would not believe. Betrayed for thirty pieces of silver that would be used to buy a potter's field. A man of sorrows. Acquainted with grief. Forsaken by His own best friends. Scourged. Spat on. Unrecognizable as a man. Crucified between two thieves. Given vinegar to drink. His hands and feet would be pierced. Others would gamble for and divide his clothes. Surrounded and ridiculed by His enemies. He would thirst, commend His spirit to His Father, and not one of His bones would be broken. Stared at in death, buried with the rich, raised from the dead, He would ascend and become a greater high priest than Aaron. He would rule the heathen. A ruling scepter. Seated at the right hand of God.

As the last word echoes off, all eyes turn toward the light several miles in the distance where a King is seated on His throne. He is resplendent. Like ten thousand nuclear bombs exploding over and over and over. He is magnificent. Splendor indescribable. Majesty on high. El Elyon. The brightness of the sun times ten trillion. To His right sits His Son. The very Word of God. Broad shoulders, the spitting image. A river—crystal clear—flows from beneath His throne. In His hand, He holds a scepter. He is radiant. Nothing has been, is, or ever will be more perfect. He is like a jasper stone and a sardius in appearance, and there is a rainbow wrapped around His throne like an emerald. From the throne come flashes of lightning and peals of thunder.[3]

Layered in the air, the several-million-voice chorus rises: "Glory to God in the highest!" The shimmering, angelic bodies below snap into unison. Twirling. Tapping. Synchronized. Each dancer has six wings. Two cover their faces. Two cover their feet. And with two more they fly. Cirque du Soleil doesn't hold a candle.

Voices sing out:

- "Only begotten Son."[4]
- "Heir of all things, through whom also He made the world. And He is the radiance of His glory and the exact representation of His nature, and upholds all things by the word of His power."[5]
- "For by Him all things were created, both in the heavens and on earth . . . whether thrones or dominions or rulers or authorities—all things have been created through Him and for Him. He is before all things, and in Him all things hold together."[6]
- "He who is the blessed and only Sovereign, the King of kings and Lord of lords, who alone possesses immortality and dwells in unapproachable light, whom no man has seen or can see. To Him be honor and eternal dominion!"[7]
- "He was in the beginning with God. All things were made through Him, and without Him nothing was made that was made. In Him

was life, and the life was the light of men. And the light shines in the darkness, and the darkness did not comprehend it."[8]

- "The Alpha and the Omega . . . who is and who was and who is to come, the Almighty."[9]
- "The Amen, the Faithful and True Witness, the Beginning of the creation of God."[10]
- "The Lion that is from the tribe of Judah, the Root of David."[11]

Then the voices hush. Every angel kneels. Bowing. Face to the floor. Twenty-four elders, each holding a harp and a bowl of incense—which are the prayers of the saints—lie on the ground in a circle around Him having cast their crowns at His feet.

The Son is quiet. Unassuming. No desire to draw attention. Not feeling that equality with the King is something to be grasped. His mannerisms are that of a dove. His presence that of a lion. His demeanor like a lamb's. His attraction like the bright morning star. Expressing both longing and joy. Both tears and a smile.

He is attended by an archangel. One of three. This angel is relatively new at his job. The other two have been here a long time. The last archangel that had attended to Jesus was described as the "seal of perfection, full of wisdom and perfect in beauty." He had been, "in Eden, the garden of God . . . you were perfect in your ways from the day you were created, till iniquity was found in you."[12] He is also described as the "son of the morning"[13] and "son of the dawn."[14] He announced the morning only to eventually grow jealous of all the praise leveled at the Son. Wanting it, he reached up, tried to grab it, and fell. Disguising himself as an angel of light, he led a rebellion, and he took a third of the other angels with him. Mutiny. God the Father would have none of it and cast the dark angel out of heaven like lightning. Hurling him earthward where he has stirred up trouble for millennia.*

---

* It is my opinion that satan was once an archangel and that his job was to attend to Jesus. I know people who disagree with this, and I admit I can't prove my opinion. Nor has anyone disproven it to my satisfaction. I cover this idea to a greater extent in a later chapter dealing with the deepest wound of the human soul: rejection.

After he left, the King made a new creation out of dust. His most stunning to date. Made in His very image. When finished, the King pressed His lips to the mouth of His creation and breathed in His very breath. The *ruach* of God. Giving man life. Angry and envious, the rebelling angel slithered in and took them all hostage. Kidnapped every one. Bondage. Slavery. Mass carnage. Things are bad. The only hope is a rescue mission. It's why the Son has to leave. Whispers are it's a suicide mission.

Slowly, the Son rises. It is pin-drop quiet. He places His scepter gently in the corner of His throne. Unbuckling His sword, he leans it upright next to the scepter. Next, He takes off His robe, folds it, and places it in the seat He just occupied. He pulls off His linen, tasseled undershirt and places it neatly next to his robe, folding the corners—or the *kanaph*, also called "wings"—gently. Finally, He removes the ring from His finger and lifts His crown off His brow, placing both atop His folded robe.

Save a loin cloth, the Son stands naked. His voice is the sound of many waters. Like Niagara. Or the break at Pipeline.

God the Father rises as His Son crosses the fiery stones. The Father hugs the Son, buries His face on His son's cheek and kisses Him. The time has come. On earth, the sons of Adam have lost their way. Each gone their own way. Astray. The entire human race has been taken captive, and the enemy is torturing them. Not one of them will survive the night. The Son has volunteered for a rescue mission, but it's a prisoner exchange. The whispers are true; their freedom will cost the Son everything.

His life for theirs.

The Father holds His Son's hands in His and tenderly touches the center of His palm. He knows what's coming. A tear rolls down the face of the Ancient of Days. The Son thumbs it away. "I'll miss you." He glances at the earth below and hell in between. Billions of faces shine across the timeline of history. He knows each by name. They are the "joy set before Him."[15] He turns to His Father, "I will give them Your word. And declare to them Your Great Name."[16] The Son looks with longing at His home.

Voices rise from every corner singing at the tops of their lungs. It is the loudest singing in the history of song. "Blessing and honor and glory and power be to Him who sits on the throne, and to the Lamb, forever and ever."[17] Angels bow. Brush the floor. He pats many on the shoulder. Kisses some. Hugs others. Long-held embraces. Kids rush forward and grab His hands as they dance in laughter-filled circles.

As He turns to leave, leaning against the two giant doors that lead out into the Milky Way, He turns to His Father. His eyes are piercing, penetrating, inviting. He smiles, "We're going to need more rooms in this house when I come back." He waves His hand across the timeline, "Because I'm bringing them with me." The Son—whose "countenance was like the sun shining in its strength"[18]—exits heaven blanketed in the singing of more than a hundred million angels and bathed in the tears of the Father.

The Word becomes flesh, and He is gone.

> In the beginning was the Word, and the Word was with God, and the Word was God. He was in the beginning with God. . . . And the Word became flesh and dwelt among us, and we beheld His glory.[19]

God with Us

The innkeeper returns as the cries of a baby pierce the night air. The child's lungs are strong. The wife clears the mucus, and the cries grow louder. The young man exhales a breath he has been holding for a little over nine months. The innkeeper stokes the fire in the corner and hugs the young man. "Come!"

The hay beneath the young woman is a mess. The baby boy has entered the world in much the same way the nation of Israel left Egypt. Through blood and water. The animals look on. The stones cry out.[20]

The woman places the baby on the mother's chest, and the two lie exhausted. The young woman is exposed, and the young man is uncertain as to his role. He has yet to know her. The innkeeper's wife leads him to the young girl's side where he cuts the cord and then slides his hand inside hers. His heart is racing. She is exhausted. Sweaty. The afterbirth arrives and the innkeeper's wife begins cleaning the woman. The young mother stares at the boy and hears the echo of the angel that appeared to her some ten months ago: "He will be great, and will be called the Son of the Highest; and the Lord God will give Him the throne of His father David. And He will reign over the house of Jacob forever, and of His king-dom there will be no end."[21]

This is a bittersweet moment because she knows well the words of both Isaiah and the psalmist. How the Messiah will suffer. Be cursed. Bruised. Pierced. Despised. Rejected. Oppressed. Afflicted. Cut off from the land of the living. He will bear our griefs. Carry our sorrows. All His bones will be out of joint. His heart will melt like wax. He will give His back to those who will beat Him, pour out His soul unto death, bear the sin of many . . . and become unrecognizable as a man.[22]

She turns to the man who did not leave her when he had every right. The honorable man who will be her husband. She hands him the boy and speaks His name, "Yeshua Hamashiach."

The young father holds his son and whispers, "The Sun of Righteous-ness shall arise with healing in His wings."[23]

The innkeeper and his wife stand at a distance. They can't take their eyes off the boy. She whispers, "Every male who opens the womb shall be called holy to the LORD."[24] On the air above them there is an echo. Faint at first, it grows louder. The innkeeper stares at heaven. The star above them is daylight bright and casts their shadows on the ground. Finally, he can make it out. Voices. Purest he's ever heard. Singing at the top of their lungs: "Glory to God in the highest, and on earth peace, goodwill toward men!"[25]

The innkeeper knows now. He bows low and speaks loud enough for the young couple to hear. "The Lord Himself will give you a sign: Behold, the virgin shall conceive and bear a Son, and shall call His name Immanuel."[26]

God with us.

But not all are so inviting. In the dark night air, invisible armies draw invisible battle lines. Forces gather. Battle plans are drawn. Even now, the boy's life is in danger.

Just over the next hill, beyond earshot, lies another hill. Mount Moriah.

It is an ancient and storied place. It is the hill where Melchizedek reigned as priest to God Most High. Where Abraham raised the knife above Isaac. The hill where Ornan the Jebusite built his threshing floor. Where the plague stopped. Where David danced before the Lord and returned the ark. The hill where Solomon built the temple. And in about three decades, forces will gather on this hill to execute this boy.

Daylight breaks the horizon, the innkeeper tends the fire, and "the people who walked in darkness have seen a great light; those who dwelt in the land of the shadow of death, upon them a light has shined."[27] Mary wraps Jesus tightly in swaddling clothes, lifts Him from the stone trough, and cradles the suckling baby, "who, being in the form of God, did not consider it robbery to be equal with God, but made Himself of no reputation, taking the form of a bondservant, and coming in the likeness of men. And being found in appearance as a man, He humbled Himself and became obedient."[28]

Joseph kneels and presses his lips to the forehead of his son. He knows the words by heart. Written 740 years ago, Isaiah was speaking about his Son. About this very moment. About this improbable beginning. About this King who stepped off His throne to become a boy who will grow into a man and walk from this cave to that hill—and down into hell—to ransom you and me.

> For unto us a Child is born,
> Unto us a Son is given;
> And the government will be upon His shoulder.
> And His name will be called
> Wonderful, Counselor, Mighty God,
> Everlasting Father, Prince of Peace.
> Of the increase of His government and peace
> There will be no end,
> Upon the throne of David and over His kingdom,
> To order it and establish it with judgment and justice
> From that time forward, even forever.
> The zeal of the LORD of hosts will perform this.[29]

A Proper Context

Most of us see Jesus as a long-haired, soft-spoken, pacifist, speaker of fables, mystic guru who never lost His cool and kept His mouth shut when the soldiers nailed Him to a tree. Nothing could be further from the truth. Jesus was "begotten." Not created like us. Big difference. Isaiah says, "a Child is born . . . a Son is given" (9:6). Meaning, He existed before the ages. Before the eons. We tend to focus on the baby in the manger, and I'm with you. But in minimizing Jesus to someone we can touch and something we can wrap our heads around, we've reduced Him. Jesus was the only begotten Son in the throne room before He arrived here as a child. Jesus Christ was, is, and forever will be King of all kings.

The One who stretched out the heavens, made the stars, and calls each *by name*. We forget this.

King David, speaking through the inspiration of the Holy Spirit, gave us insight into a conversation that occurred in heaven before the foundation of the world. It's from Psalm 110—which, incidentally, is the most quoted Old Testament verse in the New Testament. Jesus applied it to Himself[30] and it's also quoted by Peter[31]: "The LORD said to my Lord, 'Sit at My right hand, till I make Your enemies Your footstool.' The LORD shall send the rod of Your strength out of Zion. Rule in the midst of Your enemies!" (Ps. 110:1–2).

A few things strike me here. First, God the Father spoke to Jesus, the Son, and told Him to sit at His right hand. That seat of distinction has never been given to another. It also means that Jesus ruled from the throne room before He ever arrived here on earth. We also know from Stephen's speech to the high priest and leaders of the council in Acts that Jesus is still there: "But he, being full of the Holy Spirit, gazed into heaven and saw the glory of God, and Jesus standing at the right hand of God, and said, 'Look! I see the heavens opened and the Son of Man standing at the right hand of God!'" (Acts 7:55–56).

Second, God Most High made Jesus' enemies a footstool beneath Jesus' feet. That means all of them. He is the undisputed, undefeated, unconquered, unvanquished King of all kings. Speaking to His disciples, Jesus said, "If I have told you earthly things and you do not believe, how will you believe if I tell you heavenly things? No one has ascended to heaven but He who came down from heaven, that is, the Son of Man who is in heaven" (John 3:12–13).

Third, Jesus rules in the midst of His enemies. If you spend time thinking about this, it will mess with your head—and your theology. Think about it. Name any other king anywhere who rules in the midst of those who want him dead. Our definition of a ruler is one who drives out his enemies. Not lives with them. The fact that Jesus does not, to me, says much about both His power and His love—even for those who wish Him dead.

The throne room is the epicenter of the universe. It's where the decisions are made. It's where you and I were first spoken into existence. What we know of the throne room of God can be pieced together from a couple sources. Each adds another dimension to the picture. They are rich with texture and layer and worth reading.[32]

Life in the throne room is unlike anything we've experienced. There's perfect peace, perfect love, perfect everything. There is also the absence of fear. No anger. No judgments. No jealousies. Every bad emotion is not in there. Everything good is. There's no death. Only life.

Jesus gives us a peek behind that curtain when He prays to His Father in John 17. What we call the High Priestly Prayer. It's amazing—the Son speaking with unfettered intimacy to the Father, and we get to listen. His deepest and most intimate thoughts. Even as I type this, it's tough to wrap my head around. But it's still true. Everything your heart and my heart hope for—the divine search for eternity in us, the eternity that's written on our hearts—finds its perfect expression and culmination in that room. With *that* God. The reason the angels are singing, "Holy, Holy, Holy" continuously before the throne (Rev. 4:8) is because God is revealing His glory to them, anew, every few seconds. And each revelation is better than the last. It's like staring at a diamond with infinite facets and angles. And that reflection is blowing their minds.

Before we get in to the stories of Jesus' life and words and what those might mean to us, we need to first put Him in His proper context in our minds. To think rightly about Him.

Who is this Jesus?

Jesus said of Himself, "I am the way, the truth, and the life. No one comes to the Father except through Me" (John 14:6). And if Jesus is the way, then He's taking us somewhere. But where? I believe the answer is to His Father. This idea of God as "Father" as revealed by Jesus had been sparingly revealed in the Old Testament. It wasn't overly common. God refers to His people as "His children" or "His son," so the inference is made, but Old Testament writers—other than David, Isaiah, and Jeremiah—don't really refer to God as an intimate Father. The Old Testament understanding was more corporate. As in, God the Father of the nation of Israel. Of His people. He was the "God up there." Not the "God right here." Jesus turns this on its head. His revelation is individual. God is your Father. Mine.

To the apostles, this was mind-blowing.

Jesus arrived here through a gooey, humbling mess in a cave in Bethlehem. But why? What is your personal experience with Jesus? Not the one your church or your friends believe. Not the one passed to you by your parents or culture. I mean yours. The one in your gut. The one you run to when life gets tough. When things hurt.

Yes, He is my friend and the lover of my soul, but in calling Him that, have I reduced Him? Hear me: I need Jesus to be the intimate lover of my soul; I desperately need Him to whisper to me—Charles—and to single me out. But I wonder if in this need I haven't somehow forgotten that He spoke and everything I see came into existence. Including me and my ability to see it. He is eternal. He is infinite. He fashioned me from the dust. Every curve. Every wrinkle. Every hair follicle.

The books of Hebrews, Colossians, and Revelation establish Jesus as deity, anointed, Messiah, King, and Sovereign Ruler in an eternal kingdom, seated at the right hand of God, supreme, heir of everything, Creator, the radiance of God, the exact representation of God, the One who upholds all things by the Word of His power, and that He alone made purification for our sins. If we had this understanding, if we truly understood who He was and is, where He was, and what His role was before He arrived here—at least as much as our hearts and minds are capable—how would it change how we see Him and what we do with it and about it? Paul said it this way: "Now this, 'He ascended'—what does it mean but that He also first descended in to the lower parts of the earth? He who descended is also the One who ascended far above all the heavens, that He might fill all things" (Eph. 4:9–10). He alone is the first born among the dead. He alone ascended on high.

The reason the Twelve followed Jesus to the cross and died as martyrs (save John) is because they knew Him in this way. As the resurrected King of the universe. They touched the holes. Saw the light in His eyes. When they were being boiled alive, beheaded, flayed, crucified upside down, I imagine the image in their minds that spurred their faith, that got them through, was a gut-level knowing of this Jesus.

When John, the disciple whom Jesus loved and the one who reclined against Jesus' bosom at the Last Supper, encountered the resurrected King Jesus in His eternal reality on the island of Patmos, he fell on his face as though dead. And then Jesus, in beautiful Jesus fashion, touched him on the shoulder and said, "Do not be afraid" (Rev. 1:17).

Jesus is all of the above. The problem I've bumped into as I've walked with people who are wrestling with Jesus is that either consciously or unconsciously they have reduced Him to a mysterious, walk-about prophet with cool sandals and a posse. A sayer of good sayings. A soft-spoken teller of fables. A passive wimp. Just a guy whose red-printed words appear in an imposing black book.

This limitation is really dangerous. For us.

So let me come back around—what is your personal experience with Jesus? To you, who is He? No, I mean really. Spend some time here. Ask yourself, when things are bad, who holds the power? Your enemy? Or Jesus? Your enemy wants you to think he does. But your enemy was created by Your King. Uncreated vs. created. Our enemy is a footstool. And our King is on the throne. Ruling in the midst of them.

If we had this understanding, if this "knowing" was in our gut, if this was the picture we held of Jesus, if this was the truth with which we countered the lies that whisper in our ears, then the circumstances we face—no matter how horrible—would be about as powerful as gnats in a hurricane. I'm not saying our circumstances don't hurt. They can and do. A lot. Your and my pain is real. But our pain doesn't dictate our reality or the truth of who Jesus is.

I'm trying here to give you a picture that grows your faith and your hope. He is God of battle-axe and spear. God of angel armies. He holds the keys of death and hades. And when you were created, by Him, He meticulously fashioned you out of the dust, sculpted your body as it is, then knelt down, took a giant breath, placed His lips to yours, and breathed out for all He was worth. That life-giving breath made you a living, breathing soul. Your first breath started in His lungs.

That's my King.

At this point in history many of us believe the enemy (the devil) is winning and Jesus is either powerless to counter him or He doesn't care enough to do anything about it. Like He's just sitting there giving us what we deserve. Many of us point to our circumstances or to our pain or to a deep sense of powerlessness and shake our fists at the sky: "We are getting our lunch handed to us! Things are terrible! Just look around. If You are who Your book says You are, then do something about it!"

Our enemy would have us believe that our circumstances determine what is true. Our King is telling us they do not. Never have. And, He has done something about it.

Tonight, about midnight, walk outside and take a look around. Chances are good you will find the world rather dark. Sitting in that dark place you face a choice: you can determine in your infinite wisdom that this current darkness is the reality of your world and you just need to suck it up and get used to it because life's not going to get any better and only the strong survive and God either doesn't care or can't fix it anyway so you're on your own which you've known all along—or you can wait about six hours and watch the sun pierce the skyline.

I want to lift my eyes off my circumstances and onto Jesus, the author and finisher of our faith. To crush the speculations and strongholds in our minds where we've allowed the deceiver to convince us that Jesus is anything less than He is. To point out the lies that exalt themselves against the knowledge of God.

Lord Jesus, I'm asking You, by the power of Your Holy Spirit, to give me an experience with You that is new to me. Truer than I've known. Deeper than I've understood. Let me see You as You want to be seen by me. Show me who You are. And in the name of Jesus, I bind, cast down, and silence any whisper or voice to the contrary that would seek to speak lies or doubt into the reality of who You really are. I command that satan be muzzled; you may not speak lies to me about my King.

Jesus, for so long I've lived with a less-than picture of You. With a false understanding. I've let the enemy chip away at who You are and rob me of knowing You fully. I'm really sorry for doing that. I don't want to do that anymore. Please forgive me. Forgive my passive indifference. My quiet resignation. Forgive me for not bringing every thought to You and asking You if it is true.

Here and now I give my heart and mind to You, and I give You permission to paint a new picture. In 4K and technicolor. Let me see You as You are. Please reveal Yourself to me. Let me see You from King to child to Messiah to Savior to crucified to resurrected to defeater of death and the grave, to seated on high interceding for me.

And lastly Lord, I want to hear Your voice. Please. I know You are speaking. Please let me hear You. You have given me the Spirit of sonship through which I cry "Abba," and I desire nothing more than to hear You, My Father, speaking to and with me. Please let me join my voice with Samuel who said, "Speak, for Your servant is listening."[33] Lord, I'm listening.

In Jesus' Name, amen.

CHAPTER 2

We're All Bleeders

Jesus steps out of the boat, and the crowds rush the beach. The country of the Gadarenes sits behind Him. Across the water. The rumors have already spread.[1]

Even His disciples are whispering. One of them thumbs over his back. "Did you see that?"

Another nods. "Yeah, I saw it but I don't know what to do with it."

A third spoke. "I've never even thought something like that."

Jesus laughs. He has several appointments to keep. What happens in these next few minutes will upend the world.

A man runs across the beach. Robes flowing. He's wealthy. One of the rulers of the synagogue. He darts through the crowd. The apostles move to protect Jesus when Jairus falls at His feet and begs Him earnestly. "My little daughter lies at the point of death. Come and lay Your hands on her, that she may be healed, and she will live."[2]

Jesus smiles and gestures with His hand. "Take Me to her."

Moving through the street, Jairus screams at the crowd, fearing his daughter's death, "Move!" But Jesus is not hurried. In fact, He slows. Purposefully.

He chose this street. He has been waiting for this day. This moment. The crowd squeezes in, but He's not bothered. He is taking His time. He catches a glimpse of her behind Him, and His heart leaps. He knows her by name. There she is again. Weaving through the crowd, desperation painted across her face. He is her last hope, and He knows it. He smiles to Himself.

She's heard the stories. Word has spread throughout all Judea. There was the man with the withered hand. The centurion's servant. The son of the widow of Nain who was in a coffin being carried out through the gate. The paralyzed man lowered by his friends through a roof who, after the Healer touched him, walked out the front door. How He calmed the wind and the waves with just a word. How He laid His hands on those with various diseases and how He healed them all. Every one. Lastly, she's heard how He delivered the demon-possessed man of the Gadarenes. And then, just recently, she's heard how He read the prophet Isaiah in the synagogue. How the Spirit of the Sovereign Lord was upon Him. She knew the prophecy.

He was the Healer. The One the prophets talked about.

Through no fault of her own, she'd been bleeding for twelve years.[3] We're not sure why, but we do know that Leviticus 15 gives strict instructions to anyone like her. This law has declared her unclean. Everything that she touched, lay down on, sat on, or wore—and everything that touched any of these things that she touched, lay down on, sat on, or wore—was unclean. This included people. That meant whoever she touched was unclean. She was not allowed to "be with" a man or for a man to know her. The message given, the law applied to her, was, "Stay away. You are cast out." Given her condition, she was excluded from worship and from offering sacrifice—not allowed in the front door. And had been for over a decade. She could not get access to the priest, and hence, God. There was no atonement. No forgiveness. She didn't shake hands in public. She didn't kiss anyone. Didn't hug anyone. Kept at arms length.

How many times had she wondered if she'd be better off dead?

Then there was the issue of constantly having to wear a diaper. Something to soak up the blood so it didn't trickle down her leg, but sometimes it soaked through. Sometimes she left a trail. Her shame had soaked through too. In the back of her house, where she dried her laundry, she hung the stained rags. Her neighbors couldn't help but notice when they flapped in the breeze. They wished she'd do something about the smell.

She'd tried everything. Been to every doctor. Now broke, she'd traveled far and spent every penny. The problem had not improved. Only gotten worse.

Everyone knew about her condition, which also meant they knew the source of her shame. It was sin. Either hers or her family's sin had brought this curse on her. The law of Moses said so. So she lived under the constant shadow of whispers. Whatever sin she'd committed must have been significant. She's paying the penalty. And only God knows why.

She was a walking, steaming, stench-filled mess. She was also a "daughter of Abraham." We know from the narrative what's wrong with her, and to some extent, we know what she knows or has heard about Jesus. But we don't really know why she is stalking Jesus—and make no mistake, that's what she's doing.

To truly understand the depth of this woman's pain, desperation, and courage, I need to push Pause and leave her in the street for a moment. To truly "get" where she's at, we need to understand what or who has fueled the hope that brought her to this moment and has her standing in this street.

And to do that, we need to back up about fifteen hundred years.

In the Shelter of His Wings

In 1500 BC, Moses marched some three million Hebrews out of Egypt.* They were a nation of slaves. Three days out of Egypt, they're thirsty. They came upon a well, but the water was bad. They grumbled. The Lord told Moses to throw a tree in the water. He did, and the water turned

---

* Why do I say three million? In Numbers 1, during the Israelites' second year of wandering in the wilderness, Moses took a census of men over 20 who were able to go to war. That number was 603,550. From this, scholars believe the total number of men in the nation of Israel was between 1.2 million and somewhere north of that. Add wives and children, and I guesstimate three million.

sweet. (Notice deliverance here via a tree.) And then He said, "I am the LORD who heals you" (Ex. 15:26).

It is significant that one of the first names with which the Lord names Himself after His people's deliverance from generations of slavery is *Yahweh-Raphah*. It means, "The Lord—Your Healer."

Three months later, Moses stood at the foot of Mount Sinai.

> And Moses went up to God, and the LORD called to him from the mountain, saying, "Thus you shall say to the house of Jacob, and tell the children of Israel: 'You have seen what I did to the Egyptians, and how I bore you on eagles' wings and brought you to Myself. Now therefore, if you will indeed obey My voice and keep My covenant, then you shall be a special treasure to Me above all people; for all the earth is Mine. And you shall be to Me a kingdom of priests and a holy nation.' These are the words which you shall speak to the children of Israel." (Ex. 19:3–6)

Here, the Lord introduced the concept of "wings," including how He brought the Israelites to Himself and how those wings are a symbol of His protection and deliverance. The Lord continued this idea of healing and deliverance under the shadow of His wings when He gave instructions to Moses on how to build the ark of the covenant:

> And the cherubim shall stretch out their wings above, covering the mercy seat with their wings, and they shall face one another; the faces of the cherubim shall be toward the mercy seat. You shall put the mercy seat on top of the ark, and in the ark you shall put the Testimony that I will give you. And there I will meet with you, and I will speak with you from above the mercy seat, from between the two cherubim which are on the ark of the Testimony, about everything which I will give you in commandment to the children of Israel. (Ex. 25:20–22)

God's wings were a covering and a protection for His people. More than that, He invited them to come and meet with Him there, under the wings.

Psalm 91 (probably written by Moses) says it this way:

> He who dwells in the secret place of the Most High
> Shall abide under the shadow of the Almighty.
> I will say of the LORD, "He is my refuge and my fortress;
> My God, in Him I will trust."
>
> Surely He shall deliver you from the snare of the fowler
> And from the perilous pestilence.
> He shall cover you with His feathers,
> And under His wings you shall take refuge;
> His truth shall be your shield and buckler. (Ps. 91:1–4)

Note the meanings: Cover. Refuge. Deliverance. Trust.

Because God is practical and He didn't want His people to forget, He took this one step further. Brought it closer to home. He told Moses:

> Speak to the children of Israel: Tell them to make tassels on the corners of their garments throughout their generations, and to put a blue thread in the tassels of the corners. And you shall have the tassel, that you may look upon it and remember all the commandments of the LORD and do them, and that you may not follow the harlotry to which your own heart and your own eyes are inclined, and that you may remember and do all My commandments, and be holy for your God. I am the LORD your God, who brought you out of the land of Egypt, to be your God: I am the LORD your God. (Num. 15:38–41)

He said the same thing in Deuteronomy 22:12: "You shall make tassels on the four corners of the clothing with which you cover yourself."

The Hebrew word used here for "corners" in those passages is *kanaph*. It means an edge or extremity; specifically (of a bird or army) a wing, (of a garment or bed-clothing) a flap. So, the corner/border of a garment is the same word used for wings. God was making a mental connection for His people. In a sense, He was saying, "The corner of your garment should remind you of Me and My protection—of My deliverance and your healing."

This idea became a major element of the Hebrew culture.

Around 1000 BC, David was fleeing Saul in the Wilderness of En Gedi.

> Then Saul took three thousand chosen men from all Israel, and went to seek David and his men on the Rocks of the Wild Goats. So he came to the sheepfolds by the road, where there was a cave; and Saul went in to attend to his needs. (David and his men were staying in the recesses of the cave.) Then the men of David said to him, "This is the day of which the LORD said to you, 'Behold, I will deliver your enemy into your hand, that you may do to him as it seems good to you.'" And David arose and secretly cut off a corner of Saul's robe" (1 Sam. 24:2–4).

What do you think David cut off?

That tassel represented God's covering and protection. God had given Saul into David's hand. And when David held it up and showed it to Saul, and Saul glanced down at his now three-winged shirt, Saul knew it. He understood.

Then around 740 BC, the prophet Isaiah said:

> Have you not known?
> Have you not heard?
> The everlasting God, The LORD,
> The Creator of the ends of the earth,
> Neither faints nor is weary.
> His understanding is unsearchable.
> He gives power to the weak,
> And to those who have no might He increases strength.
> Even the youths shall faint and be weary,
> And the young men shall utterly fall,
> But those who wait on the LORD

Shall renew their strength;
They shall mount up with wings like eagles,
They shall run and not be weary,
They shall walk and not faint. (Is. 40:28–31)

Lastly, the prophet Malachi wrote this around 400 BC: "But to you who fear My name the Sun of Righteousness shall arise with healing in His wings; and you shall go out and grow fat like stall-fed calves" (Mal. 4:2).

The prophets fell silent for four hundred years. Then Jesus, the boy, appeared wearing a shirt with four corners. And Jesus the boy grew into Jesus the Messiah—*Yeshua Hamashiach*. How do we know this image, this idea, is important to Jesus? He told us, "O Jerusalem, Jerusalem, the one who kills the prophets and stones those who are sent to her! How often I wanted to gather your children together, as a hen gathers her chicks under her wings, but you were not willing!" (Matt. 23:37).

From Psalms to Isaiah to Malachi to Matthew, the same word was used for wings: *kanaph*. Now, let's go back to the street and our bleeding woman.

Here Is My Shame!

News has traveled and even the outcasts have heard the stories of Him. Something in her stirs. Hope? Desperation? Mixture of both. Being unclean, she cannot get to where He is. They won't let her. The law prohibits it. She knows she is not allowed around other people. She's been forced to live and sustain herself on the outskirts, and—if she knows anything at all—she is certainly not allowed to reach out and touch anyone. Most of all, Him. But, she doesn't care what they think.

She has come to the end of herself.

She doubles the cloth rag between her legs. Covers her head more so than usual, crowding her eyes and brow so that she might not be recognized. The crowd passes. He is in the middle. Everyone's attention is focused on Him. She files in behind. Out of sight. Then, gathering her nerve, she begins picking up her step, working closer. Weaving. Elbowing. If she is caught, she will be disciplined. Greater shame. Complete and total public embarrassment. Both bleeder and believer, she picks her way through the crowd.

Just a few steps away, the crowd encroaches. She has to elbow her way through. She knows she is in violation. If she's caught—she doesn't want to think about it. A few more steps and there He is. An arm's length. Standing next to him are several men who look like they are from Galilee. The loud, big one must be Cephas. She's heard of him too. The crowd shoves, and pushes, and tightens, and she is losing sight of this Man named Jesus of Nazareth. In desperation, she lunges, extends her reach, and grasps the corner of His garment. His shirt. The tassel. The wing. She clings. Holds tightly.

He feels the tug. Feels the power leave.

She feels it enter.

Now a certain woman had a flow of blood for twelve years, and had suffered many things from many physicians. She had spent all that she had and was no better, but rather grew worse. When she heard about Jesus, she came behind Him in the crowd and touched His garment. For she said, "If only I may touch His clothes, I shall be made well."

Immediately the fountain of her blood was dried up, and she felt in her body that she was healed of the affliction. (Mark 5:25–29)

Luke recorded it this way:

And Jesus said, "Who touched Me?"

When all denied it, Peter and those with him said, "Master, the multitudes throng and press You, and You say, 'Who touched Me?'"

But Jesus said, "Somebody touched Me, for I perceived power going out from Me." Now when the woman saw that she was not hidden, she came trembling; and falling down before Him, she declared to Him in the presence of all the people the reason she had touched Him and how she was healed immediately.

And He said to her, "Daughter, be of good cheer; your faith has made you well. Go in peace." (Luke 8:45–48)

Mark and Luke say, "Immediately." Or, "straightaway." Matthew says, "from that hour." Right then and there, her broken body is healed—and she knows it. Twelve years of pain and shame and anger and exasperation begin working their way out her soul. The tears begin to fall. She tries to back away. To escape. She is trembling. She is shattered. Her knees buckle.

Jesus pauses. Stops. She is fearful of what He might say next. Then He says it. "Who just touched Me?" She is discovered. Found out. More shame. Cast farther out. Will they stone her for so great a violation? Jesus raises His voice. "Who touched Me?" His friends, led by Peter, say, "Master, all these people? Everybody is touching You."

Jesus shakes His head. They don't get it. He is the Sun who has come with healing in His wings,[4] and somebody who both knew and believed that touched Him with intention. The Sun of Righteousness wants her brought before Him. Why? Because He fashioned her. Knit her together. He's known her pain. Has suffered with her. He saw her coming through the crowd. He knows she's been weakened by twelve years of chronic anemia so He slowed just enough so she could reach out and touch Him.

He's not finished with her. Not by a long shot.

He lifts a hand. "Somebody touched Me with intention. Power left My body." Everybody, all those big men, begin looking for the perpetrator in the crowd. The thief.

Trembling, having lost total control of her emotions, pleading on the inside that God would either have mercy on her in this moment or just strike her down, she falls to her knees. Soaks the earth with her tears. Bowing her head, hiding her eyes, she spills it. Lays it out there for the whole world to hear.

"Here is my shame!"

Her cries echo off the stone city walls. She is a woman undone. Laid bare.

Jesus, who knows her name, steps forward. He is so glad to see her. He has missed her and He has been looking forward to this moment for a long time. He chose this road because He knew it wound near her house. Because while her body is battered and torn, it's her heart that is broken. In this moment, Jesus has already healed her body. "The fountain of her blood was already dried up." He is calling her forward because He is about to heal her heart. Then, of all the words He could have spoken, He says the one singular word she needs to hear.

"Daughter."

The word echoes inside her. Dancing around her insides like a pinball until it comes to rest in that place in her gut. Where her soul lives. Down where her hope is buried.

Scripture doesn't say it, but I think Jesus reaches out and lifts her. Raises her up in front of everyone else. Hugs her. Tightly. While she weeps and smears snot on His shoulder, He welcomes this daughter back into the family. And then just so everybody knows and to ensure there's no doubt, no question, He says, "Your faith has healed you."

Somewhere in there it hits her. "I am healed! It's over. I am what I once was. What I've always longed to be." This knowingness spreads across her face. "I am a child of God!"

We're All Bleeders

Years ago, I was working on a book in Africa. I met up with some doctors who were treating women with obstetric fistulas. A condition caused in countries with limited medical care. Prior to birth, the baby gets stuck in the birth canal, dies, and in so doing tears a hole in either the bladder, the bowel, or both. After delivering a stillborn baby, the women are left with uncontrolled leakage of urine, feces, and blood. With no cure, the women eat and drink less to control the flow. Considered cursed by God, they are thrown out like lepers. Many sleep with the animals to keep warm. Suicide is common. The stench is significant. No, it's awful. I have walked among them so I am speaking from experience. The only thing worse than the smell is the shame carved into their faces. Few, if any, look you in the eyes. In colloquial language, these women are called "the bleeders."

For whatever reason, this tormented woman in the street was a bleeder.

I wonder how much time passed before she took off that diaper? How long before she tore down the laundry line, burning every last rag? In my mind, she stands alone in the street and screams at the top of her lungs, *"He called me 'Daughter'!"*

When I get to heaven, I want to find this woman and hug her neck. Her story knocks a few things loose in me, and I want to thank her. I want to thank her for her gumption. For her faith out of which she elbowed her way through a crowd that didn't want her. For despising her own shame. For, when all seemed lost, she reached out her hand and cried out to Jesus. Why, of all the saints in Scripture, do I want to find this one?

This woman believed the Word was more true than her circumstances.

Let that sink in.

"Thy word is truth" (John 17:17, KJV).

We're all bleeders. You, me, that person over there. All of us. We are draped in shame, bleeding out, and yes, our bodies need healing. But it is our hearts that are broken and we are in need of hearing one singular word. If you think this is an isolated event in the life of a woman that didn't and doesn't pertain to you, let me lead you to Matthew: "And when the men of that place recognized Him, they sent out into all that surrounding region, brought to Him all who were sick, and begged Him that they might only touch the hem of His garment. And as many as touched it were made perfectly well" (14:35–36).

The wings of His garment are here. Now. Will you reach out and grab hold?

Some days, I find myself at the end of myself. As Isaiah said, my "filthy rags" are hanging in the backyard and blowing in the wind. I am bleeding and I am broken and I am getting worse. But I've heard the stories, and He is passing by. I bathe quickly, wrap on a diaper. Elbow my way through. Cling to His shirttail. Plead to God to have mercy.

And then He calls me forth, saying the thing I need to hear. "Son. Charles. I've missed you. I was hoping you'd find Me today. I'm so glad to see you." It's around here that Jesus hugs my neck and I weep on His. Smearing snot.

"See how great a love the Father has bestowed on us, that we would be called children of God; and such we are" (1 John 3:1 NASB).

Children. That is what we are!

You and I are not disqualified by a decade of shame and pain. By nonstop blood. By stench and smell and filthy rags. We are not too dirty. We, each of us, and yes—that includes you—are welcomed in. Lifted up. Healed. Forever. From this very hour.

The question is this: While you are a bleeder, are you a believer?

Close your eyes. He chose this street. He's waited for this moment. He's walking slower. Taking His time. Chose this route because He knew He'd pass by you. The multitude is with Him, but there's a break in the crowd. He sees you behind Him. His heart leaps.

Go! Forget the diaper. You don't need it. Run fast. Don't worry what anyone else thinks. Throw elbows. Lunge. Reach out.

Cling! Cling.

Now, just listen.

Lord Jesus, I am a bleeder. And I am helpless to help me. I am bleeding both from what I've done and what's been done to me. I've tried everything and only made matters worse. Nothing I did changed my situation. I'm a mess, and I'm sorry.

Today, I bring my shame and my infirmity to You. All of it. Today I bring the truth of me and lay it bare before You. I don't want to live in hiding anymore. No more lies about the truth of me. Today I'm exposing all of me before all of You. I believe that You are who You say You are. You tell me that everyone who calls on the name of the Lord will be saved.

Will be delivered. You tell me that if I confess with my mouth and believe with my heart that You are the Savior and Redeemer of the world, and that You alone paid my penalty and died my death, then I am saved from an eternity without You and welcomed into an eternity with You. Jesus, this is both my confession and my belief, and here and now it is my proclamation.

You are Yahweh-Raphah. My Healer. Today I declare out across the stratosphere that I am Your child! That You are my God! The Son of Righteousness. And that You chose this road, this moment, this page, because You knew I'd pass by here and You have come with healing in Your wings. For me. Here today, I reach through the crowd and hold tightly to Your wings. To You alone I hold, and I am not letting You go.

In Jesus' Name, amen.

CHAPTER 3

The Chorus of the Unashamed

The crowds are massive. Some twenty miles down from Jerusalem, Jesus is walking into one of the oldest cities in the world. Jericho. Over a period of some five thousand years, something like twenty-six cities have been built here—one on top of another. Jericho sits in the cradle, or intersection, of ancient trade routes, so it's long been a hub of commerce, news, and information.

He's been here many times.

Due in large part to a primarily oral culture, Jericho is buzzing with rumors of a carpenter who can perform miracles. The blind see. The lame walk. The dead are brought back to life. The epicenter for all that buzz is the city gate. News travels from here to the far corners of the globe.

Sitting in the sand is a blind beggar. Given his infirmity, it's the best he can do. We don't know if he's ever been married or had children. The only definitives we have for certain are that his father was Timaeus, and that he lives in Jericho and sits daily by the gate.[1]

We don't know how long he's been there. We do know that his name, Bar-Timaeus, means "son of Timaeus." Or, "son of the unclean." The fact that he's known by any name at all suggests he's been around long enough for people to get sick and tired of the persistent rattling of his tin cup. He seldom bathes. Smells unpleasant. His hair is matted. Food particles caught in a greasy beard. Clothes tattered. Fingernails need clipping. Feet filthy. He's one of *them*.

His chosen location is strategic. This is storied ground. "The city of palm trees."[2] This is the very gate where Joshua, or Yeshua, the successor to Moses whose name means "Yahweh is Salvation," marched around the city and defeated an enemy with a shout. A spoken word. It is here that Joshua rescued the harlot Rahab, a defiled woman, and all her family because she hid the spies and believed "the LORD your God, He is God in heaven above and on earth beneath."[3] Given her public proclamation, Rahab "dwells in Israel to this day."[4]

Bartimaeus is blind, not deaf, so he sits by this same gate as another Yeshua comes near. It's also interesting that this city is under a curse.[5] Remember this. It matters. A lot.

He's no doubt heard about the lepers, now clean. About the lame, now dancing. About the demons, cast out. The five thousand, fed. The paralyzed man lowered through the roof, who walked out the front door. The lame man at the pool of Bethesda who picked up his mat. About the woman who bled. And he's heard about Lazarus and how he'd been in that stone tomb four days when the carpenter from Nazareth called him out. He's heard the power of Jesus' words and how He speaks even with the filthy and the defiled. And how He forgives sins.

To say Bartimaeus has been waiting for this day is a bit of an understatement.

As Jesus approaches, the noise of the crowd reaches Bartimaeus's ears. He knows they are still some way off but he can contain himself no longer. He stands and begins jumping up and down, waving his arms. "Son of David, have mercy on me!"[6] The root of this verbal proclamation is the same truth that delivered Rahab. A belief in the One True God. He shouts again. And again. And again. So much so that the crowd tells him, "Shut up! Can't you see He's busy?".

But that's the point. He can't see.

The term "Son of David" is a messianic claim. By saying it out loud, the speaker is stating for all who would listen that he or she believes the prophecies spoken by both Ezekiel and Isaiah about the Messiah coming from the line of David. Ezekiel says, "David My servant shall be king over them, and they shall all have one shepherd."[7] (At this point, King David had been dead for 385 years.) Isaiah says, "There shall come forth a Rod from the stem of Jesse, and a Branch shall grow out of his roots. The Spirit of the LORD shall rest upon Him."[8]

He might also have heard of the angel's promise to Mary, the carpenter's mother. "You will conceive in your womb and bring forth a Son, and shall call His name Jesus. He will be great, and will be called the Son of the Highest; and the Lord God will give Him the throne of His father David. And He will reign over the house of Jacob forever, and of His kingdom there will be no end."[9]

However he came to know it, this bold Messianic proclamation could get Bartimaeus killed because the Romans have their kings and don't like the competition.

They will prove this in about a week.

We know the other disciples are with Jesus because they are headed up to Jerusalem for Passover. Off to the side bounces Bartimaeus, screaming at the top of his lungs. Some in the crowd "warned him that he should be quiet."[10] As if Jesus has more important things to do. Another translation reads that they told him to "hold his peace." Which means to shut up.

Why? What is Bartimaeus thinking?

Undeterred. Unashamed.

Bartimaeus is thinking the same thing Isaiah thought when he said, "And in that day shall the deaf hear the words of the book, and the eyes of the blind shall see out of obscurity, and out of darkness. . . . Then the eyes of the blind shall be opened, and the ears of the deaf shall be unstopped."[11] And the same thing Joel thought when he said, "Whosoever shall call on the name of the LORD [Jehovah] shall be delivered."[12] And the same thing the psalmist thought when he said, "The LORD opens the eyes of the blind."[13] And the same thing John the Baptist thought when he proclaimed, "Behold! The Lamb of God who takes away the sin of the world!"[14]

Has Bartimaeus heard the story of the paralytic lying on a bed who was brought to Jesus? Has he heard that when Jesus met him, Jesus said, "Son, be of good cheer; your sins are forgiven you"?[15] Does he know that Jesus makes it a habit to eat with tax collectors and sinners?[16] Does he know that when questioned about this, Jesus responds, "Those who are well have no need of a physician, but those who are sick. But go and learn what this means: 'I desire mercy and not sacrifice.' For I did not come to call the righteous, but sinners, to repentance"?[17] Does he know the story of the woman with the issue of blood? Or how He raised the young girl from the dead?[18] Has he heard the story of the blind man at Bethsaida and how Jesus spit on his eyes and healed him?[19]

Truth is, I don't know what Bartimaeus knew. All I do know is that he is incredulous. He will not be quiet. Instead, he jumps higher. Screams louder. Waves his arms faster. Scripture says, "He cried out all the more, 'Son of David, have mercy on me!'"[20] Interestingly, the term "have mercy on us" is the Old Testament phrase for the forgiveness of sins. It means to make a payment for my debt—which is beyond my ability to pay. It's similar to the same phrase uttered by the humble tax collector who stood praying afar off and couldn't even lift his head.[21]

Undeterred. Unashamed. Bartimaeus shed his precious dignity for one chance at freedom. One chance to see clearly. In my mind's eye, it is here that Bartimaeus comes unglued.

Just as He purposefully intersected with the woman with the issue of blood, Jesus has waited for this day. He chose this gate. He's been waiting for this moment. I'd like to think Jesus rounded the corner, grinned, and thought, *My brother Bartimaeus, I'm coming for you.*

The sound of Bartimaeus's voice reaches Jesus' ear, and He stops walking—or "stood still"—and commands that he be brought to Him. The crowd quickly changes its disposition, "Come on. Hurry. He's calling you."

Luke and Mark record this interaction but only Mark states that

Bartimaeus threw aside his garment. Or cast it away.[22] That strikes me. He's going before the Messiah. The King of glory. The God of angel armies. The very Son of God. The Sun of Righteousness with healing in His wings. The One who called out Lazarus when he was four days dead and stinking. And yet Bartimaeus goes forward with no pretension. Nothing to cover his filth. Nothing to dress him up. If anything, he undresses.

This tells me a lot about the desperation in his heart.

He elbows his way—blindly—through the crowd. People are ushering him forward. "Hurry, He's calling you. He's very busy." Bartimaeus bounces forward like a pinball. Feet shuffling. Steps uncertain. Note the context: Jesus is on His way to Jerusalem. To the cross. Where He is going to redeem His people from the curse. He knows this. He is walking straight toward His own execution, and yet for some illogical and inexplicable reason He stops to talk with the blind, smelly beggar living under a curse.

This picture shakes some stuff loose in me. It rattles my foundation. Why? Because there is a piece of my heart that needs to know that I—with all of my filth and all that should disqualify me—matter to the God of the universe. The God who made me. That I'm worth His time when He has better things to do.

Bartimaeus makes it to Jesus' feet, but the only way he can know if he's reached a man that meets the description of Jesus is to "look" with his hands. To "read" Him with his fingers. In my mind, Bartimaeus is taller than Jesus. No, I can't say why, but I think when he reaches Jesus, he reaches out like Helen Keller at the Alabama pump house and feels Jesus' arms and face, eyes and nose, and then stands back, jaw open, realizing he'd just touched the Bright Morning Star. Living water.

Emmanuel. Yeshua. "Yahweh is Salvation." Joshua is once again standing outside Jericho, tearing down walls. Bartimaeus crumbles like a sack of potatoes. Why do I think this? If he really believed Jesus was the Son of David, he'd hit his knees. We all would.

Jesus, surrounded by a growing crowd, looks down, sort of leaning over, the smile growing on His face. Maybe He inches closer. Beneath the hovering crowd. "What do you want Me to do for you?" Jesus knows Bartimaeus is blind, but Jesus is not asking for His own benefit. And He's not really asking for Bartimaeus's benefit. He's asking for the benefit of all those people milling around. The folks with their fingers pressed to their lips or their hands in their pockets. The doubters and the haters and the debaters. Jesus wants to encourage them. Challenge them. Wake them up. Why? Because His time is growing short, and this slumbering crowd is waiting for Him to show up while the blind idiot dancing along the wall is declaring before the world that He has arrived.

Big, big difference.

Bartimaeus—forehead on Jesus' feet and lips inches from the dirt—says, "Rabboni, I want to see." That word *Rabboni* is a term of endearment. By saying it, Bartimaeus is telling Jesus, "My heart is with Yours."

Can you see the smile on Jesus' face? He knows what's about to happen. He loves this stuff. He's living for this right here. It's one of the reasons He's here. Bear in mind that another "—aeus" also lives in Jericho. A man small in stature—Zacchaeus. Does he witness this exchange with Bartimaeus? I don't know, but we do read in Luke 19 that Jesus enters Jericho, passes through, and then He looks up into the Sycamore tree. "Zacchaeus come down. Salvation has come." I tend to believe that Zacchaeus was in the crowd and witnessed the healing of Bartimaeus, but I can't prove it.

Back to the two men in the street.

Blind, smelly, begging, cloakless Bartimaeus—whose eyes are fogged over, clouded white, thick with cataracts—is piled up before the promised Messiah. Hands trembling. Maybe Jesus puts His hands on Bartimaeus' shoulders. Maybe He holds his hands in His own. I don't know but I do know that Jesus fashioned Bartimaeus together before the foundation of the world. He made his very eyes. His lens. His optic nerve. Science tells us the human eye has over two million working parts. The Carpenter standing in the street fashioned those very eyes from the dust of the earth before the foundations of the earth were laid.[23] That should mess with your brain.

Jesus has been looking forward to this moment. To set it aright. He's missed Bartimaeus.

Jesus kneels, places His fingertips on Bartimaeus' chin, and lifts his face. Then, speaking softly, He says: "Receive your sight; your faith has made you well."[24] The same words He spoke to the woman with the issue of blood.[25]

When I read that, I feel aftershocks rippling out through eternity.

Faith has made you well? Which part? His jumping up and down? His screaming at the top off his lungs? His casting away his cloak? His calling on the name of the Lord? I don't know. I just know that faith does stuff. Faith cries out. Faith acts. "For whatever is not from faith is sin."[26] And "without faith it is impossible to please Him."[27] And here in the streets of Jericho, God is pleased by Bartimaeus.

For the second time in his life, the breath of God falls on the clay that is Bartimaeus. Those words enter his ears, swim around his mind for a millisecond, and then the curtain is lifted. Technicolor, 3D, and 4K pour in. His mind is flooded with light and shape and color and depth and people and smiles and sky and clouds and perception and Bam! IMAX! 20–20! The face of Jesus.

Think about it! Bartimaeus knows the color of Jesus' eyes. You thought he was screaming at the top of his lungs before? Listen to him now.

And watch where this occurs. Near the city gates of Jericho. Why? Jesus is sending a message.

To the world.

He is standing in a "cursed city," speaking to an unclean man living under a curse. It's a good description of me. Of you.

Remember the message Jesus sent to John the Baptist some months prior: "The blind see and the lame walk."[28] Among other things, giving sight to the blind is the signature of the Messiah. And where does He sign His name? In the dirt at the Jericho gate on the road to Jerusalem.

Jesus is headed to the cross. He knows this. He is putting not only the physical world, but the spiritual world on notice. If one act served to stir the crowds into a frenzy, greater than the crowds at the World Cup, it was Jesus healing blind Bartimaeus. When He spoke to Bartimaeus, He drove a stake in the ground—"I'm coming. And I'm bringing the kingdom of God with me."

From there, Jesus walks through Jericho, through dinner with Zacchaeus, and up to Jerusalem, into the City of the Great King, where countless throngs throw their cloaks on the ground before the colt He is riding—where even the stones cry out (Luke 19:40). People are exuberant and everyone is screaming at the top of their lungs. Jesus walks from a cursed man in cursed city to a hill where the blood of Jesus redeems us "from the curse of the law" and "cleanses us from all sin." I think this is intentional (Gal. 3:13; 1 John 1:7).

Mark tells us that Bartimaeus "followed Jesus" (10:52). This is conjecture on my part, but I think Bartimaeus followed Him through that next week. I think he was in the crowd, staring at Jesus on Calvary. I think Bartimaeus saw Jesus crucified.

How could he not?

Scripture records one final interesting occurrence on that street near Jericho. Without being told, without being prompted, when Bartimaeus declared for all the naysayers, "I can see!" everyone spontaneously "gave praise to God" (Luke 18:43).

Collectively, all those doubters in the crowd, all those people with their fingers pressed to their lips, the same people who were shushing Bartimaeus and telling him to shut up, were jumping up and down, screaming at the top of their lungs. "Son of David! Son of David!" That's what happens when the blind see.

Belief was the decision. Faith the action. Praise the effect. Glory the echo through eternity—which has just rippled onto this page, and oddly enough, through your eyes.

I wonder if Jesus has just sent you a message from the Jericho gate.

Lord, Help Us to See

Several years ago, when I really read this story for the first time, it pierced me. While Lasik had freed me of glasses, I was and am still blind to myself. To my own stuff. My selfishness. Pride. Criticism. Judgment of others. Unforgiveness. The stuff about me that is not like Jesus and continues to break His heart.

It was in that instant that the Lord allowed me to see me. Albeit briefly.

My takeaway then and now is that I'm not habitually self-aware. I'm even less aware of my effect on others. More often than not, I'm not. Can't see the forest. You can ask Christy. Ask my kids. My friends. Knowing this about myself, I wanted to rattle my own chain and create something to remind myself. A marker. So, I had a bracelet made. It's like an ID bracelet except it doesn't have my name on it because I know my name. On one side, it reads: "Jesus, Son of David, have mercy on me." And on the back, the part that touches my skin, it reads: "Rabbi, I want to see."

It's become a lifelong prayer. Sometimes daily.

When I get to heaven, I plan to hug several necks, and one of them will be Bartimaeus. I want to thank him for his life. For his public proclamation. For voicing it out loud. For driving a stake in the ground and holding fast the confession of his faith. For shedding his dignity long enough to stand with the unashamed.

I pray I have the stuff inside to do the same.

With that in mind, I am taking my place along the city wall, joining my voice with the town crier—my friend, Bartimaeus—and the rest of the chorus of the unashamed and screaming at the top of my lungs that this matchless and magnificent Jesus, this awesome God of battle-axe and spear, this God of angel armies who commands his angels concerning me and mine, this Messiah, this Emmanuel, this prophecy fulfilled, this faithful One, this Truth, this Holy God who upholds all things by the Word of His power, this lover of my soul, this Alpha and Omega, this

Beginning and the End, this Brightness of the Father's glory, this firstborn from among the dead, this King of all kings, this King of glory, this Great I Am, this Son of David loves nothing more than getting down in the dirt with a blind, smelly, defiled beggar like me. That for some mind-blowing reason, He has time for me. That I matter. A lot.

There is a part of my heart that doesn't even know what to do with this revelation. What I do know is that one day I will see Him face to face—and I'll know the color of His eyes.

Jesus—Yeshua—Your name means "Salvation." You are the Lord God, You are God in heaven above and on the earth beneath. I join my voice with those who proclaim who You are. You give sight to the blind—like me. I've been blind a long time. Blind to me. Blind to who You are. Blind to my affect and effect on others. Blind to the damage and pain I cause. Blind to my arrogance and indifference. Blind to my sin.

Rabbi, I want to see. I want to see You. I want to see me the way You do. Want to see this world through Your eyes without the color and prejudice of my own lens. Jesus, I want to see. Please come touch the eyes of my heart and give me better-than-perfect vision. Yeshua, have mercy on a sinner like me and give me eyes to see You. Like Bartimaeus, I'm throwing away my cloak and I'm following You. My King.

Lastly, Lord, I know that when You left Jericho, You went up to Jerusalem where You wrapped Yourself in the sin of the world and allowed us to crucify You—the spotless lamb. Please Lord, give me eyes to see what Your blood does for me—and forgive me for being so blind that I have to ask this at all.

In Jesus' Name, amen.

CHAPTER 4

What Are You Taking
to the Grave?

I t's early. The sun is just up. Jesus is in the temple. Teaching. People are
sitting close. Packed in like sardines.

There's a commotion at the door. Loud voices. Several Pharisees
drag in a woman. Caught in the act of sleeping with a man—not her husband. Adultery. The woman is completely naked. The man, mind you, is
nowhere to be found.

They throw her down. "We caught her!" They laugh, letting their
eyes walk up and down her body. She wraps her arms around her knees,
trying to conceal herself with long hair. The scribes continue. One is toss-
ing a stone in the air like a baseball. They are baiting Jesus. Their voices
are ripe with cynicism. "Moses commands us to stone her." They have no
interest in His answer. Only their trap.

Jesus stoops down and writes in the dirt.

There's no way He can escape acknowledging so great a sin. They
know they have Him. They continue pestering Him.

Jesus continues to doodle.*

Finally, He glances at the woman, then at the men, and slowly steps

---

* I, Charles, am a writer. It's both how I think and what I do. I'd love to know what Jesus wrote.

aside. Almost as if to say, "Oh, I'm sorry, I didn't mean to interrupt you. You were saying?" Then He speaks, essentialy saying, "He who is without sin among you, be my guest. Throw the first stone."[1]

Mic drop.

It's quiet several minutes. The men file out. The temple empties. Jesus is left alone, in the temple, with a naked woman. No, I am not saying Jesus sinned in any way. Don't read that into this. He was tempted as we were, yet sinless.[2] I'm saying Jesus was and is comfortable in His house in whatever condition people come to Him.

Pause here.

Let's Deal with It

While these men and this woman may be focused on her sin and nakedness, He's not. Not in the least bit. He knows her body better than she does. He made her. Every fold, curve, and wrinkle. He's focused on her healing. The pompous men in that room are no less naked than she. Their clothing conceals nothing. Least of all their secret sins. Jesus sees everything. He knows their thoughts. Moses said, "You have set our iniquities before You, our secret sins in the light of Your countenance."[3]

You think this woman on her knees in the temple had time to get cleaned up? These self-righteous hypocrites had snatched her out of bed, and men make women messy. She was soaked in the evidence of her sin. But notice who's not there. The man.

Typical.

Sexual sin plagues many of us. Most, if not all, are guilty. Myself included. Don't think because I'm writing this book that I'm somehow better than you. If you knew my thoughts, you'd know better. Our corporate and individual sin is evident in that we don't talk about it and don't confess it. Instead we wrap ourselves in the silent shame that shackles us to it. It's an evil cycle.

Maybe you're thinking: But why is this such a big deal? Why dedicate this space to that topic? Why dredge up something that can be so painful?

Because purity was a big deal to Jesus. Later in His ministry, Jesus would tell these same men:

> Woe to you . . . ! For you cleanse the outside of the cup and dish, but inside they are full of extortion and self-indulgence. Blind Pharisee, first cleanse the inside of the cup and dish, that the outside of them may be clean also.
>
> Woe to you, scribes and Pharisees, hypocrites! For you are like whitewashed tombs which indeed appear beautiful outwardly, but inside are full of dead men's bones and all uncleanness. Even so you also outwardly appear righteous to men, but inside you are full of hypocrisy and lawlessness. (Matt. 23:25–28)

Don't think Jesus is only speaking to them. He is speaking to you and me. Here and now.

Jesus is concerned with our holiness not because He enjoys browbeating us or holding us under His thumb, but because He is taking us to His Father, and our holiness is a prerequisite to entering the Father's presence. Always has been. For those of you looking at your past and thinking, *No way*, or, *This might take some time*, or, *I don't stand a chance*, or, *I really don't feel like dragging this up out of my past*, let me speak the remedy to your heart: "The blood of Jesus Christ His Son cleanses us from all sin" (1 John 1:7).

Dealing with sexual sin comes from a desire for purity. For holiness. To confess it is the natural outgrowth of a response to the invitation into His presence. Remember that. This whole conversation is in response to an invitation. The enemy has twisted this.

So, let's deal with it.

To do so, we need to leave this naked and broken child of God with Jesus in the temple and back up. About a thousand years. To a man experienced in sexual sin.

You Are the Man!

He is facedown. Nose to the stone. He's torn his clothes. Hasn't eaten in a week. By now, the whole town knows. David, the great and conquering king of Israel, is a lying, scheming, conniving, backstabbing, murdering adulterer. Some of his own men are calling for his head on a platter.

By the hand of Samuel, he was anointed king. He defeated Goliath. Then the Philistines. Took Saul's place. Brought the ark back into the city of the Great King. But last spring, when the kings had gone to war, he had not. Instead, he walked the rooftops of his palace and spied on bathing women. One in particular. In my book, walking the rooftops staring down at Bathsheba was simply akin to a porn addiction. Why do I say this? Look at the fruit—what it cost him.

Now, soaked in his own tears, he's paying the price. A steep one.

Next door, his new wife presses the newborn to her bosom, but he will not latch on. Failure to thrive.

Last week, Nathan the prophet came to see him. Told him a story about two men in a city. One rich. One poor. And how the rich man took from the poor man the one ewe lamb which he had bought and nourished, which had grown up with his children. That had eaten of his own food and drunk from his own cup and lay in his bosom; it was like a daughter to him. David took the bait, hook, line, and sinker. He was incensed. He feigned indignation. He said, "As the LORD lives, the man who has done this shall surely die! And he shall restore fourfold for the lamb, because he did this thing and because he had no pity." Then Nathan said to David, "You are the man!"[4]

I imagine Nathan poked David in the chest with his index finger when he said that. And I imagine it stung. Deeply.

The depth of the sting had much to do with David's knowledge of God's law. Much of which he'd memorized. David would later write in Psalms, "Your word I have hidden in my heart, that I might not sin against You" (Ps. 119:11).

Three times, through the mouth of Moses, God had declared for His people to be holy:

1. "For I am the LORD your God. You shall therefore consecrate your-selves, and you shall be holy. . . . For I am the LORD who brings you up out of the land of Egypt, to be your God. You shall therefore be holy, for I am holy" (Lev. 11:44–45).
2. "Speak to all the congregation of the children of Israel, and say to them: 'You shall be holy, for I the LORD your God am holy" (Lev. 19:2).
3. "Consecrate yourselves therefore, and be holy, for I am the LORD your God" (Lev. 20:7).

David knows his sin is not holiness. It's anything but. He also knows, "The man who commits adultery with another man's wife, he who com-mits adultery with his neighbor's wife, the adulterer and the adulteress, shall surely be put to death."[5] The fact that David was not put to death for his adultery with Bathsheba is simply the unmerited mercy of God.

We also know something about David's heart which has been true from his youth. David has a heart that chases after God. After Saul—the first king of Israel—sinned, Samuel was told by God to choose a king for the nation of Israel from one of the eight sons of Jesse. While each was paraded in front of him, and Samuel was struggling with picking the right one, God told him, "Do not look at his appearance or at his physical stat-ure, because I have refused him. For the LORD does not see as man sees; for man looks at the outward appearance, but the LORD looks at the heart."[6]

The Lord has been looking at David's heart a long time.

Behind him, David hears weeping. Gut-emptying sadness. Reluctantly, his servants approach. They are afraid to speak. Finally, they muster the courage. "Your son is dead."

He peels himself off the floor and wipes his face on his sleeve. Over his shoulder, Bathsheba's cries echo off the stone walls. Cradling the limp body of her dead son, she is inconsolable.

David knows that he alone is guilty. He alone is to blame.

He bathes, anoints himself, changes his clothes, and then Scripture records an amazing thing. It says David walked into the Lord's house . . . and worshiped.

Really?

Break that down for me.

David's heart has been rent down the middle. He is shredded. He shirked his duty, stole a man's wife, killed the man, and betrayed the Lord. But, even having done all this, he is still a man after God's own heart. So, David climbs Mount Zion and walks into the tent. The Lord's house. As close as he can legally get to the very presence of the Lord Almighty. And somewhere in there, he worships. The Hebrew word translated "worship" means to depress, prostrate (especially reflexive, in homage to royalty or God). To bow yourself down. Crouch. Fall down (flat). Humbly beseech. Stoop.

Somewhere in there David fell on his face.

Wash Me

The other day, I was out running and thinking about this whole transaction. About David not going to war. Spying on Bathsheba. Ordering the murder of Uriah. The whole messy, terrible, evil thing. More than that, I wanted to know what he said. When he walked into the tent and his nose hit the floor, what'd he say? How'd that conversation go down?

A few minutes passed. And then I had a thought.

Psalm 51.

I knew David wrote Psalm 51 after he sinned with Bathsheba. But when? When in that time frame of this whole mess did he write it? Months after? The next year? I don't think so. I think it was a good bit sooner. I think David heard Bathsheba weeping, heard the words, "Your son is dead," and then bathed, clothed himself, stumbled into that tent, fell on his face, and wrote Psalm 51 through hand-trembling tears. No, I can't prove it, but look at the words and ask yourself what is the mental and emotional condition of the writer:

> Have mercy upon me, O God,
> According to Your lovingkindness;

According to the multitude of Your tender mercies,
Blot out my transgressions.
Wash me thoroughly from my iniquity,
And cleanse me from my sin.

For I acknowledge my transgressions,
And my sin is always before me.
Against You, You only, have I sinned,
And done this evil in Your sight—
That You may be found just when You speak,
And blameless when You judge.

Behold, I was brought forth in iniquity,
And in sin my mother conceived me.
Behold, You desire truth in the inward parts,
And in the hidden part You will make me to know wisdom.

Purge me with hyssop, and I shall be clean;
Wash me, and I shall be whiter than snow.
Make me hear joy and gladness,
That the bones You have broken may rejoice.
Hide Your face from my sins,
And blot out all my iniquities.

Create in me a clean heart, O God,
And renew a steadfast spirit within me.
Do not cast me away from Your presence,
And do not take Your Holy Spirit from me.

Restore to me the joy of Your salvation,
And uphold me by Your generous Spirit.
Then I will teach transgressors Your ways,
And sinners shall be converted to You.

Deliver me from the guilt of bloodshed, O God,
The God of my salvation,
And my tongue shall sing aloud of Your righteousness.
O Lord, open my lips,
And my mouth shall show forth Your praise.
For You do not desire sacrifice, or else I would give it;
You do not delight in burnt offering.
The sacrifices of God are a broken spirit,
A broken and a contrite heart—
These, O God, You will not despise.

Do good in Your good pleasure to Zion;
Build the walls of Jerusalem.
Then You shall be pleased with the sacrifices of righteousness,
With burnt offering and whole burnt offering;
Then they shall offer bulls on Your altar. (Psalm 51:1–19)

Books have been written about this psalm. Let me comment on just one word: *wash*. The Hebrew word translated here as "wash" is not the one used for the cleaning of dishes in water, but the washing of clothes by beating and pounding. Like folks do with rugs strung on lines.

Did God answer David's prayer? I believe so. The Bible says that Psalm 30 was written for the dedication of the house of David, but I wonder it if doesn't have its roots in this Psalm 51 moment.

Look at what Psalm 30 says:

O Lord my God, I cried out to You,
And You healed me.
O Lord, You brought my soul up from the grave;
You have kept me alive, that I should not go down to the pit. . . .
For His anger is but for a moment,
His favor is for life;
Weeping may endure for a night,

> But joy comes in the morning. . . .
> You have turned for me my mourning into dancing;
> You have put off my sackcloth and clothed me with gladness.
> (vv. 2–3, 5, 11)

For me, the roots of Psalm 30 lie in the soil of Psalm 51. That's my opinion. Until I know for certain, I am left with the picture of King David—a wretched, black-hearted sinner like me who even at his worst climbed Mount Zion, walked into the tent, fell facedown, and raised his hands to worship. And God, who is faithful, whose mercy is everlasting, who stretched out the heavens with His Word, who told the edge of the sea where to start and stop, who hung ten trillion stars, met him right there. In that muck and mire. That tearful, wrecked, bloodied-hands-raised sinner is a picture of both repentance and worship.

If that's not enough, here's the part that gets me. Four words. At the very beginning of Psalm 51. Go back and read it. No, before the first verse. The words, "To the Chief Musician." Let that sink in. David, King of Israel, defeater of the Philistines, the one who cut off Goliath's head with Goliath's own sword, who brought the ark back into the City of David dancing with all his might and wearing nothing but a loin cloth, who told Michal, "I will be even more undignified than this" (2 Sam. 6:22)—this great King mandated that what we call Psalm 51 be used as corporate prayer and praise in the temple. Translation? He added it to the hymnal. Then printed millions of copies and sprayed them across the globe.

When Scripture says David "was a man after God's own heart," Psalm 51 is exhibit A before the jury.

If you read further, you'll see that David never escaped the consequences of his sin. The sword never left his house. He paid a steep penalty. And what David dabbled in, Solomon made a profession, proving the exponential grip of generational sin. But here we are, three thousand years later, and that shepherd boy with a stringed instrument is still leading us in praise before his God and King. He is leading my boys. Me. You.

The command to repent was the first recorded public statement made in the ministries of John the Baptist. Jesus. Peter. Paul. And in John's letter of Revelation, God commands repentance from five of the seven churches. Repentance may be taboo in today's culture as we bathe ourselves in the half-truth of the gospel of uber grace, but despite what is popular and what makes people feel good, repentance is still the foundation of authenticity with the Father. Without it there is no intimacy. No deliverance. David said, "Deliver me from the guilt of bloodshed" (Ps. 51:14). He doesn't get to ask that without having first repented. It's the prerequisite. Step one.

When I was younger and I heard the word *repent*, I'd think about some Bible-thumping preacher spewing fire and brimstone, or some dude at a football game with rainbow hair and a sign. Maybe a billboard on the interstate. But I would do well not to allow the messenger to dull the message. God told the Israelites, "If My people who are called by My name will humble themselves, and pray and seek My face, and turn from their wicked ways, then I will hear from heaven, and will forgive their sin and heal their land" (2 Chron. 7:14). His hearing of us, and His healing of our land, begins and ends with our humbling, praying, seeking, and turning. In short, our repentance. It's why the sentence starts with "If." It's conditional. Given that, the question becomes, do we meet the condition?

When Moses lifted up the serpent in the wilderness, the Lord required the Israelites to publicly walk forward and look up: admit, acknowledge, and confess. *That* is repentance. Same applies today. When we refuse, we make a mockery of the cross. Don't miss this. If you skip repentance, you are thumbing your nose at the Savior with holes in His hands and feet and blood dripping off His toes.

The Truth Will Set Us Free

What's the closet you want to keep closed? Locked? Dark? Be honest. What's the thing you're planning on taking to the grave? Yes, I think highly of David for his kingliness and his life as warrior, but my deep admiration and great affection for him comes in the picture of the broken-hearted and contrite man who climbed the mount, fell on his face, raised bloody hands to a spotless King, and emptied himself in repentance.

But the story doesn't end there. When he walked out, he handed that written confession to the worship leader and said, "Sing this. Before everyone." It was as if he walked down into his basement with a news crew to the hole where he hid the bodies, violently tore open the doors, and screamed with a bullhorn, "This is the truth of me! The stuff I don't want you to know." I think the reason David had the courage to do this is because he knew he couldn't tell the Lord anything the Lord didn't already know. David's sin wasn't news to God. And David's deliverance came when he refused to stay silent.

We have an enemy who prowls around like a roaring lion, and he likes it when we try to keep things quiet about our sin. He is fist pumping over your and my silence. His plan is to stuff our sin in dark closets where the doors are triple locked. Lightbulb burned out. Power cut.

So, who knows what you hide in your closet? Have you led anyone into your basement where you hide the bodies?

I meet with a group of guys on Wednesday nights. Have for over a decade. Every so often, we try to do this. With each other. Sometimes corporately. Sometimes individually. We admit things like porn, lust, adultery, self-love, anger, hatred. We have a pretty long list. And when we do this, we are on our faces. Nose to the mat. We do this out of obedience to our King. In worship. Because His lovingkindness is better than life. Because better is one day in His courts than a thousand elsewhere. And because we're sick and tired of putting on the mask of the fraud that we are all so good at wearing.*

So, is this model of repentance relevant on this side of the cross? Is it really that big of a deal?

This is Paul, speaking to the church in Corinth:

---

* I also do this with Christy. And no, that's not fun. And no, I don't do it enough.

Now the body is not for sexual immorality but for the Lord, and the Lord for the body. And God both raised up the Lord and will also raise us up by His power.

Do you not know that your bodies are members of Christ? Shall I then take the members of Christ and make them members of a harlot? Certainly not! Or do you not know that he who is joined to a harlot is one body with her? For "the two," He says, "shall become one flesh." But he who is joined to the Lord is one spirit with Him.

Flee sexual immorality. Every sin that a man does is outside the body, but he who commits sexual immorality sins against his own body. Or do you not know that your body is the temple of the Holy Spirit who is in you, whom you have from God, and you are not your own? For you were bought at a price; therefore glorify God in your body and in your spirit, which are God's (1 Cor. 6:13–20).

A couple of things stand out to me. First, "flee." We have authority over principalities and powers, and yet we are told to flee sexual immorality. It means turn and run. Don't pass go. Don't collect $200.

Second, our bodies are temples of the Holy Spirit. I believe this with my whole heart, but do I treat my body as God's dwelling place? The place where He has deposited His Spirit?

No.

Do I want to?

Yes. With all of me.

When I turn to the Lord and ask Him how, He points me to His son Peter:

Therefore gird up the loins of your mind, be sober, and rest your hope fully upon the grace that is to be brought to you at the revelation of Jesus Christ; as obedient children, not conforming yourselves to the former lusts, as in your ignorance; but as He who called you is holy, you also be holy in all your conduct, because it is written, "Be holy, for I am holy." (1 Peter 1:13–16)

If you study that phrase "gird up," it means to wrap your clothes tightly around your abdomen so you can run and not be tripped up.

Around the Martin house, this is our prayer of repentance: "Create in me a clean heart. Renew a steadfast spirit within me. Cast me not from Your presence and take not your Holy Spirit from me." Our boys can quote this. It's dear to me. To us. It's our desire for purity before our Father. As our boys have grown into manhood and started dating, my conversations with them have focused on their bodies as temples of the Holy Spirit. That the girl in their car is someone's daughter and, one day, will be someone's wife and mom. And one of the most precious gifts they can each give their future wife is the gift of themselves having never been given to another.

As recently as last week, when one of them was on a date, I texted him, "Is purity somewhere near the front of your thinking?" My son knows I'm fighting for his heart. Through years of conversation, I've earned that with him.

The text was quick in returning. "Yes sir."

Have they and I made mistakes? Certainly. Does that disqualify them in any way from pursuing purity? Absolutely not.

Lastly, and I'm almost afraid to be this honest, but since my wedding day, I have declared out loud to the Lord and often in prayer with my wife and with the men who know my heart that my heart is for my wife. That my desire is for her. And that means everything you think it means. That she satisfies me completely, and I desire no other. Period.

I know the enemy will attack me because I am typing these words. But I've been saying them for twenty-five years, and it continues to be true. My desire is for my wife. And it's more so today than when I married her—and I didn't think that possible when her father gave me her hand. The enemy's attack here is relentless and he prowls around like a roaring lion looking for someone to devour, but I'd like to introduce my enemy to the Lion of Judah.

My desire is for my wife.

What About Your Basement?

One last time. Who have you led into your basement? Will you? Why not? Jesus said, "the truth shall make you free" (John 8:32). Not your new year's resolution. Not your behavior modification. Not your therapist. Not your "just say no" campaign. Not your seven habits or your twelve steps or the purposes that drive you. I'm not knocking those things. But, let's don't complicate it. Peel away the fluff. Reduce it to the nugget. What truth about you are you afraid to speak? If you're anything like me or the guys on Wednesday night, you will not want to do this. But if you skip this, then what do you do with Psalm 51?

This is the Lord speaking through the prophet Isaiah: "But on this one will I look: On him who is poor and of a contrite spirit, And who trembles at My word" (66:2).

You and I are enslaved by the stuff we keep dark. Silent. It holds us in chains until we turn on the light. Until we speak the truth of it. Words such as, "Guys, I drink a bottle of vodka a week." "A six-pack a night. Twelve-pack even." "I look at porn. Daily." "I had an affair. More than once." "I'm arrogant. All the time." "I'm a sex addict." "My phone is full of stuff I don't want my wife and kids to know about." "I think I'm better than others. Constantly." "I had an abortion." "I'm involved in some pretty sick sexual sin." "I've stolen a lot of money from my business partner."

I don't care who you are or what you've done, there is no chain, no matter how thick, that the truth won't cut.

Not only will the truth set you free, it is *the only thing* that will set you free.

Period.

When the Word says, "Confess your sins to one another" (James 5:16, NASB), He is not kidding. And He's not saying this for His benefit. It's for ours. Our backs were not designed to carry all the stuff we shove in our backpacks. His, on the other hand. . . .

Don't think I've somehow got a handle on this. You think I want to write this? There is a part of me right this very second whispering, "Control-Alt-Delete." But that whisper is not Jesus. That's my enemy. Same old tactic.

Scripture also says, "The goodness of God leads [us] to repentance" (Rom. 2:4). David knew this. I've seen this in my own life. In others. He's a good God. We can trust Him. We loved Him because He first loved us. Let that sink in too. He loved us when we were way past unlovable. "While we were still sinners, Christ died for us" (Rom. 5:8). Right now, if you've got some stuff in your basement, chances are good the enemy is whispering in your ear, "Don't do it. Just let it go. Start over. Take that stuff to the grave. Nobody will ever know and if you do tell folks, it'll only hurt some people. Better to just keep your mouth shut." There is no biblical model for this. Nowhere in Scripture can this silence be justified. On the contrary: "If we confess our sins, He is faithful and just to forgive us our sins and to cleanse us from all unrighteousness" (1 John 1:9).

If you're a dad, and you have a son, take him out for a cheeseburger and ask him how he's doing. No, I mean really. Like, with masturbation. Porn. Sex. Girls. Wrap your arm around his shoulder and wrap him in a mantle of identity as your son, not a garment of shame. Risk a tough conversation and walk him into freedom. And don't just do it once. You don't have to make it a habit, but check in with him every few months.

As I and the guys in our group have done this over the years, as we've allowed each other into our basements and opened all the closets, several guys—old and young, doesn't matter—have muttered through deep shame that they are wrestling with addictive masturbation. Can't stop. More than once a day. I've seen this enough to decide I'm not shrugging my shoulders at it. Why? Because our struggle is not against flesh and blood. That means there's something hanging on here we can't see. Something we need to fight—and we've been given authority to cast it out in Matthew 10.

Shame is heavy when it comes to sexual sin. Some guys want to pray individually with me. With no one else listening. Others in a group setting. Where everyone is listening. It doesn't matter to me. Either way, it sounds something like this: "Lord, this is my sin. . . ." And then he calls it by name and summarizes its hold on him. When, where, etc. Whenever I've stood with men praying this prayer out across the air in front of us, I've had a strong sense that we are standing on holy ground. I've also noticed that the more specific the prayer, the greater the freedom and release. Nope, it's not fun, but would you risk a few moments of embarrassment for a lifetime of freedom?

Then when he's finished praying, I place my hand on his shoulder, call the sin by its name, and cast it out. Call me crazy, but I've seen it work. "Spirit of pornography (*porneuo*), come out in the name of Jesus." "Spirit of masturbation, come out in the name of Jesus." "Spirit of lust. . . ." "Spirit of adultery. . . ." Interestingly, in more than one case, the guy I'm praying for has told me he's felt something come out his hands. I know how it sounds, but we are several years down the road and the behavior is gone. Addiction broken. We can either be embarrassed and silent or we can go to war for one another.

Sin No More

Back to the naked woman in the temple. By now, the cool air has dried the sweat on her skin. Giving rise to goose bumps. Jesus asks, "Woman, where are those accusers of yours? Has no one condemned you?" She shakes her head but won't look up. She's still too ashamed to make eye contact. I think Jesus lifts her chin. He would want her to see His face. To know the absence of shame. His acceptance. His great love. He shakes His head. "Neither do I condemn you; go and sin no more."[7]

Notice, Jesus doesn't say she wasn't in sin. Her sin was obvious. It's dripping down her leg. He tells her go and sin no more.

When Jesus sat at dinner with the Pharisees, and the woman "who was a sinner," probably a prostitute, knelt at His feet, washed His feet with her tears and dried them with her hair, and then anointed His feet with oil that cost a year's wages, the beautiful smell of that fragrance filled the room. Everyone smelled it. In truth, that fragrance was probably a tool of her trade, formerly used to attract suitors or cover up the scent of the last. But there in the room with Jesus, on her knees in confession and repentance, that scent became the smell of her purity and holiness. You and I are that woman, and our prayers are likewise a sweet fragrance that fills the room and rises up to His throne where He is pleased by you and me.

This matters to God. A lot. In Scripture, Egypt always represents sin and bondage. Slavery. Man's choice and not God's design. And yet, it is and always has been God's design to bring His people up and out of Egypt. To transform a nation of slaves into a kingdom of priests. It mattered to such an extent that when entering the Holy of Holies, the place where God's presence dwelt, the priests were required to wear a headband that read, "Holiness to the Lord." That meant when the priest bowed and walked in, the first thing that broke the plane of the room was God's written declaration of holiness. What would it look like for you and me to walk out of Egypt as slaves and into His presence as priests? To look at the inside of our cups and clean out the filth?

I know this is not easy. Some of you may accuse me of having written one more finger-pointing, guilt-focused conversation on sexual sin. That's not my heart—either for me or you. Why have I chosen this approach? Because I've seen this work. A lot. I've seen the fruit of this in a lot of men. If you're miffed by my approach, or wishing for some other call for purity, forgive me. I don't want to be one more wound, and I know these wounds are some of the, if not the, most tender. As much as I know my own heart, I am fighting for your freedom and, sometimes, for people who have been in chains such a long time they're uncertain who's the jailer and who's trying to break them out until they're outside the prison with sunlight on their faces.

You want to be a man after God's own heart? Want to know intimacy with the Father? Want to be delivered from the chains that enslave you? Want to render a spine-shattering defeat to the enemy that torments you? Want to know the childlike purity of forgiveness received? Want to sit in the Holy of Holies and know the tender fellowship of the Father? Want to feel His breath on your face? Tremble with me.

Walk down into your basement. Take somebody with you. Somebody you can trust with your heart. Then rip the doors off the hinges, turn on all the lights—and name your sins. One by one.

That prayer sounds like what's below. (And in my experience, it's better if you do this closer to the floor. Like on your knees—or face.)

Jesus, this hurts and I am ashamed, but I want to confess my sexual sin. [Now, do it. One by one. Hold nothing back. Name it all. If you question whether you ought to mention that one, the answer is yes. Definitely. Take your time. Don't skip any.]

Father, having confessed, I repent. For each act. Forgive me. I don't want this anymore. Come lift this sin off of and out of me. You made my body to be Your temple, and I have defiled both mine and others. Father, I am so sorry. Create in me a clean heart and renew a steadfast spirit within me. Cast me not from Your presence and take not Your Holy Spirit from me.

Lord, You made me a sexual person, but I've perverted myself. I want my sexual relationship with my husband/wife to be what You intend. I present my body as a living sacrifice to You. I consecrate my body, my sexual nature, to You. Lord, where I have harmed others by my words, thoughts, or deeds with regard to sex, I ask Your and their forgiveness.

Father, would You please cut me free—forever—from every unholy soul connection which was created through any and all of these acts. Cut my soul free from theirs and cut their souls free from any tether to mine. Father, I bless them in the name of Jesus. I give back to them the pieces of their souls that I've held in prison and ask You to give me back mine. Holy Spirit please fill me and heal me in every place vacated by that tie. And please fill every person now free of me and return to them the parts of them that I stole.

Lord Jesus, I thank You for offering me complete and total forgiveness. That You have wrapped me in a spotless robe of righteousness, and that when You introduce me to Your Father, He sees His spotless Son and not my filthy rags. That said, Lord, I forgive all those who harmed me sexually or took anything from me. I release them from any anger or judgment. I tear up any IOU.

Father, I break every spiritual, sexual, emotional bond with anyone whom I have ever had one and place the cross of Jesus Christ between me and that sin, declaring that You made a public spectacle of the author of that sin when You died on the cross (Col. 2:15), that You render my enemy powerless (Heb. 2), and that it was for this reason that You were made manifest so that You might destroy the works of the devil (1 John 3:8). Lord, if I've made an unholy agreements, I break them now in the name of Jesus.

Father, I ask that You would heal my relationship with my wife/ husband, completely. I consecrate our sexual relationship to You to be what You determined. I invite You into our marriage and into our bed, and I declare and decree that my desire is only for my wife/husband. Period. I desire no one else. He/she satisfies me completely, and my eyes and heart desire no other. I thank You, Father, that my desire is for my spouse alone.

Lastly Lord, I speak Your word over me; I declare it and agree with it—that it is Your blood that cleanses me from all unrighteousness. That You make all things new. That by one sacrifice, You have perfected forever those of us who are being sanctified. That You, Jesus Christ, are the end of the law for righteousness to everyone who believes. That I have been crucified with You and that it's no longer I who live but You who live in and through me, and the life I now live I live by faith in You who gave Yourself for me. And that by Your blood and in Your name, my old man is dead. That You have declared me holy and when You present me to Your Father, He, because of You, sees me washed white as snow.

In Jesus' Name, amen.

If you prayed this, a lot just happened. Don't leave this place. Thank Him.

Get on your face and worship.

Oftentimes, the confessions and repentance of sin may take a few times. Meaning, the layers of sin are more like an onion than a banana. I'd encourage you to pray this several times. How many? As many as it takes. Having said that, let me be real clear—you're not praying this several times to obtain forgiveness. You received your forgiveness the first time you prayed. It stuck then. Slate wiped clean. I'm encouraging you to stick with it and keep praying it because, in my experience, these sins are deep and they cling to us. So it can take multiple times for the reality of this grace to travel what I call the infinite migration—the distance from my head to my heart.

CHAPTER 5

Talk to the Hand—JCILOA

J esus has brought them north. Onto the green slopes of the snow-capped peak of Mount Hermon, some twenty-five miles north of the sea of Galilee.* He'd been praying alone at a high place, as was His custom. Now He's brought the disciples to Caesarea Philippi.

This is significant because the population of Caesarea Philippi is not Jewish, and Jews don't come here. They walk around it. The very city was built up and around ancient Syrian temples dedicated to Baal worship. A cave near where the disciples stand was said to be the birthplace of the Greek god Pan, hence the town's original name—Panias. The cave was cut into the side of a high cliff, at the base of which is a crystal-clear spring which forms the easternmost source of the Jordan River. Stone steps lead to a large, white marble temple which grows out from the side of the cliff. Off to one side sits a large, elaborately carved stone altar several feet tall and several feet square. Large enough to hold human bodies.

The locals call this place "the Gates of Hell." With good reason. Parents sacrifice their children here. A lot. Wishing to please the gods, they throw their babies in a bubbling, rushing spring that soon disappears below earth allowing them a few seconds to run to the river's next surface

---

* We don't know where in Caesarea Philippi they stood, but we can triangulate from three sources: Mark 8:27, Matthew 16:13, and Luke 9:18.

appearance some yards distant. If they see red, the gods have rejected the sacrifice. If no red, then they've appeased the gods. Sacrifice accepted.

The altar is stained from human sacrifice and the residue of the sex of temple priests. Along the edges, slave hands had carved a blood groove. Like a mote. Priests would capture the blood and drink it as ceremony in their orgies.

To the Hebrews—the children of the promise—this is defiled, unholy, and cursed ground. It's the worst place any of them could imagine standing, and it is arguable that none of them have ever been here.

Standing contrasted against this backdrop of idol worship, Jesus asks an amazing question, "Who do men say that I, the Son of Man, am?"[1] This is no small question. In fact, it is *the* question.

Subtle voices echo out of the twelve. "Elijah." "John the Baptist." "Jeremiah." "One of the prophets."

Oddly, the self-appointed spokesperson of the group, Peter, is silent. In fact, Peter is scratching his head. A wrinkle sits between his eyes. He can't for the life of him understand why they are standing where they are standing.

Finally, Jesus turns to him. "Who do you say that I am?"

This time Peter is not silent. He steps forward. "You are the Christ, the Son of the living God."[2]

These are no small words Peter is speaking. They are earth-shattering, stratosphere-rocking, mind-blowing words. Peter, a Jew who could probably recite by memory much of what we would call the first five books of the Bible along with much of the prophets, Psalms, and Proverbs, is saying that this man Jesus is the answer to more than six hundred Old Testament prophecies regarding the promised Messiah. That He is the long-awaited Christ. The Savior of the world.

These words could get him killed.

Later in his life, they will.

Jesus nods. They are starting to get it.

Jesus answered and said to him, "Blessed are you, Simon Bar-Jonah, for flesh and blood has not revealed this to you, but My Father who is in heaven. And I also say to you that you are Peter, and on this rock I will build My church, and the gates of Hades shall not prevail against it. And I will give you the keys of the kingdom of heaven, and whatever you bind on earth will be bound in heaven, and whatever you loose on earth will be loosed in heaven."[3]

There is a lot here. Notice this: nothing about their current environment, circumstances, or culture agrees with Peter. Absolutely nothing. In fact, everything around him is shouting the exact opposite. Peter is a man standing on a rock, alone in "hell," making his confession.

My Enemy: Resignation

The other day Christy and I were sitting in the kitchen, talking about some stuff we've been actively praying over for a long time. Fifteen years. Maybe longer. On the surface, we've seen little change. If any. She's tired. Worn down. Her Hope, capital H and her Faith, capital F, have been dinged. The look on her face spoke both frustration and hurt. "Why doesn't God do something?" I get it. Part of me was tired too.

But when she said it, something in me got pretty irritated pretty quick. Not at her. I love her. She's my precious, magnificent wife. Christy is not the problem. The problem is an unwanted guest who, over time, has crept into our house—into our language and our thinking. He is silent, insidious, crafty, and evil. Pretty good at tiptoeing. He's been whispering lies a long, long time. And he has a name. And when Christy spoke those why-doesn't-God-do-something-words, I heard his name.

It's Resignation.

Resignation is an ever-so-slight-yet-continual chipping away. His goal is to take the Rock of our Salvation, our Chief Cornerstone, our Everest, and over time, chip away at it until he hands us a river pebble about the size of the cap on a tube of Chapstick. He does this by calling into question the truths spoken in Scripture.

If you want an example of how this works, you'll find a pretty good one when satan tempted Jesus in Matthew 4. Listen to satan's words: "If You are the Son of God. . . ." The implication was that He, Jesus, is *not* the Son of God, or that He is somehow limited in His power. Jesus responded with Deuteronomy 8:3: "Man shall not live by bread alone, but by every word that proceeds from the mouth of God." The underlying message there is, "your words don't proceed from my Father's mouth, therefore, by definition, they are lies." Then satan took Jesus up to the pinnacle of the temple. Again he said, "If You are the Son of God. . . ." Jesus responded with, "Again it is written. . . ." and quoted Psalm 91. Not getting anywhere, satan said, "All these things I will give you. . . ." In response, Jesus quoted Deuteronomy 6.

That's when Scripture records an amazing thing: "Then the devil left Him" (Matt. 4:11).

Jesus countered lies with truth, and the liar left. End of story.

At its root, Resignation spins a lie that says our enemy is stronger than our King. Period.

We see this throughout Scripture. One of my favorite examples is when Joshua and Caleb returned from a land God has already given them with ten of their friends. Upon entering the tent, the ten shook their heads, "We can't win. It's a land populated by giants."[4] Their words struck fear into the hearts of the people. What they said was true—the land was populated by giants. Resignation always tells half-truths. Problem was, the God of angel armies; the God of battle-axe and spear; the God of Abraham, Isaac, and Jacob had promised them this land, that He would never leave nor forsake them, and that all they needed do was step foot on the land. Just cross the Jordan. Set out. Dip their toes in the river. In the sight of great and growing opposition, Caleb, God bless his soul, "because he has a different spirit," stood up on a table and said, "We are well able to overcome them. They will be our prey!" Notice again, nothing about his circumstances agreed with his statement.

Caleb knew the Israelites were a chosen people called to walk into a promised land. I believe you and I are a chosen people called to walk into a land of promises, and the giants we face today are the ones screaming in our ears.

Resignation is one of those voices, and he would have us resign ourselves to an impending defeat before battle is ever waged. He uses whispers like, "It's no use." "I didn't succeed before." "Nothing's changed." "Why should I expect a different outcome?" Or the classic resignation lie, "It's inevitable."

The only thing inevitable is that Jesus is coming back shining like the sun, and satan is forever defeated. Period. End of story. For me, when Jesus does come back to judge the quick and the dead and the sons of man, I don't want Him to find me resigned to the lies of the enemy.

You Get to Choose

I'm not preaching a prosperity gospel that life is all roses, lollipops, and puppy dogs. I know better. I've got a few scars to remind me. When I forget, Paul reminds me that "through many tribulations we must enter the kingdom of God" (Acts 14:22, NASB) and "we are hard-pressed on every side, yet not crushed" (2 Cor. 4:8). Our enemy would like us to focus our attention on the difficult stuff, our circumstances, and in so doing make some underhanded statement about the nature of our King. Truth is, our hardship does not determine His character or His love for us, and it doesn't make Him any less King or any less capable or any less good or any less in love with us. The choice is ours. We get to choose whether to fix our eyes on the giants—or the King on the throne. Do we focus on the white marble temples of Baal or the Messiah who rules in the midst of His enemies?

Peter and the eleven are staring down at a world which has chosen allegiance to satan and not God Most High. In contrast to Peter's confession, the world around them has chosen to proclaim, "Baal is more powerful than the God of Abraham, Isaac, and Jacob, therefore we will worship Baal." The unspoken or unwritten assumption is this: "We know this to be true because if the God of Israel were more powerful, He'd have done something about it by now."

The enemy always uses this lie to perfection. It is sneaky and slippery and finds its way into our thinking before we ever know it's there.

Think of it like propane. Propane, in its natural state, is an odorless gas. It's also explosive, which makes it extremely dangerous. In order to help consumers detect leaks, propane companies add a touch of sulfur to give it that rotten-egg smell.

Suppose for a moment you came home and smelled rotten eggs. In every room. What would you do? You probably wouldn't light a match. I hope you would open all the windows, turn on all your fans, and create a whirlwind in your house to blow that stuff out. Then, you'd find the source and cap it. Or remove it altogether.

Here's my point: I am trying to help you detect leaks in your faith. Resignation is dangerous and exceedingly evil. This thing in your hands—this book—is me adding sulfur to any whispers of resignation you might be hearing right now. I want you to realize it stinks. I want you to set up those fans and blow it out, and then I want you to cap the source for good.

How do you cap it? When Jesus sensed the same rotten smell, He capped the source with Deuteronomy 8, Psalm 91, and Deuteronomy 6. In Psalm 1:1–2, King David said, "Blessed is the man who walks not in the counsel of the ungodly . . . but his delight is in the law of the LORD, and in His law he meditates day and night." I think one of the reasons this is true is because the guy with his face in the Word has, by definition, the tools in his hand to cap the gas leak in his house. To remove the tank buried in his yard.

Let me give you another example. Imagine the son of a king inherited a hundred thousand acres. Choice land. Flowing with every good thing. Soon after, a conquered punk moved in next door. One night, with no warning, this sniveling worm relocated his good neighbor's boundary lines. Quietly acquiring a couple hundred acres. This occurred night after night. Each boundary move is a small infraction, but over the months, the loss mounts. Pretty soon, the king's son is living on a postage stamp. Unwilling to deal with the conflict of maintaining his own

WHAT IF IT'S TRUE?

boundary line, the king's son says, "No big deal, he can have it. I don't want to start a fuss. I'm a Christian and I'm supposed to love my neighbor. Do stuff for the least of these. Give him the shirt off my back and all that. I'll just reflect the person and character of Jesus." This response is called "land for peace" and it never works.

First, the encounter we find ourselves in is not a fuss. It's a fight. Stop right there.

You're in a fight.

And you're in one whether you agree that you are or not. If not, then explain Psalm 144 to me. Or Ephesians 6. Or 2 Corinthians 10. Or Psalm 91. Or Jesus' words on binding the strong man (Matt 12:29; Mark 3:27).

Second, the punk next door doesn't want part of your land. He wants it all. And once he has it, he wants to post your head on a stake outside his new city wall.

Third, there is a difference between laying down your life and being a resigned, passive doormat allowing people to walk over you because you're a spiritual wuss.

And our enemy can take you and me from warrior to wuss through our agreement with Resignation.

The enemy doesn't want land, and he's not interested in coexistence. Instead, he wants total domination. Wipe you off the planet. Eradicate your scent. Your unwillingness to engage him, your silence, is his greatest weapon.

I once said, "Indifference is the curse of this age." I still believe that, but I'd like to add to it. Indifference and resignation are two sides of the same coin. And they have real, impacting, and long-lasting ramifications.

What if Moses had resigned himself to defeat when he reached the Red Sea with a few million Hebrews in tow? What if David had resigned himself like his brothers before Goliath? Can you imagine Jesus walking up to the cross, looking into the future—to right here—shrugging His shoulders, and saying, "What's the use?" Don't skip over this. Jesus was all human and all God. What if the all-human part had stood at the foot of the cross and said, "They hadn't gotten the message since Adam.

They're not about to start now. Might as well just save Myself the discomfort and let them burn"?

Where Have You Given In?

So here's the question: Where have you resigned? Seriously. Take a walk around your spiritual house and sniff the air. Coal miners used to take canaries down into the shafts with them because they were more sensitive to gas and lack of oxygen than the miners. When the canary quit singing, the miners would surface and think things over.

Resignation is an attack against our faith. It often comes under the cover of night. Or hardship. It's death by a thousand cuts, and the fruit is always fear. Resignation is the bully in the swimming pool holding your head under the water. He's the pudgy guy on the playground who just pushed you down and stole your lunch money. Trust me, he'll be back tomorrow.

Defeating Resignation is not something we can think our way out of. Our thinking got us into this mess. Resignation is an Ephesians 6 spirit without a body. It's a 2 Corinthians 10 argument "that exalts itself against the knowledge of God." A stronghold. A speculation. A fortress in our mind. And it's time we bring it crumbling down.

Moses wanted to resign himself. He asked, "Who am I to go before Pharaoh?" God responds. "I will be with you." Moses stutters, "Well, what will I say?" God sizes him up. "What's that in your hand?"

Your weapon against the enemy is the rod in your hand. Use it to beat back Resignation. Drive it out of your house. Your heart. What's your rod? It's God's Word. His promises are yes and amen, and they are true and they will not return void. They will accomplish the purposes for which He sent them. Counter every lie with two promises of God. Make bookends.

"But, I don't know what His Word says." Then learn it.

"But, it's always been tough for me to get into. I don't really—" Stop. You've mastered the iPhone, Facebook, Instagram, Fat Chat, and online fantasy football drafts. Man up. Crack the cover and let the Word wash you from the inside out. We're sheep. He's our shepherd.. Trust me, He speaks our language.

Psalm 50:15 says, "Call upon Me in the day of trouble; I will deliver you, and you shall glorify Me."

So call.

And for those of you like Christy who have faithfully been praying for something a long time, I'm reminded of Anna. A prophetess "of a great age . . . a widow of about eighty-four years, who did not depart from the temple, but served God with fastings and prayers night and day" (Luke 2:36–37). How long had she been there praying? I don't know, but the Lord is building people of faith in a day and age when many are growing weak. And, without faith it's impossible to please Him. His Word says, "The just shall live by faith" (Rom. 1:17), and, "I have tested you in the furnace of affliction" (Isa. 48:10). Our sovereign, loving king is allowing us to know affliction because it is, as Peter says, creating in us something more valuable than gold: our faith (1 Pet. 1:6–7).

Be honest. Take an inventory. Look at your relationships. Look at your relationship with the Lord. Look at your relationship with the Word. You'll see it most evident there. Where are you living in resignation? Where have you given land for peace? Where have you resigned yourself to the lie that our enemy is more powerful than our King?

Do you really want to live that way?

Right now, a dude named Resignation is sitting in your house with his feet on the coffee table, stuffing his face with your popcorn, with this smug look on his face. He's lighting one cigarette with the glow-plug end of the other. Remote in hand, he's switching between Freddy Krueger and *Poltergeist*. "Dude . . . I got a right to be here. You left the door open. Plus, you don't really believe all that dribble about Jesus' victory. If He could do anything, He would have. You can fight all you want but what use is it? I own you. Bring me a beer."

That right there is an argument "that exalts itself against the knowledge of God" (2 Cor. 10:5).

Make a Stand

I have this thing I do in the mornings. (In truth, not every day.) After we get the kids to school, I take my Bible and walk outside with my coffee. Then I walk around my backyard reading God's Word back to Him. Usually Psalms. I do this to remind me, not Him. He knows what it says. When I've done that, I set my Bible down and I walk, praying, with my hands in the air. Doing so humbles me before God. It's how I walk into the throne room. Job said he rose early and made sacrifice to the Lord. Sounds good to me. Count me in. My neighbors might think I'm crazy. That's okay. Probably won't be the worst thing they think about me.

The thing this walk does for me is take my eyes off the waves threatening to swamp the boat and put them on the Savior who beckons me, "Come." Walking around my yard with my hands up draws me into His presence. It opens Revelation 4 to me, and I'm invited in with all the heavenly host to the courts of my King where the train of His robe fills every square inch of the room, where a river flows from His throne, where hundreds of millions of angels sing continually, where the sound of His voice sounds like Niagara, where—you get the point.

When Resignation opens its pitiful, squeaking mouth, I want the words on my lips to be: Lord, "Let Your lovingkindness and Your truth continually preserve me" (Ps. 40:11). Greater is He that is in me than he that is in the world (1 John 4:4).

I will not leave the throne room only to stare back at what's staring me in the face, scratch my head, and say, "You know what, Jesus, I don't think You've got what it takes, big guy. We're getting our butts kicked down here. Why don't You do something about it?" What I will say is this: His ways are higher than mine. I won't question Him. But I will trust Him. "Blessed is that man who makes the LORD his trust, and does not respect the proud, nor such as turn aside to lies" (Ps. 40:4).

So back to Christy and me. We were stuck. Quagmire. Christy said to me with heavy shoulders, "We've been praying about that so long. Why doesn't God do anything about it? It never changes. Never gets any better."

When Christy spoke those words of hopelessness and faithlessness, they hurt my heart. I teared up. I had literally just walked in the door from the backyard where I'd been doing laps. I said, "Honey, what you're saying doesn't come from Jesus. It's a lie from the pit of hell. I know, I've been sitting at His feet. And if you'd been there, if you had a right vision of Him, the words you just spoke would break your heart too. We need to take our eyes off our circumstances and put them on Him."

Note: I am not fighting my wife here. I am fighting something that wants her head on a platter.

Sometimes, when I say things like this, Christy rolls her eyes at me. Like, lighten up. Take a load off. Life is not always warfare. Granted, I could do a better job of laughing with my wife and kids. Guilty. But, lighten up? I think not. My job is to tend my garden. Sanctify my wife by the daily washing of the word. Be the priest of my house. Stand between her and the lies that threaten to choke her out. That's the place where I'm to lay down my life. Not when my punk neighbor wants my inheritance. My wife is a precious and magnificent daughter of the King. It should not surprise us that she has an enemy, because she reflects the Father. I'm fighting for her heart, and my enemy *cannot* have it.*

To Christy's great credit, she saw it. Despite being beat down, she mustered some gumption and grit and, while we didn't really feel all that spiritual or holy, we prayed right there at the kitchen table. The two of us, knocking on the doors of heaven. I would like to tell you that "poof," everything changed in an instant. It did not. Weeks passed. Nothing visibly changed save one thing—our view. Our perspective. The expectation in our hearts. And our unity around that. That changed a lot.

Here's what I know: I hate Resignation with a deep hatred. It can go to hell and stay there. It will not rob my wife of her magnificent heart or my children or me. Yes, it is a constant battle; yes, I get tired; yes, sometimes I feel like someone has just kicked me in the teeth; yes, writing

---

* If I've set myself up as the hero of this story, I'm not. Jesus is. I'm just—as much as I know my own heart—trying to fight for my wife because she's worth it.

this I am fully aware that I don't do this enough, that I let my guard down. But He gives us strength in the day of battle (Josh. 14:11; Isa. 40:29; 2 Sam. 22:40; Ps. 18:32). And "He delivered me because He delighted in me" (Ps. 18:19).

I don't know why God does what He does, and I don't understand His timetable, but I will not let my inability to understand the One who breathed me into existence cause me to believe for one second that He has some unspoken limitation or that our enemy is greater or stronger than my King or that He is somehow powerless to effect change in our lives.

The writer of Hebrews says, "Without faith it is impossible to please Him" (Heb. 11:6). Resignation requires no faith. If you're having trouble making a distinction between the voices in your head, let me put it this way: there are two sources of supernatural power on this earth. Jesus and satan. If what you're hearing does not come from Jesus, then, by definition, it does come from satan.

Read the great faith hall of fame in Hebrews 11. Read all the stuff those folks like you and me did with a little bit of faith. They "subdued kingdoms . . . quenched the violence of fire, escaped the edge of the sword . . . became valiant in battle, turned to flight the armies of the aliens. Women received their dead raised to life again" (Heb. 11:33–35). Resignation played no part in this.

JCILOA: Jesus Christ Is Lord of All

Sometime after my prayer with Christy, I was having a tough day writing. So I dug the label printer out of a drawer and printed a phrase to stick on the face of my computer. I wanted my confession to agree with Peter's. It's here right now as I write this. Staring at me. It reads, "Jesus Christ is Lord of All." Anything less than that proclamation, any reduction, any slighting, any chipping away, is resignation.

Since then, anytime the whisper of resignation has entered the conversation in my head, I have decided to respond with, "Jesus Christ is Lord of All." To put "this rock" between me and my enemy. Drive it like a stake in the ground.

Without Jesus, I'm a black-hearted, scum-sucking sinner, literally damned to hell and fully deserving of seeing my head on a stake. But with Him, I'm a child of the King. Heir to the throne. Clothed in a robe He gave me. "See how great a love the Father has bestowed on us, that we would be called children of God; and such we are" (1 John 3:1, NASB). I'm a child of the One who spoke Everest into existence, who dug the Grand Canyon with the words of His mouth, who set the planets in motion, who, just this morning, told the sun to wake up but stand at a safe distance, who fashioned you and me out of the dust then pressed His lips to ours and breathed life into us. And His name is Jesus and He is Lord of All. End of Story.

If your house was full of gas and you didn't know it, how would you rather I get your attention? Would you like a gentle, snively, little tug on the shirt sleeve, "Excuse me, um. . . ." Or would you prefer I use a bullhorn: "Hey, your house is filled with propane!" We're talking about your and my life. This matters. Jesus came to give us life to the full, and yet most of us have accepted life to the least—life with boundaries set by our enemy. And we've resigned ourselves not to challenge him for fear that what he's telling us might come true.

Resignation reduces. Resignation retreats.

Faith endures. Faith stands.

Both are a choice.

There is the danger in this anti-resignation rah-rah that you hear me saying, "Just try harder, little camper. Buck up." Nope. Not saying that. "When I am weak, He is strong." "He gives me strength in the day of battle." What I am saying is that you get to choose to be resigned or step foot in the river. To pick up five smooth stones. To stand on the table and shout, "We are well able. . . ."

Back to Jesus with His arm around Peter staring down at "the gates of hell." When Jesus says, "Upon this rock I will build my church; and the gates of hell shall not prevail against it" (Matt. 16:18 KJV)—what is the rock?

Yes, Peter was a rock and one of my heroes, but I don't think Jesus was just talking about Peter. I think He was talking about the foundational bedrock of the fact that He, Jesus, is Lord of all and that nothing they have, can, or ever will encounter—no matter how evil—can stand against the reality that Jesus Christ Is Lord Of All.

The rock upon which Jesus built His church was Peter's confession. Jesus echoed this to John on the Island of Patmos following His resurrection: "They overcame him [satan] by the blood of the Lamb and the word of their testimony" (Rev. 12:11). Maybe a better translation than "testimony" would be "confession."

Travel to Galilee today, into the region of Caesarea Philippi, and you'll find that pagan temple crumbled. Nothing but scattered rocks. What was once thriving is now long-since dead. Here's the truth: you and I sit at a crossroads where resignation meets faith. We get to choose. The cross placed that decision in our laps. Laid it out on a silver platter. To think less denigrates the cross. Listen to the writer of Hebrews:

> For if we sin willfully after we have received the knowledge of the truth, there no longer remains a sacrifice for sins, but a certain fearful expectation of judgment, and fiery indignation which will devour the adversaries. Anyone who has rejected Moses' law dies without mercy on the testimony of two or three witnesses. Of how much worse punishment, do you suppose, will he be thought worthy who has trampled the Son of God underfoot, counted the blood of the covenant by which he was sanctified a common thing, and insulted the Spirit of grace? For we know Him who said, "Vengeance is Mine, I will repay," says the Lord. And again, "The LORD will judge His people." It is a fearful thing to fall into the hands of the living God. (10:26–31)

See those words, "no longer remains a sacrifice," and "fiery indignation which will devour," and the most painful, "trampled the Son of God underfoot"? Resignation tramples. It has "insulted the Spirit of grace." We tend to skip scriptures we either don't understand or don't like, so don't miss that last one: "It is a fearful thing to fall into the hands of the living God."

To remind myself, I had a bracelet made. Actually I ordered a couple thousand. They're crimson red, rubber, and stretchy, easy enough to order online, and printed with the letters, "JCILOA."

If I really believed—like Peter—that Jesus Christ is Lord of all, I would approach conversations a little differently. When someone looked at me and shrugged, bubbling disbelief and doubt, saying, "Charles, you can't . . ."

Before they finished the sentence, I'd be shaking my head and showing them my bracelet: "Stop! Jesus Christ is Lord of all."

"Hah. Funny. Nice gimmick. But let's be serious a minute, you won't ever . . ."

"My Redeemer lives. Jesus Christ is Lord of all" (Job 19:25).

"Charles, saying a bunch of mumbo jumbo changes nothing. Look at history . . ."

"My God is able to make all grace abound to me, and He will supply all my needs according to His riches in glory, and He gives good gifts to His children, and He speaks that which is not as though it is, and He will never leave me nor forsake me, and—Jesus Christ is Lord of all" (2 Cor. 9:8; Phil. 4:19; Matt. 7:11; Rom. 4:17; Deut. 31:6).

"Okay, but you've been praying this a long time, and He's never done anything about it."

"Thank God we're that much closer to an answer. The testing of our faith produces perseverance. Perseverance, character. Character, hope. And hope does not disappoint—Jesus Christ is Lord of all" (James 1:3; Rom. 5:3–5).

"You'll never find . . ."

"Get off my couch. Get out of my house. Jesus Christ is Lord of all."

"Don't set such high expectations. It'll never get . . ."

"Be quiet. Jesus Christ is Lord of all" (Luke 4:35).

"But, God didn't . . ."

"Get behind me. Jesus Christ is Lord of all" (Matt. 16:23).

"But, God hasn't . . ."

"Jesus Christ is Lord of all."

"But He was absent when you needed Him . . ."

"I know that Jesus can do all things and no purpose of His can be withheld from Him. Jesus Christ is Lord of all" (Job 42:2).

"Charles, you are feeding people false hope. You should know better. How can you prove any of this?"

"I'm not offering proof. If you have proof, then you don't need faith. The name of the Lord is a strong tower, the righteous run to it and are safe. Jesus Christ is Lord of all!" (Pr. 18:10).

How Will You Respond?

Just this moment, Jesus has sidled up next to you. The two of you are staring down at your circumstances. Things look bad. In fact, they're horrible. Jesus wraps His arm around you. His eyes are gentle. Brimming with hope. You can feel His breath on your face. He leans in and asks you, "Who do *you* say that I am?"

How will you respond?

Six days after this event at Caesarea Philippi, in the very next chapter in our Bibles, Jesus led Peter, James, and John up on a high mountain. While I can't prove it, I believe this occurred on Mount Hermon given its proximity. We read in Matthew 17 and Mark 9 that, inexplicably and out of nowhere, Elijah and Moses appeared. Then, before their very eyes, Jesus was transfigured. His face shone as bright as the sun, His clothes became white, a bright cloud overshadowed them, and a voice sounded from the depths of the cloud, "This is My beloved Son, in whom I am well pleased. Hear Him!" (Matt. 9:5).

Why does this matter? Because the confession came before the revelation. Peter made His claim about who he believed Jesus to be *before* he saw the evidence that proved he was correct.*

So, you want the revelation? Want to see Jesus shine like the sun in all His glory? Then make the confession: "Jesus Christ is Lord of all."

Lord Jesus, I confess that I have given in to resignation. I have listened to his lies and given in to his claims on more than one occasion. Actually, I've done it a lot. Today, even. I've bowed my heart to his babbling rather than surrender it singularly to Your truth. I'm sorry. Please forgive me. I've been giving more air time to the enemy's blue sky than Your Word. I want to take back that ground. I want to hold up a stop-sign hand and declare, "Jesus Christ is Lord of all!" I want to believe Your word more deeply.

So, Holy Spirit, come make it so. Take the Words of my King and sow them deeply in my soul. Say to my soul, "Jesus Christ is Lord of all." Lay the axe to the root of any lie to the contrary. Any whisper. If there are doors in me, in my life, in what I do, or in my soul, that leave room for his pitiful voice to squeak through, close them now in the name of Jesus. I give You my physical ears and my spiritual ears. Sanctify them. When the enemy whispers lies, give me Your Scripture to speak out loud and proclaim over my circumstances. No, I am not falling prey to the name-it-and-claim-it false prosperity gospel, but I am saying with my actions that if it was good enough for You, it's more than good enough for me.

And if I and my spouse have fallen into this pattern in our lives where we've grown tired, given in, thrown in the towel—Lord, I'm so sorry. I don't want to live that way. So, come in like a flood. Renew our strength. Let rivers of flowing water bubble up in, through, and out of us. Let us speak Your promises over and to each other. Let me be used by

---

* We also see this pattern when John baptized Jesus. John confessed, "Behold the Lamb of God, who takes away the sin of the world." Following his confession, he baptized Jesus. And only then did God the Father speak from heaven, "This is My beloved Son, in whom I am well pleased." Confession first. Revelation second.

You to build up and encourage my spouse and those You've given me to encourage and love. Let me be like Caleb and declare across the ages, "We are well able!"

Father, touch my lips with the burning coal and set Your words on my tongue. I say to the spirit of resignation sitting on my couch, "Get out in the name of Jesus! Get out of my heart. Get out of my wife's/husband's heart. Get out of my children's hearts. You are a liar from the pit of hell. You're a defeated punk. Shut up!"

Lord Jesus, I give You, and You alone, permission to speak what is true to me. Tear down any and all strongholds in my mind that would argue with You. Please seal me—all of me—and grow me into a man/woman who will stand beneath Your word and declare, "Jesus Christ is Lord of all!"

In Jesus' Name, amen.

CHAPTER 6

What's That You're Carrying?

N ight has fallen. Darker than usual. Turning cool. Jesus has just finished the Passover dinner. Given His betrayer permission. Watched
Judas walk out. Washed His disciples' feet. Taken the cup.

The end has come.

The unsuspecting eleven follow Him through the quiet city streets.
Flying high on the heels of the triumphal entry, they are giddy with what
might be. The conquering Son of David soon to sit on His rightful throne.
Somewhere a candle flickers. Then another. They descend the hill of the
City of David, and Jesus approaches the Brook Kidron. Higher on the
hill above them, the clear spring bubbles up out of the earth, circulates
through the grounds of the temple, and fills the ceremonial cleansing
pools. From there it washes out the blood of the morning and evening
sacrifices before it descends the hill.

When it rolls beneath their feet, it smells of death.

Jesus stands on the stone bridge that crosses the brook. Glancing over
His shoulder. The smell fills His nostrils. Fitting.

He enters the Garden. Gethsemane. This is the place where the olives
are crushed. Where the oil is poured out. This too is fitting.

A thousand years before Jesus, Absalom, King David's son—his own
flesh and blood—betrayed him. Turned on him. David was forced to flee
the city. "All the country wept with a loud voice, and all the people crossed

over . . . the Brook Kidron . . . toward the way of the wilderness." Seven verses later, it reads, "So David went up by the Ascent of the Mount of Olives, and wept as he went up; and he had his head covered and went barefoot. And all the people who were with him covered their heads and went up, weeping."[1]

One of the things I love about Scripture is that nothing, and I do mean nothing, is wasted. David did what Jesus is doing. Took the same path.

When David fled from Absalom, he wrote, "But you, O LORD, are a shield for me, my glory and the One who lifts up my head."[2] Did Jesus whisper this to Himself as He crossed the brook? I like to think so. I'm also pretty sure He was thinking about Psalm 22. Why? Because He is about to live it. Line by line.

Jesus enters the garden with the eleven. Stomachs full of food and eyelids heavy with wine. "Sit here while I go and pray over there."[3] He took with Him Peter and the two sons of Zebedee. "My soul is exceedingly sorrowful, even to death. Stay here and watch with Me."[4] Despite His pleas, they sleep. Snoring. Smiling smugly. Remembering how all the city laid down their cloaks and sang, "Hosanna to the Son of David! Blessed is He who comes in the name of the LORD!"[5] A song so loud that had they been silent, even the stones would cry out.[6] The eleven are dreaming of their conquering King. A political solution. But their dreams will not come true.

Jesus separates Himself. Prays. He knows the end from the beginning. He is in agony. Listen to King David again: "O My God, I cry in the daytime, but You do not hear; and in the night season, and am not silent."[7]

Jesus returns to His friends only to find them crashed out. Oblivious. Drool running out the corners of their mouths. He shakes their shoulders. They momentarily rally. "Oh . . . so sorry, Lord. You were saying?" He returns to His prayers. Behind Him, they return to their snoring. Face to the ground, Jesus' blood vessels burst and He sweats blood. His heart knows, before His ears can hear them. "Be not far from Me, for trouble is near; for there is none to help."[8]

In the distance, the air is filled with the sound and flickering firelight of soldiers. "Rise, let us be going. See, My betrayer is at hand."[9] The stone bridge carries the echoes of swords and shields and whispers. Judas, thirty pieces of silver richer, emerges, smirking. He slithers forward. Grabs the Master, and then presses his lips to the face of Jesus.

The seal of betrayal. Of the King of the universe. Of the "heir of all things, through whom also He made the worlds . . . being the brightness of His glory and the express image of His person, and upholding all things by the word of His power."[10] Don't miss this: that very same Jesus—the Ancient of Days—who fashioned Judas out of the dust of the earth and then pressed His lips to Judas's face and breathed in the breath of life, the *ruach*, has just allowed the created to betray the Creator.

What kind of a king does this?

The prophets had said this was coming. None better than Isaiah:

Who has believed our report?
And to whom has the arm of the LORD been revealed?
For He shall grow up before Him as a tender plant,
And as a root out of dry ground.
He has no form or comeliness;
And when we see Him,
There is no beauty that we should desire Him.
He is despised and rejected by men,
A Man of sorrows and acquainted with grief.
And we hid, as it were, our faces from Him;
He was despised, and we did not esteem Him.

Surely He has borne our griefs
And carried our sorrows;
Yet we esteemed Him stricken,
Smitten by God, and afflicted.
But He was wounded for our transgressions,
He was bruised for our iniquities;
The chastisement for our peace was upon Him,
And by His stripes we are healed.
All we like sheep have gone astray;

We have turned, every one, to his own way;
And the LORD has laid on Him the iniquity of us all.

He was oppressed and He was afflicted,
Yet He opened not His mouth;
He was led as a lamb to the slaughter,
And as a sheep before its shearers is silent,
So He opened not His mouth.
He was taken from prison and from judgment,
And who will declare His generation?
For He was cut off from the land of the living;
For the transgressions of My people He was stricken.
And they made His grave with the wicked—
But with the rich at His death,
Because He had done no violence,
Nor was any deceit in His mouth.

Yet it pleased the LORD to bruise Him;
He has put Him to grief.
When You make His soul an offering for sin,
He shall see His seed, He shall prolong His days,
And the pleasure of the LORD shall prosper in His hand. . . .
Therefore I will divide Him a portion with the great,
And He shall divide the spoil with the strong,
Because He poured out His soul unto death,
And He was numbered with the transgressors,
And He bore the sin of many,
And made intercession for the transgressors. (53:1–10,12)

The History of the Cross

We talk a lot about the cross. Wear it around our necks. Print it on our letterhead. Chisel it in stone. Genuflect. It's *the* symbol of Christ. But what's it mean? I mean, really? When we wear it, what are we saying? What are we agreeing with?

To understand the cross, we need to back up four thousand years from our present day—or about two thousand prior to the cross. Somewhere between 2000 and 1800 BC. To Abraham.

Long story short, when Abraham was seventy-five, God promised him a son. Abraham scratches his head because Sarah is post-menopausal. "Um, Lord. . . ." Eleven years pass and nothing happens. So Sarah, tired of waiting and feeling like a failure as a wife, pushes him toward Hagar. Nothing wrong with that in their culture, except God said Sarah. Not Hagar. Ishmael is born. The son of his flesh. Fourteen years later, when Abraham is a hundred, Isaac is born. The son of his love. Twenty-five years after the promise. Years pass. Scripture doesn't say how many. I think Isaac was a teenager but that's just a guess.

Let's pick up the story there:

Now it came to pass after these things that God tested Abraham, and said to him, "Abraham!"

And he said, "Here I am."

Then He said, "Take now your son, your only son Isaac, whom you love, and go to the land of Moriah, and offer him there as a burnt offering on one of the mountains of which I shall tell you."

So Abraham rose early in the morning and saddled his donkey, and took two of his young men with him, and Isaac his son; and he split the wood for the burnt offering, and arose and went to the place of which God had told him. Then on the third day Abraham lifted his eyes and saw the place afar off. And Abraham said to his young men, "Stay here with the donkey; the lad and I will go yonder and worship, and we will come back to you."

So Abraham took the wood of the burnt offering and laid it on Isaac his son; and he took the fire in his hand, and a knife, and the two of them went together. But Isaac spoke to Abraham his father and said, "My father!"

And he said, "Here I am, my son."

Then he said, "Look, the fire and the wood, but where is the lamb for a burnt offering?"

And Abraham said, "My son, God will provide for Himself the lamb for a burnt offering." So the two of them went together. (Gen. 22:1–8)

Every time I read that, my eye focuses on "rose early." I cannot imagine. In that predawn light, how did he make himself climb out of bed? Scripture records that Abram "believed in the LORD, and He accounted it to him for righteousness" (Gen. 15:6).

Let that picture focus. There's Isaac. Broad-shouldered. Bright-eyed. Carrying the wood—and his own life. Everything before him. There's Abraham. Heavy-hearted and carrying the knife. Death before him. He'd made sure the knife was sharp. So it would be quick. Less suffering. In his other hand, he carried the fire for the sacrifice.

Isaac bounds up the trail. Abraham drags his heels.

The story continues: "Then they came to the place of which God had told him. And Abraham built an altar there and placed the wood in order; and he bound Isaac his son and laid him on the altar, upon the wood. And Abraham stretched out his hand and took the knife to slay his son" (22:9–10).

Scripture records these events in less than two sentences, but back up. Look closer. There's a "binding." Abraham wrestles his son to the ground and forcibly hog-ties him. Imagine Isaac's surprise. His dismay. Utter unbelief. Can you hear his cries, "But Abba, what!? Why are you . . . ?" Can you see Abraham's tears? See his quivering hands fumbling to tie the rope? He is near to losing his mind. His brain is throwing out a thousand questions such as: How is he going to explain this to Sarah? Will his son suffer? And somewhere in that moment, he raises the knife—above Isaac's screams. "No, Abba!"

Isaac's eyes are wide. Frantic. Searching. Abraham's hand is shaking uncontrollably. His knees are buckling. He has lost it. His heart is already broken. Rent down the middle.

But the Angel of the LORD called to him from heaven and said, "Abraham, Abraham!"

So he said, "Here I am."

And He said, "Do not lay your hand on the lad, or do anything to him; for now I know that you fear God, since you have not withheld your son, your only son, from Me."

Then Abraham lifted his eyes and looked, and there behind him was a ram caught in a thicket by its horns. So Abraham went and took the ram, and offered it up for a burnt offering instead of his son. And Abraham called the name of the place, The-LORD-Will-Provide; as it is said to this day, "In the Mount of the LORD it shall be provided."

Then the Angel of the LORD called to Abraham a second time out of heaven, and said: "By Myself I have sworn, says the LORD, because you have done this thing, and have not withheld your son, your only son—blessing I will bless you, and multiplying I will multiply your descendants as the stars of the heaven and as the sand which is on the seashore; and your descendants shall possess the gate of their enemies. In your seed all the nations of the earth shall be blessed, because you have obeyed My voice." So Abraham returned to his young men, and they rose and went together to Beersheba; and Abraham dwelt at Beersheba. (22:11–19).

Walk with Abraham and Isaac down the mountain. See Abraham's hand resting on Isaac's shoulder. Listen to their voices. I'd like to know what that conversation sounded like.

Now turn the camera. Change the perspective. From up top. Looking down. Jesus/God the Father/the Holy Spirit are staring down from the top of Mount Moriah. Watching Abraham and Isaac descend. I'd really like to know what their conversation sounded like.

Note: What I'm about to suggest is not in Scripture, but this is what I imagine the rest of this story looked like. Also, while I'm painting this picture as occurring on the mountain while Abraham and Isaac are walking down, in truth, I think it occurred much earlier. Before the foundation of the world. Before time was set in motion. I don't understand that, and I can't wrap my head around it, but God knew this long before it happened.

So, back to the mountain.

Jesus and the Father watched in silent admiration and affection. The Father nodded and spoke what Paul would later write. "In hope against hope he believed . . . he did not waver in unbelief but grew strong in faith, giving glory to God." (Rom. 4:18–20, NASB). A long pause followed as the three of them looked out across time. Out to you and me. The Father continued, "Son, there's going to come a time when he needs Us. When his sons and daughters don't love Us the way he does, when they bow down to other gods and sell themselves into slavery and Our enemy puts them in prisons of their own building. Shackles them. He won't sell them cheap. Matter of fact, only one thing will buy them back."

Jesus thought about this a long time. Isaac was hugging his dad as they neared the bottom of the hill. Arms around his waist. They were laughing. Abraham's cheeks had almost dried. Jesus turned to His Father, nodding. "I know." A tear trailed down His cheek. Jesus was weeping. The Father thumbed it away. Jesus whispered, "I'll go. I'll buy them back."

Abba raises an eyebrow. "With what?"

Jesus tilts his head. Staring past Abraham. Past Isaac. To you and me. To us right now. "With all that I have."

For those of you who doubt that this has been the plan from the beginning, we need to back up even further. To Genesis 3:15. After the fall, God is speaking to the serpent, who just deceived Adam and Eve. He is speaking about His Son, about Jesus: "And I will put enmity between you and the woman, and between your seed and her seed; he shall bruise you on the head, and you shall bruise [crush] him on the heel" (NASB). Theologians call this text the *Protoevangelium*. It's the first time the gospel is proclaimed. Three chapters into Scripture and God already has an answer for our problem.

And that answer is the execution of His Son.

Seven hundred and forty years before Christ, the prophet Isaiah said it this way:

And in this mountain
The LORD of hosts will make for all people
A feast of choice pieces,
A feast of wines on the lees,
Of fat things full of marrow,
Of well-refined wines on the lees.
And He will destroy on this mountain
The surface of the covering cast over all people,
And the veil that is spread over all nations.
He will swallow up death forever,
And the Lord GOD will wipe away tears from all faces;
The rebuke of His people
He will take away from all the earth;
For the LORD has spoken. (25:6–8)

Follow Him Where?

Jump forward two thousand years. Back to the garden where that same Jesus is making good on His promise. Over the course of His three-and-a-half-year public ministry, Scripture records that Jesus said "Follow Me" over twenty times. We know we're supposed to follow Him. He's our Shepherd. We're His sheep. But *where* are we going? Where *exactly* is He asking us to follow Him?

All roads only lead to one place. The cross.

If that's the case, do I, do you, really understand what we're saying when we hang that thing around our necks and sign our name on the dotted line to follow Jesus? Where did the road to the cross take Jesus? What did it cost Him?

From the garden, Jesus is arrested and brought to the court of Caiaphas, the high priest. Matthew, an eye witness, says this: "They spat in His face and beat Him with their fists; and others slapped Him" (Matt. 26:67, NASB).

The thought of someone actually clenching his fist and striking my King in the face, busting His lip—something in me wants to look away.

Psalm 22:12–13 says it this way: "Many bulls have surrounded Me. . . . They gape at Me with their mouths, like a raging and roaring lion."

The prophet Micah, some eight hundred years before it happened, foretold this: "With a rod they will smite the judge of Israel on the cheek" (5:1, NASB). Isaiah said this: "I gave My back to those who struck Me, and My cheeks to those who plucked out the beard" (50:6).

How'd they hit Him? Haymaker? Jab? Superman punch? Elbow strike?

Unable to decide what to do with Jesus, they bring Him before Pilate who orders Him flogged and scourged (Matt. 27:26). This was not a cow whip. Not Indiana Jones. The Roman scourge was a tasseled whip studded with metal, glass, or bone. Whatever was available. The whip didn't so much slap the skin, or even cut it, as sink into it. The tassels wrapped around the back, chest, neck, and face—embedding into them. Buried. When removed, it peeled chunks of skin and flesh with it. It carved away tissue. Divinely inspired, Isaiah described Jesus this way: "His appearance was marred more than any man and His form more than the sons of men" (52:14 NASB). Another translation says, "He was unrecognizable as a man."

Unrecognizable.

That means all those pretty and priceless paintings depicting the loving Savior staring down upon the world could not be further from the truth. By the time Jesus was hung on the tree, He'd been shredded.

Following the scourging, they crowned Him, "King of the Jews." Only this crown was a little different. If you've ever traveled the Rift Valley in Israel, you know that most every bush or tree there has a thorn on it. And these aren't uncomfortable little stickers that hinder your meander through the blueberries. Bigger than sewing needles, these are one-to-three-inch-long stilettos that grow on acacia trees. They are often used as darts in blow guns. They will punch through leather, tennis shoes, and rubber tires. "And after twisting together a crown of thorns, they put it on His head, and . . . they spat on Him, and took the reed and began to beat

Him on the head" (Matt. 27:29–30, NASB). Can you see the rods beating down? Driving the thorns in deeper?

Back to Psalm 22:

> I am poured out like water,
> And all My bones are out of joint;
> My heart is like wax,
> It has melted within Me.
> My strength is dried up like a potsherd,
> And My tongue clings to My jaws;
> You have brought Me to the dust of death. (22:14–15)

Blood vessels burst, beard plucked out, struck in the face, beaten with rods, flesh ripped off His back, crown shoved onto His skull and thorns pressing into His temples, the soldiers drop a cross on His hamburger back and point outside the gate to the top of the hill. "Walk!" In truth, Jesus probably only carried the crossbar and not the entire cross. Soldiers were lazy and tended to reuse the post.

Having lost a lot of blood, His blood pressure dangerously low, Jesus began trudging up the hill. Painting a trail behind Him. Taking too long, the guards spot a healthy bystander. Minding his own business. Simon of Cyrene. "You! Carry that!" Simon shoulders the cross and then hooks one hand under Jesus' armpit to help Him stand. It is there, in my mind, that Jesus clings to Simon's sleeve, lifts Himself, and looks into Simon's eyes. Scripture is silent on this, too, but I'd like to know what He said. I'd like to know what Simon knew in that moment.

Add in a hostile crowd, ill-tempered soldiers, and a host of salivating spiritual forces of wickedness, and I think that walk took a while.

Reaching the top of the hill, Simon drops the cross and steps aside. Pause right here. That blood-smeared, splintered thing on the ground? That tree? That method of execution? That murder weapon. That death sentence? How many of us wear a small, shiny one around our necks? I'm not knocking it. I do it too. I'm just wondering if we really understood what happened on it, if we'd still be so eager to display it. What part of this are we identifying with when we do that?

The next step is so understated in Scripture. So without comment. Very simply it reads, "They crucified Him."[11] Let the reader understand. New Testament Scripture is relatively silent on the single most important event in the history of humanity. On the sound of the hammer hitting the spike head. Or, the echo off the stone city walls. And the blood-curdling screams of Jesus as they crossed His feet and drove rusty spikes through each.

Remember, He stepped off His throne for this.

No matter how hard I try, no matter how many times I read this or try to write it better, I cannot wrap my mind around this. I shake my head. Stare at the heavens. "Really?!" This wrecks me. I'm totally undone. Unworthy.

Having skewered Him, they drop the cross into its hole, jolting the rag-doll, hamburger-meat body of Jesus. Suspended between heaven and earth—between throne and grave—there hangs Jesus.

> For dogs have surrounded Me;
> The congregation of the wicked has enclosed Me.
> They pierced My hands and My feet;
> I can count all My bones.
> They look and stare at Me.
> They divide My garments among them,
> And for My clothing they cast lots. (Ps. 22:16–18)

The Old Testament does a much better job of describing the death of Jesus than the men and women who watched it happen.

Another myth that needs exposing are all those paintings of Jesus wearing a loin cloth. Covering His privates. I wish it were so, but it wasn't. Jesus had been stripped and hung naked. Fully exposed. This is why Scripture reads, "And many women who followed Jesus from Galilee, ministering to Him, were there looking on from afar."[12]

If you live with shame because of your sin, if you think to yourself, *Jesus can't possibly know the depth of my embarrassment and depravity*, it is here that Jesus wore it for you.

> But I am a worm, and no man;
> A reproach of men, and despised by the people.
> All those who see Me ridicule Me;
> They shoot out the lip, they shake the head, saying,
> "He trusted in the LORD, let Him rescue Him;
> Let Him deliver Him, since He delights in Him." (Ps. 22:6–8)

In a crucifixion, there is a constant struggle between your chest and your legs while your lungs combat your writhing body for air. During this, fluids build up in your chest cavity. Filling your lungs. Producing a slow drowning.

The carpenter lasted three hours.

During those three hours, God the Father laid on Jesus every sin of mankind. One by one. Yours and mine. All of it. Piled on. Not one was left out. God the Father clothed His Son in the sin of humanity. Wrapped it around Him like a blanket. Or shroud. And while I think the weight of that was killing Jesus, I don't think it was the final straw. I think the killing blow—what broke the spirit of Jesus—was rejection. When God saw the sum of that sin, He turned. And Jesus, able to see into this world and the world to come, saw it happen. He saw His Father, His Abba, turn away. That's why He asked Him, "My God, My God, why have You forsaken Me?" (Matt. 27:46). And when He did, every Jewish man and boy in the crowd would have known the reference and could have finished it for Him: "Why are You so far from helping Me, and from the words of My groaning?" (Ps. 22:1).

I believe that's the moment that killed Jesus. Because it was there that He knew the rejection of His Father.

I want to pause here and speak to all of you who were put up for adoption, or who have suffered an equally great rejection, who have known loneliness of the soul—you are not alone. What you feel in your gut, what you sense in your DNA, the absence, the void, Jesus felt first. There on the cross, He knew your rejection.

> But You, O LORD, do not be far from Me;
> O My Strength, hasten to help Me!
> Deliver Me from the sword,
> My precious life from the power of the dog.
> Save Me from the lion's mouth
> And from the horns of the wild oxen!
> You have answered me. (Ps. 22:19–21)

Answered me? Think about it. The Father's answer—is a dead Jesus.

What were Jesus' last words? "It is finished." And the last words of Psalm 22? "He has done this." Jesus spoke an entire psalm with just a few words.

A few hundred yards away, at 3:00 p.m. in the temple, the high priest was slicing the throat of the Passover lamb.

Dead on the cross, "One of the soldiers pierced His side with a spear, and immediately blood and water came out" (John 19:34). If you doubt that Jesus drowned, here speaks evidence to the contrary. Again Isaiah, "He poured out His soul unto death" (53:12). The Hebrew word for "flesh" is translated here as "soul." Jesus poured out His flesh.

Payment made in full.

Sixteen hundred years prior, God told Moses, "The life of the flesh is in the blood, and I have given it to you upon the altar to make atonement for your souls; for it is the blood that makes atonement for the soul" (Lev. 17:11).

What's Your Isaac?

Here's the nugget, and this is what gets muddled when we read and re-read this story. This is the part that satan has and is actively working to draw your attention away from. That's because he wants you to miss this. To water this down:

The cross is a crucifixion, an execution. Something and someone is being put to death. And just as the Father required it of Abraham, He is requiring it of you.

Those blows Jesus took, the thorns that pierced His head, that scourging, that flesh removed in chunks, those nails, that spear in His side, that shame, that rejection, that death—that should be you and me. That's the cross we deserve. Instead, Jesus—the spotless Lamb of God—gave us what we did not deserve and withheld from us what we did. Theologians call that unmerited grace. I scratch my head and ask myself, *What kind of king would do such a thing—for me?*

When Jesus walked with His disciples, He was and is speaking to us: "If anyone desires to come after Me, let him deny himself, and take up his cross daily, and follow Me" (Luke 9:23).

So, in order to follow we must first deny and take up? Here's what that means—you can't pick up your cross if you're carrying your Isaac. Let me say that again.

You can't pick up your cross if you're carrying your Isaac.

So, what's your Isaac? What is that thing that prevents you from denying, taking up, following, daily? If you're going to keep reading, walk out the rest of this, it will help you (and me) to approach this whole conversation with some gut-level honesty. Real truth. Revealing all. Even the stuff you want to keep hidden.

The rest of this will require that you and I admit our own sin.

For those of you who really know the Word, please don't get hung up on my equating Isaac with sin. I realize Isaac is the son of promise and Ishmael the son of the flesh. What I'm asking you to consider is the same thing God asked Abraham: Who (or what) do you love, are you holding onto tightly, are you unwilling to trust Him with, and will you offer it up to Him? For you and me, here and now, this can be sin (and most often is), or it could be something as awesome as the gifting He's given us. It can be anything that has become an idol. That's the way the enemy works.

Our enemy has been waging war against the likes of us for at least five thousand years (probably a lot longer), and he knows the weaknesses in our walls. Given that, he will use anything to draw our affection away from our Father. For me, the most obvious place to start is my sin. Looking beyond that and into my gifting is a bit more tricky, but I have my idols here too. Think about it this way: What if Abraham had not offered Isaac? What if he had clutched him tightly to his chest and said, "Nope. Too painful. Waited too long. I can't live without him. Ask me anything but that. I'd rather die than. . . ." What would Isaac then represent in the life of Abraham if Abraham had not offered him up?

That's what I'm asking you to lay bare.

Want some help? Ask for the Spirit of truth. Jesus said, "When He, the Spirit of truth, has come, He will guide you into all truth; for He will not speak on His own authority, but whatever He hears He will speak; and He will tell you things to come" (John 16:13). If you and I are to survive the rest of this, we need truthfulness—the same spirit of truthfulness the Israelites needed when they had to look upon the bronze serpent lifted high on a pole in the wilderness (Num. 21:9). Their healing required an honest and public admission of their guilt. Same goes for us.

Let me encourage you. You can't tell Jesus anything He doesn't already know. You're not telling Him for His benefit. You're telling Him for yours.

So, be gut-level honest about your sin. No pretending. No blue sky. Isaiah said, "All our righteousnesses are like filthy rags" (Isa. 64:6). The words he used describe a woman in her customary impurity. That means the best we have to offer of our own accord is of no more value than a bunch of bloody maxi pads. Paul recognized his own unworthiness when he said this: "Christ Jesus came into the world to save sinners, of whom I am chief" (1 Tim. 1:15). If we're honest, we all have "gone astray . . . every one, to his own way" (Isa. 53:6).

When I've taught this message to (mainly) groups of men, it's at this point that their eyes tell me their minds have started to wander. To their Isaacs. Their strongholds. The things they love more than God. And, if I'm honest, as I'm writing this, my mind has wandered there too. Maybe some of you are starting to think, *Okay, Charles, I'm with you. I need to clean house a bit. Sweep out a few closets. Smoke out the cockroaches, so I'll offer up these three. Possibly four.* You, like the rest of us, sacrifice the easily expendable. Those closest to the door. That which you can possibly live without. But then there's the secret hold in your basement. The bar across the door. The triple locks. Your eye wanders there. You shake your head, *Nope. Not going to happen.*

We covered this in chapter 4, but it's huge for many men so I'm not skipping over it simply to save space. For some of you, "that" is sexual sin. And don't think you get off the hook if you're not physically touching someone else. John on the island of Patmos, writing his Revelation about the judgment and outcome at the end of the age, said, "Then one of the seven angels who had the seven bowls came and talked with me, saying to me, 'Come, I will show you the judgment of the great harlot who sits on many waters, with whom the kings of the earth committed fornication, and the inhabitants of the earth were made drunk with the wine of her fornication'" (Rev. 17:1–2).

The Greek word translated as "committed fornication" is *porneuo* (porn-yoo-oh). From it we get "pornographic" and "pornography." It means to engage in illicit sexual intercourse, be unfaithful, play the harlot, prostitute oneself. The word is used literally and metaphorically to describe spiritual fornication, which is idolatry. One of the biggest idols of the men reading this is *porneuo*.

Am I trying to shame you? Guilt you? No. I am fighting for your freedom and speaking light into dark places, because if we don't we are just like those hypocrites who punched Jesus in the teeth. And believe me, I'm hypocritical enough without adding to it. Over the last couple of years, as the Lord has revealed the cross to me and what His blood accomplished, I've been trying to ask myself some real honest questions: What, or who, do I lean on other than Him?

Note: This has not been a fun process, and it will lick the red off your lollipop. But it has been freeing. And freedom is better than slavery. And no matter how I try to weasel my way out, I have found that only one thing will cut you and me free. It's not mercy. Not good intentions. Not warm, fuzzy, positive feelings sent some place safe. "You shall know the truth, and the truth shall make you free" (John 8:32). The truth frees us. The kind that comes out of our gut. That's His promise. So welcome the truth. Don't fear it.

In considering my own Isaacs, here's some of what I looked at:

- *Alcohol:* I want to know if this is an idol. And you don't have to be a drunk or an alcoholic for it to be an idol. You may brush me off, but don't drink it for a week or two or three, and then honestly ask your response to its absence. How's the craving? Where do your thoughts go? When you see it advertised or see others drinking it, do you think "good time"? And what else causes you to think "good time" with the same excitement? Do you escape into it? Just something to take the edge off? To medicate your pain? Admittedly, I have. Jesus drank wine when here, and He's already said He's drinking it when He returns. Alcohol is not bad in and of itself. It's what it becomes in our lives.
- *Food:* for me, food can be an idol. What about you? How grumpy do you get when you don't get what you want when you want? If you really want to know to what extent food is an idol, just fast a day or two or three. Won't take long to find out.
- *Caffeine:* definitely. For some of you this might not be an issue. For me, it is.
- *Money:* and you don't have to have a lot of it for it to be an idol. If you want to know if this is an idol, ask yourself if you lean on it to provide your comfort, to bail you out. Is it your go-to? How tightly do you control it? How much time do you spend thinking about it? Do you spend more time in the *Wall Street Journal* or your monthly statements than the Word? When you think about that sum sitting wherever it sits, do you think "safety"? "Provision"? If you want to go deeper, ask yourself, honestly, do you think your money somehow makes you better than the guy sitting next to you?

Does it elevate you? You may answer no, and I might have once said the same—but I travel to Nicaragua once or twice a year, and every time I step foot off the plane, I am pierced with the knowledge that I am exceedingly guilty of all of this. Do you tithe? Do you tithe willingly? Scripture is clear that if you don't, you're robbing God and by definition, your money is an idol.

- *Your children:* this is a biggie, and we're all guilty. All of us attempt to control every circumstance of their lives so they don't suffer what we've suffered. Or, because we're fearful that they'll get hurt or not make the right choice or . . . name your own fear. One of the reasons the Lord gives us children is to allow us to know the love of parent for a child. We have a better knowledge of His heart through interacting with our kids. The enemy knows this and hates it, so he uses this relationship, or relationships, to cause us to distrust our Father. He twists it. Whispering lies. Doubt. His attacks usually start with the same phrase he spoke to Eve in the garden: "Did God really say?" We take over from there. It is no exaggeration to say that God requires us to lay our kids down at His feet in the same way that Abraham laid down Isaac.

- *Sports/football:* this was a biggie for me. If you need more on this, read my novel *A Life Intercepted.* And don't think I'm talking only to athletes. What do your weekends look like? Do you raise your hands in triumph when your fantasy football star scores but keep your hands in your pockets in church? I've spent some time studying worship in the Bible, and I can find no place where the mention of or description of worship does not include some motion or action of the body. Whether hands raised, head bowed, dancing, or body lying prostrate on the ground, worship is an act of the body. Problem is, I often see more worship at a football game than church.

- *Writing:* yes, it could be an idol for me. I had to and continue to have to check this. Asking, "Lord, have I made this more important than You? Do I like being called a *New York Times* bestselling writer more than I desire being called Your child? Or, even more, a bondservant of Jesus Christ? Have I found my identity in the pen or the cross? Could I walk away from writing if You called me?" Just being honest, this is a toughie.

Hear me when I say this: I'm not telling you that all these things are evil. Certainly, our kids are not evil. Football is a great game, Scripture says wine is good for the heart (Ps. 104:15), and the Lord made me a writer in the same way He made Abraham a father. I'm asking you to examine whether or not you've made these things into idols. Are they preventing you from picking up your cross? Daily?

Here's the truth: your idols are what you run to when you are afraid or you need comfort. What you hide behind. When you want to be made to feel the way that you want you to feel. Read that again. Your idols are what you turn to when you want to be made to feel the way you want you to feel.

Let me ask it this way: What in your life do you hold closer to your chest than Jesus? Long cut Skoal? Chardonnay? Single malt? Vodka? Those pictures on your hard drive? The power of your Amex Card? Three squares a day of meat and potatoes and just the right type of dessert? The comfort you find in the balance in your account? Your car? The image you project to the world? Will you let Him show you?

If you're game, I have a suggestion: put this book down, grab a notecard, go for a walk, and get real honest. Spend an hour. Maybe two. Write down what comes to mind. Be honest—what are the things that have your attention? That have captured your heart? Where do you not trust Him? What have you hidden in your basement? What do you turn to when you want to be made to feel the way you want to feel? Come back when you've thrown open the cellar door and clicked on the light.

I mean it. Put this down, grab a notecard, and spend some time writing down your go-tos.

If you did this and if you were honest, chances are good your Isaacs are now written on the card in your pocket. For lots of reasons, I've had some rather truthful and intimate conversations with different groups of men from all over. Hundreds of men. Times of conversation where we've gotten past the walls and broken through the BS, and the pretensions and the lies we project and masks we hide behind. Throughout those conversations of more than a decade, I've kept a running tally of the words on our cards.

That list of possible idols reads something like this:

- my pride
- my fear
- my girlfriend (the one my wife doesn't know about)
- the substance I'm addicted to
- my sex addiction
- my deviant sexual practices
- my porn addiction
- my porn addiction
- my porn addiction—yes, I've listed this three times.
- my anger
- my depression
- my pain
- my money
- my money
- my money—yes, three times.
- my success
- my accomplishments
- my wall of plaques
- my position
- my career—and the power I can and do exercise because of it
- my bitterness
- my inadequacies
- my prescription meds
- my lies
- my shame
- my gambling

- my secrets—those I'm taking to the grave
- my guilt—the skeletons in my closet
- my habits that my wife doesn't know about—and the lies I keep from her
- my hopelessness
- my rejection
- my abandonment
- my self-sufficiency—the idea that if it is to be, it's up to me
- my false identity
- my false self
- my kids
- my wife
- my performance meter
- my measuring stick with which I measure myself and beat down others
- my failure
- my fear
- my vodka
- my DUI
- my drugs
- my anxiety
- my food
- my broken heart
- my Plan A
- my Plan B
- my I-want-to-do-what-I-want-to-do-when-I-want-to-do-it-just-'cause-I-want-to-do-it
- my hatred
- my pissed-off-ness
- my racism
- my unbelief
- my fear of being found out
- my doubt

- my unworthiness
- my what I thought I should have been, could have been, would have been
- my reasoning
- my intellect
- my soul wound
- my unforgiveness
- my unforgiveness
- my unforgiveness—yes, I said this one three times too.
- Now you write down your own:

_____

_____

Peter was talking about these places in our lives when he said, "For we have spent enough of our past lifetime in doing the will of the Gentiles—when we walked in lewdness, lusts, drunkenness, revelries, drinking parties, and abominable idolatries" (1 Peter 4:3).

Whatever you're holding onto, whatever you're afraid to let go of, whatever you're taking to the grave—that's your Isaac.

Jesus' question for you is this: Will you lay down your Isaac and pick up your cross?

Like Abraham, like Jesus, this is a decision of your will, not your emotions. Will you deny yourself and sacrifice what you love for the One who loves you more? When Paul said in Romans 12:1, "Present your bodies a living sacrifice," I think he was talking about this process right here. I'm not asking you to want to. I'm asking you to choose to.

Twenty-six hundred years ago, God spoke through the prophet Jeremiah about us. He's talking about you and me. "My people have committed two evils: they have forsaken me, the fountain of living waters, and hewed out cisterns for themselves, broken cisterns, that can hold no water" (Jer. 2:13, RSV). What's your broken cistern? Most of us are holding spaghetti colanders. Paddling Titanics.

Paul put it this way to the church in Ephesus:

And you He made alive, who were dead in trespasses and sins, in which you once walked according to the course of this world, according to the prince of the power of the air, the spirit who now works in the sons of disobedience, among whom also we all once conducted ourselves in the lusts of our flesh, fulfilling the desires of the flesh and of the mind, and were by nature children of wrath, just as the others.

But God, who is rich in mercy, because of His great love with which He loved us, even when we were dead in trespasses, made us alive together with Christ (by grace you have been saved), and raised us up together, and made us sit together in the heavenly places in Christ Jesus, that in the ages to come He might show the exceeding riches of His grace in His kindness toward us in Christ Jesus. For by grace you have been saved through faith, and that not of yourselves; it is the gift of God, not of works, lest anyone should boast. For we are His workmanship, created in Christ Jesus for good works, which God prepared beforehand that we should walk in them. . . .

But now in Christ Jesus you who once were far off have been brought near by the blood of Christ. (Eph. 2:1–10, 13).

I love that: "brought near by the blood of Christ."

To the church in Colossae, Paul wrote:

And you, being dead in your trespasses and the uncircumcision of your flesh, He has made alive together with Him, having forgiven you all trespasses, having wiped out the handwriting of requirements that was against us, which was contrary to us. And He has taken it out of the way, having nailed it to the cross. Having disarmed principalities and powers, He made a public spectacle of them, triumphing over them in it. (Col. 2:13–15)

The most powerful weapon in the universe is not a gun or a bomb or a president with his finger on a button. It's one drop of Jesus' blood. "And they overcame him by the blood the Lamb and by the word of their testimony" (Rev. 12:11).

I'm betting my life on His blood, and what you're reading is my testimony.

Jesus again: "He who does not take his cross and follow after Me is not worthy of Me" (Matt. 10:38). I desperately want to be worthy of Him. But here's the tricky part. Jesus will not take from you and me what we do not offer. That's right. He won't take what you don't give Him.

Some of you are feeling weighed down. Your list is long. Your Isaac is precious to you. Maybe you need some encouragement. The writer of Hebrews knew this:

> Therefore we also, since we are surrounded by so great a cloud of witnesses, let us lay aside every weight, and the sin which so easily ensnares us, and let us run with endurance the race that is set before us, looking unto Jesus, the author and finisher of our faith, who for the joy that was set before Him endured the cross, despising the shame, and has sat down at the right hand of the throne of God. (Heb. 12:1–2)

What that means is you're not alone. There's a host cheering you on. And they are raucous.

I'm not saying it's easy. But it is simple. Here's what's involved. "If anyone desires to come after Me, let him deny himself, and take up his cross daily, and follow Me" (Luke 9:23).

Try this. Hold out both your hands. In one, you hold your idol. Your Isaac. Or Isaacs. In the other, Jesus. Now extend your arms. Hold them both up to the light. Which do you want more? Your money or Him? Those glossy pictures or Him? The touch of a girlfriend your wife doesn't know about or Him? Your power? Your identity? Your career? Want me to keep going?

And don't accuse me of telling you that this whole exercise is a function of good works and working your way to Jesus, and you're somehow saved by your own bootstraps. That I'm one more Bible thumper giving you one more list of things to do, one more set of boxes to check, en route to righteousness. Stop. That's baloney. I am telling you to walk up to the throne of God, lift your hand up, uncurl your fingers, and give Him the opportunity either to take what's in it or give it back. But leave the taking and the giving to Him. Your job is obedience, lifted hand, and open fingers. It's an offering. That's it. You let Him decide whether you keep it or it dies. We carry the wood and our lives. He carries the knife and the fire.

Want to call yourself a Christian? Follow Jesus? Hang that shiny thing around your neck? Then there is a cross in your future. An execution. The road you're on will take you there.

What hangs on your cross is up to you, but something and someone is going to be put to death. Your choice. But take heart. Jesus has been here before us. It's the very same choice He faced in the garden: Deny. Take up. Daily. Follow.

God Wastes Nothing

One last thing. I started this by saying that to understand the cross we needed to back up. To Mount Moriah. It has a historic past. It's the same hill

- where Abraham raised the knife above Isaac,
- where King David built an altar on the threshing floor of Ornan the Jebusite,
- where Solomon built the temple,
- and it's also called Calvary—where Jesus poured out His blood.

I want to make sure you get that: the hill where Abraham offered his son, where He provided the lamb for the sacrifice, is the same geographic hill where God the Father offered His Son two thousand years later.

God wastes nothing.

I quoted this before. It's Isaiah. Seven hundred years before Christ. See if it means more the second time around:

> The LORD of hosts will prepare a lavish banquet for all peoples on this
>   mountain,
> A banquet of aged wine, choice pieces with marrow,
> And refined, aged wine.
> And on this mountain He will swallow up the covering which is over
>   all peoples,
> Even the veil which is stretched over all nations.
> He will swallow up death for all time,
> And the Lord GOD will wipe tears away from all faces,
> And He will remove the reproach of His people from all the earth;
> For the LORD has spoken. (Isa. 25:6–8, NASB)

Let me end with Psalm 22 one last time:

> All the ends of the world
> Shall remember and turn to the LORD,
> And all the families of the nations
> Shall worship before You.
> For the kingdom is the LORD's,
> And He rules over the nations.
>
> All the prosperous of the earth
> Shall eat and worship;
> All those who go down to the dust
> Shall bow before Him. (vv. 27–29)

"Shall remember . . . shall turn . . . shall worship . . . shall bow. . . ." Each of us is headed to the foot of the throne. No escaping that. Like it or not, we will all fall at the very real and very resurrected feet of Jesus—the firstborn among the dead. Seated at the right hand of God Most High. So, you can either extend your arms and uncurl your fingers now, at a date and time of your choosing, or you can do it later at a date and time of His choosing.

This thing I'm talking about is a surrendering. A giving up. A throwing away. A yielding to. A coming under. When I do this, because it humbles and shreds me, I get on my knees. Literally. Sometimes I sink to my face. Then I raise my hands. I offer it. Push it away from me and toward Him. Then I say, or scream, something like this. Feel free to join me and make it your own.

Lord, here. Take it. I don't want it anymore. I want to give You my Isaac. It's separating me from You. Killing me slowly. Forgive me. Please. I am so sorry for putting it between us. For preferring it over You. For running to it rather than You. For clinging to it and not You. For trusting in it and not You. For wrapping myself in these chains.

Lord, I run to You. Cling to You. Trust You. When I hang this shiny thing around my neck, I want to be identified with You, not my Isaac. I bow down to You, not it. I worship You, not it. I deny myself. Right now. This very second. And every second to come. And I want to pick up my cross and follow You. To lay it across my shoulders and walk like Simon. Not out of obligation or guilt or duty or shame, but because I love You.

I desire to be like You. Walk with You. Because Your lovingkindness is better than life. Because one day in Your courts is better than a thousand elsewhere. Because You're my glory, my shield, and the One who lifts up my head. Because I'd be lost without You. Because I'm no longer a slave, but a son—and if a son, an heir. Because I don't want to ever do anything that diminishes the truth about Your blood and what it accomplished for me. Because I don't know how else to say thank You for dying my death so that I might share in Your life. Because I just can't get past the fact that You, perfect and sinless, went through all that You

went through for a wicked, black-hearted sinner like me. Jesus, I lift my
hands and praise You with all that is in me. Today, I lay down my Isaac
and pick up my cross and follow You.

    In Jesus' Name, amen.

Sometimes I say this prayer two or three times. Or ten times. Usually, when I do, tears follow.

Note: Don't beat yourself up if you wake tomorrow and find your hands and heart clutched around something that is not splintered wood and you've got to come back here and offer it up again. These things can have deep roots. Sometimes they come up all at once in one big clump and sometimes it takes a while to uproot them. We have a tendency to take back what we've offered up. That's why Jesus said "daily." But don't lose heart. "Even now the ax is laid to the root" (Matt. 3:10). Remember, God blessed Abraham after he offered up Isaac—and when He did, the blessing stretched beyond his wildest imagination.

If you're having trouble, invite a friend. Two lights in the basement are better than one. Don't be ashamed. Remember, satan is using that against you. On purpose. For those of you who are married, invite your wife or husband. I know, it's painful. But the Lord will honor and bless that. Grab her hand. Grab his. Hit your knees. Spill the truth from your gut.

Last thought: when Simon shouldered the cross, and Jesus looked into Simon's eyes, that look pierced eternity. Jesus was looking through Simon, all the way to you and me, here and now. His last step onto that cross purchased your and my eternal, irrevocable redemption. There will come a time, when our time here ends, when each of us will look into those same eyes. And this is the crux of the matter, this is *the* question—the hinge pin—when that time comes, and you stare into those eyes, what will He find on your shoulder?

What's that you're carrying?

Welcome to the cross.

CHAPTER 7

The Toughest Thing You and I Will Ever Do

At 3:00 p.m., as the high priest is sacrificing the Passover lamb in the temple, Jesus lifts Himself and tries to inhale but His lungs have flooded and there is no room. Only a gurgle. Having "poured out His flesh," He lets go and exhales for the last time.

There on the cross, Jesus—the Lamb upon the throne—dies.

An earthquake shakes Mount Zion. The ancient stones cry out. The veil in the temple is torn in two. The crowd falls pin-drop silent. Many cry. Groups huddle together. All shake their heads. "Surely, He was the Son of God."

Their eyes focus on Him. Lifted high. Silhouetted against the sky. Just "as Moses lifted up the serpent in the wilderness, even so must the Son of Man be lifted up."[1] He hangs unrecognizable. Bloodless. Crushed. Lifeless.

Sabbath is approaching. If they don't get Him off the cross soon, He'll have to hang, by law, until Sabbath is over. Their hearts are shredded. Mary Magdalene is weeping uncontrollably, clawing at the dirt.

A rich man, Joseph of Arimathea, who had become a disciple, uses his status to gain access to Pilate. "I am here to ask for the body of Jesus."

Happy to be rid of him, Pilate waves him off. "Take Him."

In muted whispers, and careful not to rock the body, the men slide the cross out of its hole and set it down. They peel off the crown, pull out the nails, and some brave soul reaches up and closes His eyes. One by one, they stare at Him. The absence of His voice is unbearable. How could this be?

The soldiers are impatient, and the time for goodbyes is over. With an armed escort, they carry Jesus' body to a new tomb, which Joseph had hewn out of the rock. Inside, they lay the very dead and now decaying body of Jesus down on a cold shelf. His skin is pale, grayish in hue; His lips are purple, and His face ashen. Dark, caked blood trails down his legs and toes. The hour is late. Long shadows stretch along the ground. No time to wash the body. Through tears, they kiss His forehead and wrap Him in clean linen grave clothes. When they'd said their goodbyes and prayed over the body, they walked out only to watch a large stone rolled against the door of the tomb, leaving Jesus' flesh and bones to lie in darkness.

Walking away from the tomb, the images flashed back across their minds' eyes. The depth of their sorrow was more than their minds and hearts could grasp. "How could this have happened? How did He let it? He healed the sick. Raised Lazarus. Why?" Their last image of Jesus was a man dying in anguish and torment, screaming out at the top of His lungs. Seemingly helpless. Powerless. His body ripped and torn. Inhuman suffering. In their minds, the unfathomable had happened. Jesus had lost.

In the minds of those who loved and followed Him, Jesus had lost everything.

Walking away from the cross, from Jesus' tomb, as they wiped away tears and swore at the memory of the soldiers, as they plotted and planned, each asked one impossible question: "What now!?"

For these simple two words, they had no answer. No game plan. All they could do was shake their heads and fists. No one, not even Peter, James, or John, had an answer. They did not know what we know. All they knew was that the Lamb of God who takes away the sin of the world, the hope of all mankind, the One who came to sit on the throne of David, the One who healed the sick, walked on water, drove out demons, the One who raised the dead to life—could not defeat death. Could not save Himself. He was gone. And they were left to mop up the mess.

Three days pass.

Three silent, long, dark, lonely, angry, and tear-filled days. Everything they'd hoped for, and everything they'd dreamed about, has vanished.

Given the timing of Jesus' death and the beginning of the Sabbath, they did not have time to wash and prepare His body. In haste, they pulled Him down, wrapped Him in grave clothes, and laid Him in the tomb. Now, on the first day of the week, at early dawn, they have brought spices which they prepared to properly embalm the body. They intend to do now what they could not do then. And, maybe spend a few more moments with His body. To comprehend the incomprehensible.

Mary Magdalene, out of whom Jesus had driven seven demons, is there. Her deliverance is significant because it demonstrates that nothing in her past excluded her from being first to the tomb. Nothing about her history limited her love of or intimacy with Jesus. Mary arrives while it's still dark, but there's a problem. She squints her eyes. The six-foot round stone, sealed by Roman decree, has been rolled away. The tomb door is open. Evidence that grave robbers got here first. She tiptoes forward.

When she slowly pokes her head in, she is met by two men. "Two angels in white sitting, one at the head and one at the feet, where the body of Jesus had been lying."[2]

Two angels. One left and one right. They are book-ending the space where the body of Jesus had lain. They are doing so in much the same way the cherubim covered the lid, or mercy seat, of the ark of the covenant— with their outstretched wings. Since Moses gave the law to the nation of Israel, the high priest entered once a year into the Holy of Holies and sprinkled the mercy seat with the blood of the sacrifice to make atonement for the sin of the people. Every time he did this, the priest would sprinkle or spill or smear the blood over the lid seven times to "cleanse it, and consecrate it from the uncleanness of the children of Israel."[3] And every time he did this, the golden wings of the angels covered his hands. Just as they are doing right this moment. The mercy seat of the ark isn't so much a seat as it is a lid and a place of atonement. It is *the* place where God received payment for the sin of humanity.

When Paul, the writer of Hebrews, and John describe Jesus as our "propitiation," they are making this visual connection. Jesus, who is both just and the justifier, the propitiation for our sin, has entered into God's presence with His own blood, and made payment once and for all. These glowing angels, sitting in an empty tomb, are God's unspoken declaration that payment has been received, that the "Sun of Righteousness shall arise with healing in His wings" and forever heal those who fear His Name.[4]

Staring at the two of them, Mary is perplexed. Growing angry. And more than a little afraid. But before she or any of the women with her can utter a word, an angel poses one of the greatest questions ever asked in the history of spoken language: "Why do you seek the living among the dead?" After a short pause, he says what may well be the seven best words ever heard by the human race: "He is not here, but is risen!"[5]

Seeing the confusion on the faces of the women, the other angel explains with great patience: "Remember how He spoke to you when He was still in Galilee, saying, 'The Son of Man must be delivered into the hands of sinful men, and be crucified, and the third day rise again.'"[6] *

Somewhere in here, Mary Magdalene thinks for the first time, *What if Jesus is alive?* She steps out of the tomb as the first rays of daylight streak across the horizon and whispers, "He's alive?"

The women return to Jesus' other disciples and spread the word, but no one believes them. "Their words seemed to them like idle tales."[7] Like nonsense. To the heartbroken, their words are too good to be true, and even the thought that they might be true is too painful to entertain. Yet slowly, as the fog of pain lifts, the disciples remember the words Jesus spoke to the Pharisees when they told Him that Herod wanted to kill Him: "Go, tell that fox, 'Behold I cast out demons and perform cures today and tomorrow, and the third day I shall be perfected."[8] And the words of the prophet Hosea: "On the third day He will raise us up."[9]

Could it be?

In the hours following, two men are traveling to a village called

---

* I laugh every time I see this verse and chapter reference: Luke 24:7. As in 24/7. To me it's a sign of God's sense of humor. It's always true.

Emmaus, seven miles outside Jerusalem. One of the men is Cleopas, whom an early tradition holds was the brother of Mary's husband Joseph. It might be that Paul tells us the identity of the second man when, in 1 Corinthians 15:5, he tells us Jesus first appeared to Peter. Whatever the case and whoever they were, "While they conversed and reasoned . . . Jesus Himself drew near and went with them."[10] They walk awhile, talk about the last few days' events and yet their eyes are blinded. They don't know it's Him. Only when they sit to eat and Jesus takes the bread, blesses it, breaks it, and gives it to them are their eyes opened.

His last act with His friends was to break bread and offer the cup of the new covenant. His first act when returning is the same. Maybe it was here that they remember what He told them after He'd walked on the Sea of Galilee: "I am the living bread which came down from heaven. If anyone eats of this bread, he will live forever; and the bread that I shall give is My flesh, which I shall give for the life of the world."[11]

Notice where they are as He breaks bread. Seven miles outside of Jerusalem. The last time they saw Jesus, He was stone-cold dead in a sealed tomb in Jerusalem. The fact that He's no longer there means—if nothing else—that He's been somewhere . . .

Party's Over

By the time they took down the body, Jesus' spirit was long gone. The moment He died here, His work wasn't over. Jesus' spirit climbed down off that cross and—cloaked in the sin of all mankind, starting with mine and yours—He descended into hell where there was a party underway, an orgy, unlike any seen in the history of this world or any other.*

Jesus descends and walks through the gates of hell, where demons and spiritual forces of wickedness throw blood-stained metal and bronze and run out of the crowd and punch Him or stab Him with swords or

---

* I realize what I'm suggesting here is not in Scripture and may be theologically suspect, but just work with me for a moment.

whip Him or thrust spears completely through Him. The road is littered with bones and maggots and rotting flesh. The pandemonium rises as He approaches the throne where satan has placed himself. The raucous party is at a climax. The noise deafening. The stench nauseating. The evil horde has created a mosh pit and they are foaming at the mouth because they think they are about to feast on the body and blood of Jesus the Christ.

The only one not enjoying the party is satan.* he knows the prophecies; he knows the Word; he was there when God spoke it. Don't think so? Read Ezekiel 28 and Isaiah 14. Want further evidence? When he tempted Jesus just three and a half years prior to His crucifixion, he quoted verbatim from Psalm 91:11–12. satan is not happy. In truth, he is squirming; he's been dreading this day. Trying to find a way out. A way around. A legal loophole. his eyes are frantic. he is looking for a way out because he knows he is about to be exposed as the fraud he is—and always has been.

Jesus walks down the road to satan's court. Hordes of demonic entities hang on the rafters and balconies around Him. They are taking turns on the ceiling fans that do little to alleviate the heat. Everything that is evil is in attendance and salivating at the coming final blow which they know will eradicate Jesus once and for all. Total, universal, otherworldly domination! In their minds, they have salted and peppered the body and are turning Him over the spit. They can taste Him.

But a funny thing happens here.

It is here—in the pit of hell—that Jesus strips off the sin of humanity that has masked Him. Like a dark blanket, or cloak, He rips it off His shoulders and hurls it like Halley's Comet at the skeletal throne comprised of skulls and vertebrae on which satan has parked his fat self. The light shoots forth from Jesus' body, and the darkness rolls back like a scroll. Demons screech and writhe. Those closest to Him go up in smoke. Literally. Ten

---

* These aren't typos. I refuse to capitalize the name "satan," and I refuse to capitalize the word "he" when it refers to satan—even at the start of a sentence.

thousand degrees Fahrenheit in less than a second. Just dark spots on the dirt where their souls once stood.

Party's over. satan turns and kicks it into high gear, cowering. he's defeated. Powerless.[12] Dethroned. Destroyed.[13] Disarmed. Having been made a public spectacle.[14] Exposed as a punk whose kingdom is crumbling all around. Jesus, the Word made flesh, who upholds all things by the word of His power says, "Stop!" and lucifer can't move. he knows what Jesus came to get. Jesus lifts the keys dangling on lucifer's belt. "I'll take those." Then He places His heel on satan's neck and speaks for all eternity to hear. All of this universe and every other can see and hear His proclamation. His thundering voice sounds like many rushing waters. Like Niagara. Or the waves breaking at Pipeline. Right here and right now, Jesus is ruling in the midst of His enemies, who have been made His footstool.[15]

The Lion of Judah roars, "All debts are paid. All past, present, and future claims are cancelled. Forever. 'The life of the flesh is in the blood, and I have given it to you upon the altar to make atonement for your souls.'[16] I have bought mankind back with My blood. My children are justified, redeemed, sanctified. No longer slaves. I have snatched them back out of the hand of the deceiver. Sin no longer has dominion. My children are no longer under law but under grace!"[17]

Face down, satan lies in excruciating pain. he writhes as Jesus' foot presses his mouth into the maggot-filled, worm-crawling dirt of hell. satan raises a finger. "But, what about that scum-sucking sinner, Charles Martin?"

Jesus nods and considers me, then He squeezes His hand like a sponge. Given the hole, it should have produced blood. At least a drop. But there was none. Not one single drop. "Nope."

satan protests. "But, what about that thing he did . . ."

Another squeeze. Nothing. Evidence that on the cross, Jesus held nothing back. He'd left it all topside. Bled out. "Paid in full."

satan reaches in his pocket and holds up the record of my wrongs of which I was and am guilty. Every last one. The claims were true then.

They are true now. I'm guilty as sin. Jesus reads it. "You got them all. Even missed a few. But. . . ." Again, He holds His hand. One last squeeze of the sponge. The hole is dry. Veins empty. "Your claims are revoked."

Jesus, dangling the keys, makes one final declaration, carving it into the walls of hell with His very voice. (Here He speaks in King James English.) "Be it known this day—all is forgiven. I have redeemed mankind with My blood on the altar. It is finished."

Upon hearing the words of Jesus, the foundations of hell crack and crumble. satan's throne crumbles. The kingdom is in chaos.

This is the moment in which Jesus has made good on His promise. Gone is the tortured carpenter. Gone is the heavy, lumbering, splinter-laden cross, the nails still dripping. It's been snapped like a toothpick. Reduced to splinters. It doesn't hold Him anymore. Neither does the grave. This right here, this is Jesus, the firstborn among the dead, the victorious conquering, undefeated King—who holds the keys to death and hades—and this is the moment in which God the Father has officially and once and forever transferred you and me from the kingdom of darkness to the kingdom of the Son of His love. This is *the* moment when "you who once were far off have been brought near by the blood of Christ."[18]

In Leviticus 17:11, when God said, "the life of the flesh is in the blood, and I have given it to you upon the altar to make atonement for your souls," this is the moment where we begin living in the truth of that. satan's defeat was absolute. The victory complete. Eternal. Irrevocable.

This is that moment.

As Jesus walks out of hell, He exits through the prison of cells—the Alcatraz of hell—where His people have been held in bondage. Slavery. Every form of addiction. Every sin. And as He walks by, every lock clicks, shackles fall off, gates of bronze are ripped off their hinges, bars of iron cut in two.[19]

Prisoners, long held captive, begin screaming at the top of their lungs. "Freedom!" and "Long live King Jesus." "Worthy is the Lamb that was slain!" "Worthy to receive honor and glory and praise." And then my favorite, "And the King of glory shall come in"![20]

Love with Legs

Scripture tells us that upon His resurrection, Jesus appeared to Mary; Peter; his brother James, who later founded and led the church in Jerusalem, and who wrote the book of James; to the eleven where He invited Thomas to stick his hand into the hole in His side; to over five hundred brethren; and to Paul. The last recorded appearance we have in Scripture is with John on the island of Patmos.

Here's what I'd like to know—what did Jesus do when He met them? He had just defeated death. Evil. Sin. He just gave the most resounding and obliterating defeat to the enemy in the history of history. I think it's worth asking, "What did He do when He returned? What did He say?"

John gives us at least a partial answer:

> Then, the same day at evening, being the first day of the week, when the doors were shut where the disciples were assembled, for fear of the Jews, Jesus came and stood in the midst, and said to them, "Peace be with you." When He had said this, He showed them His hands and His side. Then the disciples were glad when they saw the Lord.
>
> So Jesus said to them again, "Peace to you! As the Father has sent Me, I also send you." And when He had said this, He breathed on them, and said to them, "Receive the Holy Spirit." (John 20:19–22)

Then Jesus said this: "If you forgive the sins of any, they are forgiven them; if you retain the sins of any, they are retained" (v. 23).

Two things: First, in the same way Jesus was sent, He is sending us. But sent to do what? The answer is quick in coming. Forgive.

Ouch.

If forgiveness is not the signature piece, the anchor, of a walk with Jesus, then tell me why it's the first word out of His mouth when He returns from hell?

The bedrock of the resurrection of Jesus Christ is forgiveness. Forgiveness is love with legs. Period. The mushroom cloud rising out of hell was caused by three words: "Father, forgive them." And for that, hell had no answer. Death lost its victory. No sting. Captives set free.

If life for the unbeliever on that side of the cross is, "Lord, please forgive me," then life for the believer on this side begins with, "Lord, I forgive _____." You fill in the blank.

Here's the truth about the resurrection, and it flies in the face of much of contemporary preaching: the resurrection does not guarantee you a life free from hardship and suffering. The resurrection guarantees you the power to die Jesus' death and live Jesus' life. Read that again. It's a paradigm shift.

The resurrection does not guarantee you a life free from hardship and suffering. The resurrection guarantees you the power to die Jesus' death and live Jesus' life.

And that power and that life start with forgiveness.

How sure am I that Jesus is serious about forgiveness? Let's look back at His words:

- "Judge not, and you shall not be judged. Condemn not, and you shall not be condemned. Forgive, and you will be forgiven. Give, and it will be given to you: good measure, pressed down, shaken together, and running over will be put into your bosom. For with the same measure that you use, it will be measured back to you" (Luke 6:37–38).
- "And Jesus answered saying to them . . . 'Whenever you stand praying, forgive, if you have anything against anyone, so that your Father who is in heaven will also forgive you your transgressions. But if you do not forgive, neither will your Father who is in heaven forgive your transgressions'" (Mark 11:22,25–26, NASB).

Don't skip over the "whenever you pray" part. It means, whenever. Or, every time. The Lord is encouraging us to take a quick inventory. Check our own pulses. Sniff out any unforgiveness.

Secondly, see those words "and," "so that," and "if"? They are conditional. Maybe they stand out to me because I'm a writer. These words connect two phrases. The second is conditioned upon the first. That means that certain conditions must be met in order for the second half of the equation to come true.

Don't miss this. "If you do not forgive . . . neither will your Father . . . forgive you."

This is nonnegotiable. If it feels like a kick in the gut, I can't help that. But regardless of how you feel about it, it begs the question: Do you meet the conditions?

I want to pause for those of you who have been dinged by legalism—meaning you grew up somewhere with somebody thumping you over the head with Scripture and a long list of don't dos, or you were taught that your salvation and happiness and worthiness are somehow tied to your deeds and how well you measure up and check all the boxes and obey all the commandments, or you've been beat over the head with the idea that Christianity is nothing but a list of rules. If that's you, take a deep breath. I'm not hitting you with a list of don't dos or thou shalt nots. satan has twisted this.

Instead, I am echoing an invitation offered by Jesus: "But I say to you, love your enemies, bless those who curse you, do good to those who hate you, and pray for those who . . . persecute you" (Matt. 5:44).

Accepting the invitation to forgive is a choice. We either accept it or not.

Let's look at the Lord's Prayer—Jesus is teaching His friends how to pray: "And forgive us our debts, as we also have forgiven our debtors. . . . For if you forgive others for their transgressions, your heavenly Father will also forgive you. But if you do not forgive others, then your Father will not forgive your transgressions" (Matt. 6:12,14–15, NASB).

There it is in black and white: "if you do" and "if you do not." I can't water that down for you so it doesn't hurt less. It means what it means.*

This requires an honest look in the mirror. A truthful glance at your soul and my soul. Do I meet the condition? Do you?

---

* Look also at Matthew 18:21-35.

But Charles, that's a hard word.

Yes. It is. But, let me encourage you with this: our choice to forgive is the beginning of our own healing. The opposite is also true—the choice not to forgive will delay our healing. Unforgiveness eats us from the inside out. It's like pouring gasoline in a Styrofoam cup. Forgiveness is the stake in the ground that Jesus drove into the floor of hell. And it stands there today. It's is how He, Jesus, made a "public spectacle" of the enemy (Col. 2:13–15). It is where He, Jesus, was made manifest so that He might "destroy the works of the devil" (1 John 3:8). And it is here that He, Jesus, rendered powerless the enemy (Heb. 2:14). And from heaven's perspective, the cross of Jesus looks a lot like a peg, driven into the face of earth, on which everything hangs.

Those of you who are really hurt might cry out, "But Charles, that's not fair." I know. Trust me, I feel your pain. Or, at least some of it. But let me take you by the hand and lead you back to the cross. Nothing about the cross was fair. We—through your sin and my sin—crucified the very Son of God.

Jesus, who is both "just and the justifier" spent His life focused on redemption (Rom. 3:26), not fairness. To be honest, He's far more concerned with our holiness.

In contrast, the enemy is focused on fairness because he knows if he can get you stuck there, he can take your eyes off Jesus. Unforgiveness is a trap. It's one of the enemy's strongest weapons. If not the strongest. Before the enemy shoots this arrow at your chest, he dips it in gasoline and lights it. But when we forgive, we douse the flame with water and render it impotent.

Look again at John 20:23: "If you forgive the sins of any, they are forgiven them; if you retain the sins of any, they are retained."

In Greek, to "forgive" or "remit" means to send forth or send away. To let go from oneself. The same word was used to describe when Jesus "gave up His Spirit" (John 19:30). It means to let go from one's power or possession. To let it go free. To let go from obligation. To remove the sins from someone. To liberate a person from their guilt and their power. And in my mind, there's some energy behind this when it happens. Jesus didn't just whimper out His spirit on the cross. He yelled at the top of His lungs for all He was worth.

Forgiveness is not freedom in sin, but freedom from sin—to thrust away, to loose, to send forth as a voice, to leave or let alone, leave behind, to remove the sins from another. The toughest part for most of us is "to let go from obligation." To tear up the IOU we carry in our back pockets.

Now let's look at "retain." It means "to use strength, seize, hold fast, to hold as in the hands, to have power over, rule over, to hold by the feet, to cleave to, hold fast in mind, to hold a prisoner."

Have power over? Rule over? Hold a prisoner? You mean, when I don't forgive someone, I do this to them? Yes. And what's more, that same power imprisons you, rules over you, and holds you a prisoner.

When we don't forgive someone, we retain. Forgive versus retain. That's it in a nutshell.

The Hard Truth

Unforgiveness is the anchor in us where hatred, bitterness, racism, envy, self-pity, jealousy, anger—it's where they attach. It's where they purchase. It's like rotten meat in our spirits. Velcro of the soul. You can shake those surface things loose till you're blue in the face, but until you remove the rancid stuff, you're just swatting flies.

At its most basic, forgiveness is an attitude of your heart toward another. It is an act of your will. Not emotion. It is often in direct opposition to your emotions.

Does this sound familiar?

As you've been reading this, many of you have been having internal dialogues. I have and I'm writing it. They sound like this: *Do I really need to forgive that person?* Their face keeps flashing in the corner of your mind. You're trying to talk yourself out of it. I'm trying to as well. *No, I don't really need to forgive them.*

Yes, you do. You and I need to start with *them*.

"But," I can hear the objection, "I don't feel like forgiving them." Entirely natural. Chances are good that we are not going to "feel" like forgiving. Our souls are seldom in agreement with our spirits. This is why King David often commanded his soul. Just read the Psalms.

I started this chapter with a few heartbroken men and women appearing at an empty tomb. Let's go back to that same moment. Imagine we are sitting alongside the disciples. In their minds, Jesus was battered, beaten, and died a gruesome and undeserved death. After three years of hope and planning, the movement is dead. Hopes dashed. Can you see the long faces? Can you hear the hearts breaking?

Then we get word. Stone rolled away. Body stolen. "They've taken Him." We are livid. We, like Peter, run to the tomb. Out of breath, we jump in. Ready to go to fisticuffs. "Where is He!?" The angel casually smiles as if he's filing his nails with an emery board. "He is not here. He is risen!" It is the best news any of us have ever heard. Hope bubbles to the surface. We step into the first rays of daylight and whisper to ourselves, "What if He's alive?"

As we walk away, whistling and doing fist pumps, we hear the faint echo of Jesus' voice. He is issuing an invitation. "Follow Me." We want nothing more. So we, like giddy school children, shoulder that splintery thing and take a step like Simon of Cyrene—and we immediately bump into resurrected Jesus who is staring at us. He is mopping up the ooze spilling out of our heart. His eyes are sympathetic. "What's this?"

We stammer, wrapping our cloak tighter about us. "Oh, hello, Lord. It's an old wound. . . . I was wronged. Somebody hurt me—"

He cuts us off. He knows the answer. The pus is proof. But He asks anyway, "Have you forgiven them?"

We shake our heads. Throw up our hands. "You don't understand. I was wronged. Deeply."

He holds out His hands. "You mean like Me?"

Now He's starting to get it. We smile. "Yes! Exactly!"

He glances behind us. "What's that you're carrying?"

We proudly boast. "Your cross."

He sniffs the putrid stuff spilling out of our chests and shakes His head. "No. No, it's not."

He touches our wound with His finger. "Why don't you let Me have that?"

We recoil. "Because it'll hurt."

His eyes show the depth of His compassion: "It'll hurt a lot more if you let it stay there."

We protest. "But Lord, it's all I have. . . ."

He wraps His arm around us. "How about you give it to Me, and I'll give you Me in exchange."

Maybe we in the church, as we've taught this, have turned this whole forgiveness thing into a "thou shalt not." Yes, it is a command. But the reason it is commanded is because, at the root, it is an invitation to climb up into Abba's lap. If you're a parent, and your child came to you with a telephone pole stuck through his chest, how many of us would just cuddle alongside them and ignore the pole? Of course not.

Will the pulling out of the pole hurt?

Yes. No denying that.

But it's going to hurt a lot more if it stays there.

If we're honest, our problem is a deep-seated desire for people to get what they've got coming. For justice. And because we are in pain, the enemy reminds us of the IOU tucked in our back pocket, of the long list of wrongs committed against us, and he convinces us that the only way for justice to be served—to our satisfaction—is for us to serve it on our terms and in our timing.

But, that's not justice. That's vengeance. And that doesn't belong to us.

The truth is that Jesus wants justice too. It's the foundation of His throne. He just wants you to let Him administer it.

Note: I am not telling you to be a doormat and let someone continue to walk all over you. Nor am I telling you to continue to suffer abuse at the hand of someone else. Don't hear that. Nor am I telling you that a desire for justice is somehow wrong. That desire is entirely right and in perfect alignment with the heart of Christ.

I'm trying to make the case—and I realize this can be painful—that if you are walking in unforgiveness, you are not carrying the cross of Jesus.

Maybe you're still struggling. Giving rise to another honest and heart-felt objection. "But, if I show compassion I appear weak. Like they've won. Like I'm letting them off the hook."

Forgiveness is not weakness. It's a stake through the heart of the enemy. It is entirely possible to forgive someone and seek justice. The two are not mutually exclusive. I am simply holding up the Word of God and showing you that the centerpiece, the epicenter, to the gospel of Jesus Christ is forgiveness. We are commanded to forgive.

Straight up—forgiveness is an act of obedience.

Forgiveness doesn't let them off the hook. Forgiveness is just handing them, still dangling on the hook, to Jesus.

Note: While I'm working on this, I am involved in a situation where someone is maliciously trying to hurt me and others I love. It's painful. My anger bubbles. An injustice has been committed. And trust me, I want justice. The Perry Mason moment. I have had lots of those silent conversations in my head. Where I've rehearsed all the words I'd like to tell them.

Then I hear the whisper, feel His breath on my face: "You gonna give Me that? Charles, it'll kill you."

So, here I am, facing a choice. Staring me in the face. "I'm sorry, Lord. Here. You take it." And don't think it's any easier cause I'm sitting here writing about it. If anything, it's amplified. Proving I'm no expert and need to listen to my own teaching.

The Power of Forgiveness

When we forgive, we proclaim the resurrection to this world and to every other.

Let me say that again: When you forgive, you proclaim the resurrection to this world and to every other. It echoes through eternity. When we forgive, Jesus wins again, and the doors are torn off prison cells. Chains broken. Captives set free. You are used to usher in the kingdom of God.

Don't believe me? Forgive someone who doesn't deserve it.

Maybe you're not yet at this place. It's okay. Forgiveness is a process. And it can take time. The wound took time to fester. Sometimes the unpacking of those layers takes time. For some of you, your wound is Mount Rushmore and it's crushing your chest. You can think of little else, and you're not real interested in proclaiming the resurrection. The only thing you want to echo through eternity is vengeance. I get it. I do. So does Jesus. I am not denying the pain or severity of that. But His command is not conditional upon the depth or age of your and my pain.

Regardless of our objections, forgiveness is still a commandment. Here's the rub. Just as Jesus will not take your Isaac by force, He will not make your choice for you. We choose to forgive. And we can choose not to.

In my own life, I've learned that while forgiveness is an act of obedience, obedience itself requires something. And that something is the same thing Jesus did before He ever walked this earth. Paul describes it writing to the Philippians:

> Let this mind be in you which was also in Christ Jesus, who, being in the form of God, did not consider it robbery to be equal with God, but made Himself of no reputation, taking the form of a bondservant, and coming in the likeness of men. And being found in appearance as a man, He humbled Himself and became obedient to the point of death, even the death of the cross. (Phil. 2:5–8)

The fruit of forgiveness is rooted in the soil of humility. Without humility, there is no forgiveness.

Sometimes we just need reminding, in real simple terms, that the King of all kings—the very Son of God, the One who fashioned us from the dust of the earth, who pressed His lips to our mouths and breathed in the *ruach* of God—stepped off His throne to forgive you and me. He didn't have to. He had a choice. How can we look on Him and not do the same?

If you're wrestling with forgiving *that* person, the answer is yes. You need to start with them. And they don't have to be alive. They can be stone-cold dead. Whether they are alive or dead matters little. The question is this: is the wound healed or still festering?

Here are some of the names I've heard when people describe *that* person. I list them because some have surprised me:

- Father, mother, dead father, dead mother, wife, ex-wife, ex-wife's boyfriend or spouse, ex-wife's attorney, the biological parents who abandoned you at the hospital, brother/sister, children, mother-in-law, father-in-law.
- Current boss, former boss, opposing counsel, that guy who didn't hire you, the guy that fired you without cause, that former partner who sued you for ownership—and won.
- The man who molested you when you were a kid, the drunk driver that killed your loved one, the person sitting next to you, the person who sleeps in the same bed with you.
- That white guy, that black man, that Jew, that Muslim, that Mexican.
- The IRS, the Democratic or Republican or Tea Party, Fox News, the president, Congress.
- God.
- Or—and this is a biggie—yourself.

Sometimes the worst damage to our own soul is that which we've caused ourselves. The enemy tricks us into thinking if we punish ourselves, we can somehow beat out the pain or purify the sick place. Not true. We need to forgive ourselves.

Scripture says the Holy Spirit is the finger of God. So, if you want to walk in the power of the resurrection and the love of Christ, give Him permission to point out those people to you. Can you pray this: "Lord, I give You permission to point out to me every person I need to forgive"?

True forgiveness includes releasing someone from our judgment. Doing this sounds like, "Lord, I forgive so-and-so. *And* I release them from my judgment."

When I've suggested this to folks, the response I've often heard is, "Well what do you mean?"

The best way I can describe it is that it's a heart thing. It means giving them all the way up. Otherwise—and I don't really understand this other than to know that it is true—the people are forgiven but they remain in some sort of emotional probation. When we release them from our judgment, we also free ourselves from future false expectations. If we don't, we walk into future relationships unconsciously expecting the same thing.

If you're really struggling here—staring up at the El Capitan towering before you—God knew this about you, so He made a provision here too. And listen to this because it frees you up. The power to forgive others does not start with you. It starts with Jesus.

And just as His forgiveness of you is a gift, so is your ability to forgive others.

Here is Paul, and he spoke as one of us: "The love of God has been poured out in our hearts by the Holy Spirit who was given to us." (Romans 5:5). Poured out means I'm filled up. So, what do I do with the reservoir? Jesus' answer is, "He who believes in Me . . . out of his heart will flow rivers of living water" (John 7:38). Will flow? Why is this? Because water that doesn't flow stagnates. We'll talk more about this in a later chapter, but this is Jesus speaking during the last time He ate with His closest friends: "A new commandment I give to you, that you love one another, even as I have loved you" (John 13:34, NASB).

What kind of love is this? To begin with, it is forgiving.

Your ability to forgive does not depend on your size, strength, speed, intellectual smarts, good looks, money, the power you wield in the corporate world, who you know, or what your father did or didn't do. You have everything you need. The question is not can you forgive but will you. Are you willing? If you're looking at your wound and you're still not quite sure, let me pose it this way: Are you willing to be willing? The gift is yours for the taking. Will you ask Him to give you this gift? His answer is clear: "If you ask Me anything in My name, I will do it" (John 14:14, NASB). Forgiveness is an unmerited gift. And just as we desperately need it from Jesus, there are people who, whether they know it or not, need that gift from us.

Here's where it can get messy and the rubber meets the road. In some cases, we need to go to that person and verbally forgive them. Face to face, if possible. It's a spiritual transaction. In the same way we need to hear it from Jesus, they need to hear it from us, and we need to hear it from us.

In every case, whether we meet with that person face-to-face or not, we need to give that person audibly and out loud to Jesus. Words matter. Especially when we speak them out loud. "By your words you will be justified, and by your words you will be condemned" (Matt. 12:37).

Whether today or seventy years from now, you and I will stand in judgment before the King. No one escapes this. Remember Matthew 7:2 about how with the measure we use, it will be measured back to us? This is where it comes home to roost.

Taking Up the Cross vs. Walking with It

Paul tells us we must all stand before the judgment seat of Christ (2 Cor. 5:10). Because this is true, it's worth considering that moment. My image is rather simple: I die here and wake up in the throne room. Blink to blink. God the Father—the Ancient of Days—is seated. His Son, My Redeemer, is seated at His right hand. The Holy Spirit is sort of hovering in the background.

Revelation 19:11–16 describes my Judge in this way:

> He who sat on [a white horse] was called Faithful and True, and in right-eousness He judges and makes war. His eyes were like a flame of fire, and on His head were many crowns. He had a name written that no one knew except Himself. He was clothed with a robe dipped in blood, and His name is called The Word of God. And the armies in heaven, clothed

in fine linen, white and clean, followed Him on white horses. Now out of His mouth goes a sharp sword, that with it He should strike the nations. And He Himself will rule them with a rod of iron. He Himself treads the winepress of the fierceness and wrath of Almighty God. And He has on His robe and on His thigh a name written: KING OF KINGS AND LORD OF LORDS.

This is the King who judges us.

As I imagine this scene, God is staring at a giant PowerPoint presentation on the back wall of the Milky Way. Every sin I've ever committed is listed in detail for all humanity. A wrinkle between His eyes. He points to the list. "You do all this?"

There's no denying it. "Yes, Sir."

"What defense do you offer?"

I point to Jesus. "Him."

He raises an eyebrow. Long pause. He turns to Jesus who whispers in His Father's ear.

God turns back to me. "My Son tells Me that in the time He's known you, you've repented. Of everything. And—by His unmerited gift of grace— you have forgiven. Everyone. Of everything." He leans back. "Is this true?"

The enormity of this is more than I can understand or bear. Maybe for the first time, I can see the whole of it. I speak softly. "As much as I know my own heart, yes . . . Sir."

Jesus whispers again. God nods. Returns to me. "He tells Me that you believe and have openly confessed Him before men." I am trembling and I can't stop shaking. God stands, and the entire host of heaven bows. His voice thunders. "Is this true, Charles?"

This will either be my end or my beginning. So, I tuck my knees beneath me, press my face to the floor of heaven, and raise my hands to God Most High. "Yes. Yes, that's true! I did all that. I'm guilty." I point to Jesus who I can't look at because He's shining like the sun. "But, I know Him and I have not denied Him. He knows me. And my wife and kids know Him. And people who know me know I know Him. Your Son withheld from me what I deserve and gave me what I did not. He forgave me. He's my king. My redeemer. My sanctifier. My justifier. And the lover of my soul." I pause. "Your Word tells me that He endured the shame for the joy that was set before Him. . . .[21] Well, I am the cause of that shame and the source of that joy."

The Ancient of Days scratches His beard, pivots, and stares intently at the wall of heaven, which, once covered in pages and pages of ink, is now blank. White as snow. Control-Alt-Delete. He stands, sucks through His teeth, steps down off that throne, and walks forward. My body gives way, and I crumble. Kneeling, He lifts my chin, breathes on my face, and whispers the words my spirit has been dying to hear since He spoke me into existence. "Well done, good and faithful servant."[22] *

The way to "good and faithful"—to eternity with the Father—is through repentance on one side of the cross and forgiveness on the other. Neither of which Jesus will do for you. They are flip sides of the same cross, and they require a daily choice. A daily humbling. And it may well be the toughest thing you and I ever do.

Taking up the cross is saying, "Please forgive me."

Walking with it is saying, "I forgive."

Don't let your eyes pass over that—taking up the cross of Jesus is saying, "Jesus, please forgive me." Walking with it is saying, "Jesus, I forgive."

If the struggle of that causes you trepidation or concern, keep your eye focused on the prize. His "lovingkindness is better than life" (Ps. 63:3). I know of no more powerful force in the universe than the power to forgive. The blood of Jesus cries a better word than that of Abel (Heb. 12:24). And each of us wields it. Abel's blood cries out, "Guilty!" Jesus blood whispers, "Not guilty." The blood of Jesus is the antidote to the blood of Abel, and by speaking it out loud we inject it into the wound.

Don't let satan twist this. Forgiveness is not a "thou shalt not." It's a "get to." It's an invitation. When we do this, we get to be like Him and with Him.

Inside each of us is a deep-seated desire for justice. A reckoning. A hope

---

* Father, forgive me if this is presumptuous. It is my hope and prayer.

that others get what they've got coming. But, truth be told, if justice is going to be leveled, then we've got it coming too. Let's not lose sight of the basics. The King of the universe stepped off His throne, disrobed, laid down His crown, and walked your death for you. For me. He gave us what we did not deserve and withheld from us what we did. Now, He's alive, seated at the right hand of God Most High, and beckoning. "Child, I've prepared a place for you. Come join Me in My Father's house." Entrance into His kingdom, passage through the gates, starts with repentance. "Please forgive me." Residence in His kingdom, the process of sanctification where we become more like Him, occurs with "I forgive _____."

If you're still reading, then you've shouldered that splintery thing and you're carrying your cross. The fact that your eye is resting on this word is evidence to this. In the same way that He met His friends after He walked out of hell shining like the sun, He is here. Right now. Face-to-face. With me. With you. For some reason I think His breath smells like mint—but maybe that's just me.

Some of us are carrying shrapnel we have yet to let Him cut out. Some of us know people who are bleeding and need triage. Whether yours, mine, or theirs, Jesus eyes the wound and says to us what He said two thousand years ago:

- "Thus it is written, and thus it was necessary for the Christ to suffer and to rise from the dead the third day, and that repentance and remission of sins should be preached in His name to all nations, beginning at Jerusalem. And you are witnesses of these things" (Luke 24:46–48).

- "'Peace to you! As the Father has sent Me, I also send you.' And when He had said this, He breathed on them, and said to them, 'Receive the Holy Spirit. If you forgive the sins of any, they are forgiven them; if you retain the sins of any, they are retained'" (John 20:21–23).

We are standing on the precipice of His kingdom. His last step onto that cross purchased your and my redemption. Our first step walks it out. The same power that raised Jesus from the dead rests on the tip of your and my tongue and it begins with the words, "I forgive."

The last thing Jesus did with His friends before His crucifixion, and the first thing He did upon His return, involved bread and wine. It's important to Him. So, before we pray, take bread and wine and set if before you. If alcohol is a problem, grape juice works fine. Find some place quiet, bless the bread and wine, break it, and then lift the cup. Eat the body and drink the blood of Jesus. Proclaim the resurrection.

As you do, let this prayer echo through eternity. This is what it sounds like:

Lord, what I am about to do is not easy for me. In fact, it's one of the toughest things I've ever done. Help me do this. This entire act of forgiveness is contrary to my nature, but You humbled Yourself coming here, and I want to do the same. So, regardless of how I feel about this at this moment, I yield to You. I surrender to Your righteous reign and sovereign dominion. You alone are God.

Lord, You know what I'm about to tell You, but I'm going to say it anyway: I have been hurt deeply and I am hurting. As a result, I am hurting others. When I look inside, I feel like parts of my soul have been stolen. Like parts of me are missing. As a result, there is unforgiveness in me. I can feel it. It doesn't like my praying this prayer. Paul told us in Romans that sin dwelt in him. I can feel this dwelling in me. And I don't want it there anymore. So Father, here's my heart—take this stone from me. I forgive _____ [name them out loud one by one]. I forgive them for what they did to me. [If you want to name the acts, do it.]

Lord, I give every hurtful act to You. I also give justice to You. I take my hands off the outcome and release them from my judgment and into Your hands. Completely. [It may be cheesy, but take your hand, pick the stone out of and off your heart, place it in your other hand, and offer it up to God.] Having done so, Lord, I ask that You release me from these chains. As I have cut them free, I ask that You cut me free. I declare that I have forgiven them, that their sins are forgiven them, and that You have forgiven me. I declare that no matter the injustice, no matter the pain, no matter the hurt and anguish they have caused me, I forgive them outright and completely. I tear up the IOU. They owe me nothing from this day forward. As You forgave me unconditionally on the cross, I forgive them. Your Word says for us to pray for those who persecute us and bless those who curse us, so in obedience to Your Word, I pray for them and I bless them in the name and by the blood of Jesus.

And, Lord, just being honest, when I grow weak in my conviction, and the pain of the memory returns, and I shake my fist and want to turn the screws, see justice done my way, or take back the IOU, please forgive me. Let me return here, give me this grace again, and I will give them to You again and again. I know me, and this might happen. Please forgive me when it does.

Lord, there is now this place in me. You know the one. It's the vacant place where the wound of unforgiveness festered. It's raw. Painful. It needs You. And I can't heal me. I am in desperate need of You. So, please send Your Holy Spirit right now, into the deepest, darkest, hurting, wounded places in me and bring healing. Restore to me my missing pieces. Make me whole again. By Your stripes I am healed, and I need that healing. Jesus, I know that it is Your heart to forgive. I want that. Today. Tomorrow. Every day. Pour it out on me. Give me Your heart. A new heart.

Lastly, Lord, if You've really done what I've just asked You to do, and I believe You have, then it would be rather unthoughtful of me not to thank You. So, I do. Really. I thank You, Lord. Where else can I take this? Who else has any power to do anything with any of this? No one. Thank You for healing me, releasing me, and restoring me. For returning the pieces of me that were lost or stolen. In the name of Jesus, I release Your Holy Spirit to abound and grow and heal me, now.

In Jesus' Name, amen.

If you're one of those people who started reading this with shrapnel on the inside, and you prayed this, let me echo the words of Jesus: "Your sins are forgiven you." For those of you with tears streaming down your face or snot pouring out your nose, a pile of tissues in your hand, be encouraged; all are evidence of a deep work of forgiveness having taken place. I pray the Lord bless you and seal His work in you this day and forever.

CHAPTER 8

Choose This Day

Jesus is preaching the kingdom of heaven in a home church in Capernaum. Possibly in the house of Peter's mother-in-law. The house sits within earshot of the synagogue and crowds have packed the interior. They are spilling out the doorway. A mob has surrounded the exterior. No one can easily get in or out.

Four men carry their friend, a paralytic, but they can't get near. Desperate, they climb up on the roof and begin tearing off the thatching. Making a hole. They've heard the stories. The lame walk.

Jesus looks up through the falling dust and debris into the new skylight as they lower the man on his bed. Note: the man is paralyzed. Adult diapers don't exist. This is not a sterile situation. Might not smell too great either.

The man lands in a limp pile before Jesus. Only his eyes move. He stares at Jesus.

The crowd is stunned. Astonished. Quiet. They crane their necks. Whispers spread. What will Jesus do?

Jesus marvels at the faith of the four holding the rope ends from the roof. He looks down at the paralytic. "Son, your sins are forgiven you."[1]

Why, when the man has obviously come for physical healing, does Jesus speak of his sins? Can't He see the man is paralyzed?

Fast forward. Jesus has been teaching in the temple, and the Pharisees have just tried to stone Him because He rattled their thinking with,

"Before Abraham was, I AM."[2] Scripture doesn't record where He "passed by," only that He did and He saw a man born blind. "From birth."[3] Seeing the man, the disciples ask, "Rabbi, who sinned, this man or his parents, that he was born blind?" Jesus responds, "Neither this man nor his parents sinned, but that the works of God should be revealed in him."[4]

We tend to focus on the second part of that exchange. But don't look past the disciples' question. It's important. Not just for them or for the man born blind, but for us. Today.

For the disciples, it was a given that either the blind man or his parents sinned. They are saying this based on Deuteronomy 28:28, "The LORD will smite you with madness and with blindness and with bewilderment of heart" (NASB). In their Jewish mindset, infirmity and sickness—in the cases above, both paralysis and blindness—were considered a curse and the direct result of either the individual's sin or the sin of his ancestors. This was the result of the law of Moses. God had ordained in His law that a person's ancestors' actions affected and effected them. God blessed the descendants of those who obeyed His law, and He cursed the descendants of those who disobeyed His law.

At the Jerusalem council, Peter describes this very thing as the "yoke on the neck of the disciples which neither our fathers nor we were able to bear" (Acts 15:10).

Let's look briefly at what the disciples believed and why.

Blessings and Curses in Israel

Both blessings and curses are words spoken. And each contains power. God is the author of most of them.* In order for a blessing to exist and be passed down, it must first have a cause: obedience. God blessed Abraham and his descendants because Abram believed God, and God credited it to him as righteousness. This meant the descendants of Abram experienced

---

* I'll talk about the others shortly.

blessing not because of their own faith but because of Abram's faith. Their blessing had nothing to do with them. Totally unmerited.

A curse is the reverse of that. Like a blessing, in order for a curse to exist, it must first have a cause. "Like a flitting sparrow, like a flying swallow, so a curse without a cause shall not alight" (Prov. 26:2). Meaning, something set it in motion. While this is difficult for some to hear or understand, most curses originate with God the Father. For those of you who are logically minded, both curse and blessing are the result of an if-then statement.

- If you listen and obey, then blessing follows you.
- But if you don't listen and disobey, then curse overtakes and devours you.

This was the mindset through which the disciples and every child of Israel since Moses gave the law, understood and interacted with God. It was how they knew Him. Through this filter, they knew His goodness and mercy. And they knew His wrath and judgment. But where did this understanding of God come from?

God affirmed this mindset of sin-caused infirmity when He described His own name. Four times God named Himself as the One who carries the sin of the fathers to the children. The first two times occurred just after He had delivered the nation of Israel from slavery in Egypt. Here, He had just given them the first of the Ten Commandments: "You shall not bow down to them nor serve them. For I, the LORD your God, am a jealous God, visiting the iniquity of the fathers upon the children to the third and fourth genera- tions of those who hate Me, but showing mercy to thousands, to those who love Me and keep My commandments" (Ex. 20:5–6).

See those words, "visiting the iniquity of the fathers upon the children to the third and fourth generation"? This was the crushing weight of the law from which there was no escape. The disciples knew this. As did the four guys holding the ropes. And the paralyzed man. And every Jewish boy since Moses.

The second time God named Himself, it was back up on the mountain when Moses asked to see Him. In short, Moses was asking God—this great and awesome God who had just delivered them through the most miraculous signs and wonders any group of people had ever thought of—"God, who are you?" God answered in what are some of the most important words in Scripture. They are His covenantal name:

> Now the LORD descended into the cloud and stood with him there, and proclaimed the name of the LORD. And the LORD passed before him and proclaimed, "The LORD, the LORD God, merciful and gracious, longsuffering, and abounding in goodness and truth, keeping mercy for thousands, forgiving iniquity and transgression and sin, by no means clearing the guilty, visiting the iniquity of the fathers upon the children and the children's children to the third and fourth generation." (Ex. 34:5–7)

The third time this name occurred was from the mouth of Moses as he begged God not to kill the entire nation of Israel when they refused to enter the land of Canaan after the twelve spies returned. God was annoyed and ready to strike them with pestilence and disinherit them when Moses prayed: "The LORD is longsuffering and abundant in mercy, forgiving iniquity and transgression; but He by no means clears the guilty, visiting the iniquity of the fathers on the children to the third and fourth generation" (Num. 14:18).

The last time occurred when Moses called all Israel together, reminding them of the covenant God made with them as he reviewed the Ten Commandments:

> You shall not make for yourself a carved image—any likeness of anything that is in heaven above, or that is in the earth beneath, or that is in the water under the earth; you shall not bow down to them nor serve them. For I, the LORD your God, am a jealous God, visiting the iniquity of the fathers upon the children to the third and fourth generations of those who hate Me, but showing mercy to thousands, to those who love Me and keep My commandments. (Deut. 5:8–10)

Don't miss this: four times God promised to visit or repay the iniquity of the fathers upon the children—for disobedience. And then just to make sure His people didn't forget, He sent His prophets to remind us that He never changes. Some eight hundred years after the law was given, Isaiah reminded God's people: "The earth is also defiled under its inhabitants, because they have transgressed the laws, changed the ordinance, broken the everlasting covenant. Therefore the curse has devoured the earth, and those who dwell in it are desolate. Therefore the inhabitants of the earth are burned, and few men are left" (Isa. 24:5–6).

Fifty years after the death of Isaiah, Jeremiah picked up the torch: "Ah, Lord GOD! Behold, You have made the heavens and the earth by Your great power and outstretched arm. There is nothing too hard for You. You show lovingkindness to thousands, and repay the iniquity of the fathers into the bosom of their children after them—the Great, the Mighty God, whose name is the LORD of hosts" (Jer. 32:17–18).

And then four hundred years before the birth of Christ, as the prophets were about to go silent, Malachi reminded the people that they serve an unchanging God: "For I am the LORD, I do not change" (Mal. 3:6).*

Pragmatically, how did this law work itself out in the Israelites' lives? Four generations is thirty people. (That's your mom and dad, plus your grandparents on both sides, plus your great-grandparents on both sides, plus your great-great-grandparents on both sides.) This meant in order to escape living under a curse, all thirty preceding people in a generational line had to live completely obedient lives, never disobeying the voice of the Lord.

Bottom line: no one escaped this.

But what were the results of obedience and disobedience? The genesis of this understanding comes straight from Moses:

If you diligently obey the voice of the LORD your God, to observe

---

* On this side of the cross, the writer of Hebrews reminds his first-century brothers of this same truth: "Jesus Christ is the same yesterday, today, and forever" (Heb. 13:8).

carefully all His commandments which I command you today, that the LORD your God will set you high above all the nations of the earth. And all these blessings shall come upon you and overtake you, because you obey the voice of the LORD your God. (Deut. 28:1–2)*

Moses then laid out twelve verses of blessings and instruction on how to receive the blessing of the Lord. It was simple. Listen and obey. If they did, blessing would overtake them. Notice the verb *overtake*. There's nothing you can do to avoid it. Blessing is coming whether you want it or not. The obedience of your forefathers will result in your experiencing blessing.

Then in Deuteronomy 28:15, Moses said, "If you do not obey the voice of the LORD your God, to observe carefully all His commandments and His statutes which I command you today, that all these curses will come upon you and overtake you." In verse 45, Moses said, "All these curses shall *come upon* you and *pursue* you and *overtake* you, until you are *destroyed*, because you did not obey the voice of the LORD your God, to keep His commandments and His statutes which He commanded you" (emphasis added). Then he listed a whole string of verses filled with curses. All total, there are more than two hundred curses pronounced in the Bible. Many occur between Deuteronomy 27:9 and 30:19.

This was life "under the law." This was the "yoke on the neck of the disciples which neither our fathers nor we were able to bear" (Acts 15:10). What Paul described as being "sold under sin" (Rom. 7:14). Everyone lived under a curse of some sort which had been sent down to them by those who had come before. It was there when they opened their eyes at birth. In return, they sent it to their children.

It was like swimming with weights.

With all that in mind, go back to Jesus' disciples as they question Him about the man born blind. As Jewish boys, they knew the verses I've just described. They could probably recite them from memory. For them,

---

* A better translation of "diligently obey" is "listen listening." It means to listen with both your ears and your heart.

physical sickness and infirmity was the direct result of disobedience—of not doing what God said. It was as natural a law as gravity.

For the disciples, living under a curse was inevitable. Therefore, one of the questions of their lives, if not *the* question, was: What do I need to do to come out from underneath this curse? How do I get back to blessing?

Why else did Jesus stand on the mountain and begin the most famous sermon in the history of sermons with the words, "Blessed are . . ."? He said it nine times.

The people sitting at His feet on that mountain knew they were living cursed lives. When Jesus said to the paralyzed man, "Your sins are forgiven you," He was removing the curse that caused the paralysis. And this was not a singular event. In over 60 percent of Jesus' healings, He first forgave sin and removed the curse before He brought healing.

Do Blessings and Curses Apply Today?

Okay. Why am I traveling down this rabbit hole?

I have walked intentionally with a group of men for over a decade. With a few for several decades. My desire for them and me has been closer intimacy with Jesus and greater freedom from the stuff that hinders us. During that walk, we've routinely fallen on our faces before the King and repented of everything we know to repent from. Whole-heartedly. Often with tears.

Yet, despite years of repentance, many Christians are still suffering chronic, relentless, illogical events in their lives. It's as if no matter what they do, how many times they repent, or how sincerely they might come back before the throne, they can't seem to come out from underneath whatever is hounding them. (I would include myself in this group.)

I knew Scripture tells me that by the blood of Jesus I'm more than a conqueror (Rom. 8:37). But I had to ask, how do I become a conqueror when my circumstances suggest I'm being conquered?

So, I began asking the Lord, "What is at work here?" From there, the Lord led me through a process of understanding blessing and curse as defined in His Word. But at that time I still saw those themes as Old Testament stuff. So I asked, "Is that Old Testament stuff really at work in our New Testament lives today?"

In order to answer that, let me take us back to His Word. We've seen that disobedience was the primary source of curses according to the law—but what kind of disobedience? What are the causes of curses? Here's an overly simple summary of the *causes* of the curses listed in Deuteronomy:

- false Gods—this can include going to see a witch doctor or fortune teller, palm reader, tarot card reader, or seeking any source other than God Most High for supernatural power or knowledge
- idolatry, including involvement in cults that worship other gods
- disrespect for parents
- treachery against a neighbor
- injustice to the weak or poor
- unnatural sexual relations, including incest or bestiality
- stealing
- perjury
- striking someone in secret or murder for hire
- stinginess—an unwillingness to give
- twisting the gospel

In summary, if someone had dabbled in any of those things, they would be overtaken by a curse. So what did a curse look like in someone's life? Many of the curses in Scripture are defined in Deuteronomy 28:15–54. In general terms, they look like:*

- humiliation, mental or emotional breakdown, which can include mental illness.
- barrenness—unable to have children, miscarriages, female problems, chronic bleeding, male problems

---

* Remember, these are things God declares He will cause to happen to His people if they don't listen and obey Him.

- sickness of all kinds, disease, especially if other members of your family have it
- poverty or continued insufficiency—even when the income would seem to cover expenses
- defeat, never feeling like you can succeed at anything
- helplessness
- weakness, constantly feeling beneath your circumstances
- breakdown of marriage or family, divorce
- accident-prone
- suicide or unnatural death

I realize we live in a fallen world and that the gospel of Jesus does not guarantee us a life on this earth free from suffering and hardship. We will not experience paradise until we are in heaven with Jesus. But as I walked with the men in my group, I started to wonder if there was something else going on. And if so, did we have the authority to overcome it? Is there some suffering which we don't have to suffer? And if so, how?

Keep in mind, I'm not talking about salvation. Our salvation is guaranteed and secure. Nothing can separate us from the love of God (Rom. 8:39). I'm talking about our lives here, on this earth.

One way to check if you might be living under a curse is to ask yourself if you see these conditions in your own life or in the lives of those you love. According to Scripture:

- Curses cling to you.
- You feel like there's no one to save you.
- You long for your children, but there's nothing you can do for them.
- You're driven mad by what you see.
- You feel sick in your eyes, your heart.
- You are seldom happy; one word describes you: frustrated.
- You've said, "The same thing happened to my father."
- Your goals feel like they are within reach, but you are never able to achieve them.

- You feel like you are wrestling a giant shadow, and life constantly slips like water through your fingers.

Living under a curse feels like a giant cloud that follows you. Or a giant hand out of the past that controls your present and future. No matter what you do, you just can't seem to shake it. Nothing ever changes. This cloud and this hand have a source.

If you've ever said, "It runs in the family," that family might be living under a curse. (Notice: I said "might.") I had a friend once tell me he didn't believe curses were still passed down. Days later he described his daughter as having her mother's eyes. I responded, "How can you understand and even agree with the idea that physical traits are passed down from parent to child, but not the spiritual consequences of sin?"

Here's my point: you and I, for reasons I don't entirely understand, do and can live under the lingering effects of generational sins and curses.

Maybe you're wondering how it's possible for us, on this side of the cross, having been redeemed from the curse, to still be living under the effects of one, or many. Maybe you're asking, *If I'm suffering the consequences of generational sin, and according to Scripture repentance is the remedy, do I have a responsibility to repent for sins I didn't commit? And why am I held accountable for something I didn't do?*

To answer, let's figure out what the Word says.

The Example of Nehemiah

I started this conversation showing four times where God promised to curse succeeding generations because of the sin of the fathers—to pass down the consequences of disobedience and of not listening to His voice. He put that same word in the mouths of the prophets and then, just before He closed the Old Testament, He told us that He never changes.

So, does the merciful God I know and love require repentance for sins

I didn't commit but were committed by my family? And if there's not been repentance, does His wrath still extend to me here and now?

I believe so.

And to explain why I believe so, let's look back to God's Word. Specifically, let's look at the story of Nehemiah.

Nehemiah was cupbearer to the Persian king Artaxerxes. This was decades after the people of Judah had been conquered and taken as exiles into Babylon. When Nehemiah heard of the condition of the remnant in Jerusalem (446 BC), with its walls torn down and a city lying in rubble, he wept. He fasted and mourned for many days. Then he prayed, "Please let Your ear be attentive and Your eyes open, that You may hear the prayer of Your servant which I pray before You now, day and night, for the children of Israel Your servants, and confess the sins of the children of Israel which we have sinned against You. *Both my father's house and I have sinned*" (Neh. 1:6, emphasis added).

Do you see it? When Nehemiah heard about the terrible conditions in Jerusalem, the city where God's Name dwelt, he knew sin was the cause. But not just his sins and the sins of his generation—the sins of "my father's house" as well. The sins of previous generations.

Nehemiah returned to Jerusalem, the people busied themselves with rebuilding the walls, and Ezra the scribe "prepared his heart to seek the Law of the LORD, and to do it, and to teach statutes and ordinances in Israel" (Ezra 7:10). Once the wall was complete, Ezra stood on a platform and read to all the people "distinctly from the book, in the Law of God; and they gave the sense, and helped them to understand the reading" (Neh. 8:4, 8).

But that wasn't the end of the story. Look at what Nehemiah and the people did in the very next chapter:

> Now on the twenty-fourth day of this month the children of Israel were assembled with fasting, in sackcloth, and with dust on their heads. Then those of Israelite lineage separated themselves from all foreigners; *and they stood and confessed their sins and the iniquities of their fathers*. And they

stood up in their place and read from the Book of the Law of the LORD their God for one-fourth of the day; and for another fourth they confessed and worshiped the LORD their God (9:1–3, emphasis added).

Do you see it again? The people knew they needed to break the curse that had overtaken them. And they broke it by confessing their sins and the sins of their fathers. This desire to repent for ancestral sin is the same belief that drove the disciples to ask Jesus, "Who sinned, this man or his parents?" (John 9:2).

When I see this evidence in Nehemiah, and when I understand it was that mindset that spurred the disciples' question to Jesus, I have to ask myself, *Why don't we do that?*

I think we should.

Of all the chapters in this book, I have wrestled most with this one and how to communicate it. I believe this teaching puts a sword in your hand, which the tradition of our churches and teaching hasn't given us. Mark 7:13 tells us that the traditions of men, those we pass down, make "the word of God of no effect." The NASB says, "invalidating the word of God." I can think of nothing else on earth that does that, and I believe something in our tradition has nullified and silenced this teaching for a long time.

One of the arguments I've heard from Bible-believing, Jesus-loving people is, "Charles, I feel like you're telling me the blood of Jesus hasn't done something." No. That's not what I'm saying. If anything, I'm arguing that Jesus' blood will do more than you think. I'm also not suggesting this is a "work" required of you. Breaking a curse and walking in blessing is not a work. It's an expression of faith.

I believe we play a role in our own freedom. Jesus has given us spiritual weapons and authority, and He's commanded us to use them—here and now. Most of us act as if we don't really believe this. We are afraid to use the weapons given to us, or we don't understand the authority we carry.

Too many Christians have limited the cross to a single-use tool. We are quick to say the cross is the guarantor of our salvation in the next life. And it is. Period. But it has more than one use. What does it do in this life?

Not only do we hold it before us as the guarantor of our salvation, but we can also drive it like a stake into the ground behind us to cut ourselves free from the stuff in our past that plagues us.

I am writing this to encourage you to place the cross both before and behind you.

For a long time, we have been taught in the church that we have been freed from the prison of sin. My problem is that I don't see people living in freedom. We've convinced the inmates they've been set free while never giving them the keys to unlock their own cells. As a result, they stare through prison bars and accept a false freedom, or an incomplete freedom. We have an enemy who relishes this deception.

Despite our public repentance and expressions of faith, when I look around at the church—including myself and the guys I do life with—I see people who are still living in prisons. And when I take a step back, those prisons look like the outworkings of a curse.

For example:

- Alcoholism—when fathers and grandfathers were alcoholics.
- Diabetes—when parents and aunts and uncles were diabetics.
- Mental illness, anxiety, or depression—when parents and grandparents suffered the same.
- Obesity—when much of the family is grossly overweight.
- Cancer—interestingly, it's often the same type of cancer.
- Sex addiction—which is often true of fathers and others in the family.

All of these things "run in the family." Am I saying that all of them are absolutely the result of a generational curse? No. But they might be.

One of the distortions of this idea—one of the accusations against this message—is the claim that I'm suggesting we are all just victims and not responsible for our own actions and sin. Nothing could be further from the truth. I am preaching a gospel of repentance. We need to own and repent for our own sin. And, we need to repent for the sin of our ancestors.

Why? Because God said so.

And until we do, we could be living under a curse.

Not to Destroy, but to Fulfill

Many in the church would say I'm describing the God of the Old Testament. A God of wrath. They believe He changed at the cross. Or, to put it another way, they just can't believe He would curse anyone. That doesn't gel with their view of God.

But Scripture is clear: "The entirety of Your word is truth, and every one of Your righteous judgments endures forever" (Ps. 119:160). Beginning with Moses, God set up a law that has not changed. This law is as real as gravity. In it, He said, "If you do this, I will bless you. And if you don't do this, I will curse you. You choose."

Many believers today would say all that ended with Jesus. But in Matthew 5, Jesus Himself said, "Do not think that I came to destroy the Law or the Prophets. I did not come to destroy but fulfill" (v. 17). Still not convinced? "Assuredly, I say to you, till heaven and earth pass away, one jot or one tittle will by no means pass from the law till all is fulfilled" (v. 18).

So, what does it mean that Jesus didn't destroy the law, but He did fulfill it?

The answer has everything to do with our connection to the law today. Specifically, has anything happened to take its requirement of us out of the way? The answer is no. The law still stands.

You raise a finger and say, "Charles, that's heresy!" Let me ask this: Is it okay for you to murder someone? How about sleep with someone else's wife? How about steal your neighbor's house and everything he or she owns? Worship another god? Of course not. The requirement of the law on us hasn't changed. What has changed is the means by which we can obey the law. Jesus didn't come to abolish the law, but fulfill it. All of the law and the prophets is summed up in this: love the Lord your God with all your heart soul and mind and love your neighbor as yourself (Matt.

22:37–40). We now relate to and obey the law not through the blood of bulls and goats but through the shed blood of Jesus.

Speaking of Jesus' blood, many Christians choose to ignore the real-world consequences of sin because they believe those consequences were abolished at the cross. Or, they don't believe they have a responsibility to do anything about those consequences—or that they can do anything about them. This mentality is something akin to saying, "Jesus did it all, and all I have to do is rest in Jesus." Or, "This is just the fallen world we live in."

Yes, we live in a fallen world, and yes, we will not escape the curse of death and we will all die (unless Jesus returns first), and no, I am not preaching a name-it-and-claim-it prosperity gospel. But what if the blood of Jesus does more than guarantee our salvation? What if the blood of Jesus works for us here in this life? What if I can overcome generational curses because "He who is in you is greater than he who is in the world" (1 John 4:4) and He "trains my hands for war and my fingers for battle" (Ps. 144:1) and "the weapons of [my] warfare are not carnal" but spiritual (2 Cor. 10:4) and I "wrestle not against flesh and blood, but against principalities . . . against the rulers of the darkness of this world" (Eph. 6:12, KJV)?

What if curses really have been passed down and we, through the blood of Jesus, have been given the ability to break them? What if you and I have been given the authority and weapons necessary to cut ourselves and our children free from the bondage of generational sin and curses? What if we don't have to live this way?

Most of us evangelicals are fond of quoting this:

For with the heart one believes unto righteousness, and with the mouth confession is made unto salvation. For the Scripture says, "Whoever believes on Him will not be put to shame." For there is no distinction between Jew and Greek, for the same Lord over all is rich to all who call upon Him. For "whoever calls on the name of the LORD shall be saved." (Rom. 10:10–13)

Look closely: with the heart we believe unto righteousness. And with the mouth, we confess to salvation. That means Jesus shed His blood for all. Salvation is available for all who would come to Him. No one is excluded. But, not everyone is saved. Only those who do something—who believe and confess—are saved.

I'm suggesting that the same is true with curses.

Yes, Jesus has broken the power of sin and generational curses on a grand or corporate scale. But we still need to do something to apply that power to our own individual lives.

With this assumption as my basis, and motivated by my love for my brothers mixed with my experience of praying through stuff with no breakthrough over long periods of time—and my very real desire that they experience freedom from whatever was hounding them—I began asking the question: *What if something had happened or was currently happening that gave the enemy entrance to continue hounding us?* Our enemy is a legalist, and a legal loophole gives him legal entry to attack us. A legal loophole would be sin. Unrepented sin. he attaches himself to unrepented sin, digs in, entrenches himself, and gains legal entry into our lives.

I come at this life through the understanding that we are at war. Period. You and I have been at war from the moment we opened our eyes—at war with an enemy we cannot see—and we are in it whether we agree we are or not. Saying, "I'm not at war," or, "I don't have an enemy" is naïveté. An ostrich sticking his head in the sand. You are and you do. Ignoring it and him emboldens your enemy; he loves it when you think he's not real.

I believe Paul when he said, "We do not wrestle against flesh and blood, but against principalities, against powers, against the rulers of the darkness of this age, against spiritual hosts of wickedness in the heavenly places" (Eph. 6:12). And, "The weapons of our warfare are not carnal but mighty in God for pulling down strongholds, casting down arguments and every high thing that exalts itself against the knowledge of God, bringing every thought into captivity to the obedience of Christ" (2 Cor. 10:4–5).

I take this to mean that in this life I have been given armor and authority and power to use it—and that I'm not wrestling a physical human, but a spirit without a body who is just as real as me, if not more. And these spirits without bodies have powers, and they make up hosts who rule. In this war, I have been given spiritual instruments of warfare with which to pull down and cast down all arguments and anything which exalts itself against the knowledge of God.

The Example of Joshua

I hope you're getting really excited as you read this, because you're starting to see a way out. That something might possibly be able to lift that giant cloud off you and your family.

I am trying to make the case that curses affect you whether you like it or not, and that the cross, the shed blood of Jesus, offers you the remedy to free yourself on this side of the grave. That, because of the blood of Jesus, you can do something about it.

The example of Joshua and the Israelites taking possession of the promised land is a great illustration of this principle.

When Joshua stepped foot in the Jordan, he and three million Hebrews were walking into the promised land. It had already been given to them. Generations ago. By deed, it belonged to them. Legally. God said so. End of story. But they didn't take ownership of the land until they drove out all the "ites" who lived there: the Canaanites, Hittites, Hivites, Perizzites, Girgashites, Amorites, and Jebusites. These nations were, in effect, squatters.

Don't miss this: God left the driving out of those nations to the Israelites. "But if you do not drive out the inhabitants of the land from before you, then it shall come about that those whom you let remain of them will become as pricks in your eyes and as thorns in your sides, and they will trouble you in the land in which you live" (Num. 33:55, NASB). He legally gave them a land of blessing and healing, but they had to take action in order to receive that blessing and that healing.

I believe the same is true for Christians today. While we are not walking into a promised land, we are walking into a land of promises. God's

Word. And in this land, the spiritual squatters who reside in or about us—meaning, the consequences of our sin and the forces of evil who seek to destroy us—don't care who owns the deed. They don't want to give up control. It's our job to take possession of our land (that is, us) and drive them out.

As believers, we often act like people who have picked up the Sunday paper with all its coupons, but have never gone to the store to redeem those coupons. When it comes to blessings and curses, we are resting on a tradition that says just because you receive the paper means you've redeemed the coupon. That doesn't make sense to me.

When the angel of death passed over the Israelites living in Egypt, he passed over those who had painted their doorframes with the blood of the lamb. They appropriated the blood. This means they took the blood of the sacrifice out of the bowl and painted their doorframes with it. Blood in the bowl did them no good. Blood on the doorframes saved their and their families' lives. I'm encouraging you to take the blood out of the bowl and paint your house.*

Let's look back at Moses and the Israelites in the Old Testament:

> Then they journeyed from Mount Hor by the Way of the Red Sea, to go around the land of Edom; and the soul of the people became very discouraged on the way. And the people spoke against God and against Moses: "Why have you brought us up out of Egypt to die in the wilderness? For there is no food and no water, and our soul loathes this worthless bread." So the LORD sent fiery serpents among the people, and they bit the people; and many of the people of Israel died.
>
> Therefore the people came to Moses, and said, "We have sinned, for we have spoken against the LORD and against you; pray to the LORD that He take away the serpents from us." So Moses prayed for the people.
>
> Then the LORD said to Moses, "Make a fiery serpent, and set it on a pole; and it shall be that everyone who is bitten, when he looks at it,

---

* The blood of Jesus redeems us from the curse of the law, not the curse of the fall. We won't escape the curse of death until Jesus returns.

shall live." So Moses made a bronze serpent, and put it on a pole; and so it was, if a serpent had bitten anyone, when he looked at the bronze serpent, he lived. (Num. 21:4–9).

So, the people sinned, God sent serpents, and many died. But then He offered a remedy. Bronze serpent on a pole. God required that the Israelites admit their sin, walk forward, stare up (thereby acknowledging their sin), and live.

Three questions:

1. What was required of them?
2. When they met the requirements, what were they freed from?
3. When were they free?

Now, fast forward to the gospel of John:

And as Moses lifted up the serpent in the wilderness, even so must the Son of Man be lifted up, that whoever believes in Him should not perish but have eternal life. For God so loved the world that He gave His only begotten Son, that whoever believes in Him should not perish but have everlasting life. For God did not send His Son into the world to condemn the world, but that the world through Him might be saved.

He who believes in Him is not condemned; but he who does not believe is condemned already, because he has not believed in the name of the only begotten Son of God. (John 3:14–18)

We all know this. It is *the* salvation scripture. That said, four questions rise to the surface:

1. What is required of us?
2. When we meet the requirements, what are we freed from?
3. When are we free?
4. Is this limited only to our salvation?

The rebuttal I often get is this: "But, I've already done that. I'm saved. It's a one-and-done-thing, Charles." I'm not questioning your salvation. Nor am I doubting it. But, while we're on this side of the grave, I'm trying to point out that your enemy, the cunning one that prowls around looking for someone to devour, is a legalist. And legally, sin—whether yours or your ancestors'—gives him a door to access you in this life.

Jesus has given us His blood to close that door. Here and now. Sin requires payment, and we get to apply the blood of Jesus as the payment for our ancestors' sin. Notice, I'm not saying we obtain their salvation. We are simply holding up the remedy to free ourselves from those consequences.

An analogy might be that we live every day drinking from living waters. The enemy uses our ancestors' sin—through the legal loophole of God's spoken law—to poison the water upstream. So, in order to make the water clean again, we must remove the source of that poison. By appropriating the blood of Jesus and cancelling the curse, we in effect dig up the nuclear waste upstream and burn it.

When Moses brought the people of Israel out of Egypt, he brought them three days into the wilderness of Shur and found no water. When they came to Marah, the water was bitter and they couldn't drink it. The people complained, Moses prayed, and God told him to throw a tree in the water. He did, and the water became sweet and drinkable. As the Israelites were drinking, God told them—and He is telling us—"If you diligently heed the voice of the LORD your God and do what is right in His sight, give ear to His commandments and keep all His statutes, I will put none of the diseases on you which I have brought on the Egyptians. For I am the LORD who heals you" (Ex 15:26).

The Lord used a tree to heal the waters then, and He is using a tree to heal now. The cross.

If you and I are living under the weight of generational curses, the cross is the remedy—always has been. "The life of the flesh is in the blood, and I have given it to you upon the altar to make atonement for your souls; for it is the blood that makes atonement for the soul" (Lev. 17:11).

Read these scriptures through the lens of breaking the curse and how completely and perfectly the blood of Jesus breaks the curse:

- "Reckon yourselves to be dead indeed to sin" (Rom. 6:11).
- "For sin shall not have dominion over you, for you are not under law but under grace" (Rom. 6:14).
- "You also have become dead to the law through the body of Christ" (Rom. 7:4).
- "But now we have been delivered from the law, having died to what we were held by, so that we should serve in the newness of the Spirit and not in the oldness of the letter" (Rom. 7:6).
- "For the law of the Spirit of life in Christ Jesus has made me free from the law of sin and death" (Rom. 8:2).
- "If the Spirit of Him who raised Jesus from the dead dwells in you, He who raised Christ from the dead will also give life to your mortal bodies through His Spirit who dwells in you" (Rom. 8:11).
- "For Christ is the end of the law for righteousness to everyone who believes" (Rom. 10:4).
- "Christ has redeemed us from the curse of the law, having become a curse for us" (Gal. 3:13).
- "For by one offering He has perfected forever those who are being sanctified" (Heb. 10:14).
- "For by your words you will be justified, and by your words you will be condemned" (Matt. 12:37).
- "Assuredly, I say to you, whatever you bind on earth will be bound in heaven, and whatever you loose on earth will be loosed in heaven" (Matt. 18:18).

I've included more in Appendix B in the back of this book. Often, when I'm praying with someone to come out from underneath a curse, we will pray these out loud.

What Now? Repent.

Stop reading for a moment and take an inventory. Do you see evidence in your or your family's life of a curse at work? Does a specific type of cancer run in your family? Mental illness? Heart disease? Suicide? Obesity? Certain types of arthritis? Divorce? What plagues you? Look honestly at your family line and discern if you see patterns across generations. If you do, there might be a curse at work.

What if we humbled ourselves and approached the cross of Jesus with His Word held high and said, "Lord, I'm looking into my family situation, and I'm seeing some things that look suspicious. I'd like to yield to You, repent for whatever sin caused it, and bring myself specifically under Your dominion in all of these areas of my life. I'm making a specific confession, a specific repentance, and seeking specific deliverance. I'm not questioning my salvation, I'm just beginning to believe that Your blood can do more in this life than I've previously given You and it credit."

Often I think our posture toward Jesus is that we stand there with this how-about-giving-us-a-break-Big-Guy? look on our faces. I think His response in return is to point at His Word with a what's-that-in-your-hand? look on His face. The same way He responded to the staff in Moses' hand. As if to say, "I gave you My Word and My blood. Now put them to work."

As I look at those I love and those who love Jesus, people are still suffering. Still bound up. And as much as I know my own heart, I believe every word of His Word. As I have dissected it, I feel like He takes joy in our specific repentance for our families' sins, and His Word tells me that His blood was then and is now the remedy—and that we can appropriate it to bring His freedom in our lives.

If I'm reading God's Word rightly, just because I didn't commit a sin and just because it didn't occur in my lifetime doesn't mean He doesn't require repentance. Sin sits outside of time. I believe specific repentance brings specific forgiveness. Specific deliverance. So, based on His Word, I want to repent for my extended family's sin and—by His blood—break those curses that hold influence over our lives.

We know God carries the consequences of sin down through generations:

> But if they confess their iniquity and the iniquity of their fathers, with their unfaithfulness in which they were unfaithful to Me, and that they also have walked contrary to Me, and that I also have walked contrary to them and have brought them into the land of their enemies; if their uncircumcised hearts are humbled, and they accept their guilt—then I will remember My covenant with Jacob, and My covenant with Isaac and My covenant with Abraham I will remember. (Lev. 26:40–42)

When did He stop doing this? Never. Paul affirmed this when he wrote, "Do we then make void the law through faith? Certainly not! On the contrary, we establish the law" (Rom. 3:31).

Through the blood of Jesus, we can place the cross between ourselves and that sin by repenting of it. This is the expression of faith that imparts the righteousness He has imputed to us. The blood does what the blood does when we move it out of the basin. Legally, His righteousness was ours before the foundation of the world. Experientially, it becomes ours when we repent for their sin and confess that it is only His blood that cleanses us. This is an argument for active expression of faith versus passive acceptance of someone else's. This is an argument which states we play a role in our own deliverance. And being freed from a curse is just that. Deliverance.

Curses come from our roots and they often act like roots. If you've ever tried to dig up a tree, you understand. Roots are stingy, tough to get rid of, and don't like sunlight. John the Baptist, knowing the time for Jesus had come, told the Pharisees, "Bear fruits worthy of repentance . . . even now the ax is laid to the root" (Luke 3:8–9). The fruit of what I'm preaching here is continued repentance for both my and my ancestors' sins. How often should you do this? I can't answer that. But I would suggest you start with repentance and be obedient until you sense blessing.

Let me end with this: we know God carries the sin down to the third and fourth generations for sexual sin. When did He stop doing that? At the cross? He made the remedy available at the cross; He left the timing up to you and me. If you were thirsty and I gave you a glass of water, when is your thirst satisfied? When the water is in your hand in the glass or when you drink it? This is true with our salvation—we believe and confess and are saved—and it is true with generational sin.

When did God tell us to stop asking forgiveness for the sins of our forefathers? Many of us believe today that we no longer need to because of the cross. We believe that our faith has nullified the law and that it no longer pertains to us. And yet Paul says, "Do we then make void the law through faith? Certainly not! On the contrary, we establish the law" (Rom. 3:31). We treat the cross as if it were a blanket get-out-of-jail-free card. If it is, then is everyone going to heaven?

I am not making a statement about something the blood of Jesus hasn't done or can't do. I am describing what we have not done with it. So, here's what we are going to do:

- Pray.
- Confess faith in Jesus.
- Repent of rebellion and sin.
- Claim and receive His forgiveness.
- Forgive all who have wronged you.
- Renounce any contact or agreement with any god that is not Jesus Christ.
- Release yourself in the name and by the blood of Jesus.

If you want to kneel, I think it's a good idea. It's a sign of submission and yielding. I'm a big fan of it and I do it a lot.

Lord Jesus Christ, I believe You are the Son of God and the only way to God, and that You died on the cross for my sins and rose again from the dead. I believe that Your blood redeems, justifies, forgives and sanctifies me, and pays the complete penalty for all my sin.

Today, for me and my family, I refuse death and curses, and I choose life and blessings. I give up all my rebellion and all my sin, and I submit myself to You as Lord.

I confess all my sins before You and ask You for forgiveness, especially for any sins that have exposed or do expose me to a curse. Father, I feel like I have been pursued and overtaken by a curse or curses due to generational sin, so even though I don't know the cause, and even though some of this language sounds kind of old or foreign and we don't really talk this way today, I want to act in faithfulness to Your Word. Even though the grass withers and the flowers fade, Your Word stands forever. Because of that, I want to renounce and repent for my and/or my ancestors' sins.

Specifically:

- I repent for any sin committed by either me or my ancestors, knowingly or unknowingly, in which any of us made or worshiped an idol of any kind, or practiced any form of satanic or occult worship. Father, if any of us ever bowed down to or worshiped anyone but You, I'm so sorry, and I turn 180 degrees away from that.
- I repent where we did not honor our mother and father and/or treated them with contempt.
- I repent where we moved our neighbor's landmark.
- I repent where we made the blind to wander off the road.
- I repent where we perverted justice due the stranger, the fatherless, or the widow.
- I repent where we had sex with any family member or any person other than our wife/husband in the right covenant of marriage, and this includes adultery, fornication, incest, homosexuality, bestiality, or sexual perversion of any kind. And Lord, I include in this any place in which any of us have sinned not just in our actions, but with our eyes, including taking in any pornographic image.
- I repent where we attacked our neighbor in secret.
- I repent where we took a bribe to slay or hurt an innocent person.

- *I repent for any ungodly behavior, words spoken, divorces, thoughts, and/or negative emotions.*
- *I repent of all word curses spoken over or to others, including myself, especially the word curse of "I wish I were dead," which I do not agree with. I declare Your Word as the antidote: "I will not die, but live and declare the works of the Lord."*
- *I repent for any place where I or we have operated in or through the wound of rejection.*
- *I repent for any compulsive addictions, whether they be of substance (drugs, alcohol, etc.) or practice (sexual, eating, and so on).*
- *I repent for any suicide or abortion.*
- *I repent for any place I or we have perverted the gospel of Jesus Christ.*
- *I repent for any place where I or we have stolen from You and not brought our firstfruits to You—for not tithing. I also repent for any place where I or we have acted in greed or covetousness, stinginess or self-reliance.*
- *I repent where we did not confirm all the words of Your law by observing them—and Lord, that includes blessing Your chosen people, the nation of Israel. You told Abraham, "I will bless those who bless you and curse those who curse you." So Father, if I or anyone in my family has ever cursed Your people, I am sorry. For myself, my family, and my generations, I repent for any racist thoughts, words, actions, or deeds spoken or committed against the Jewish people. I ask for Your and their forgiveness. I am a wild olive shoot, grafted in, and the root supports me. I thank You that I am grafted in, and I bless Your people today in and by Your great name.*

By and through the blood of Jesus, I now break and renounce all blood oaths, blood covenants, blood dedications, blood ties, and all blood bondages to satan and any other false god by my family or myself. I cancel any ungodly documents, agreements, and assignments against me and my family past, present, and future, and I appropriate and apply the blood of Jesus to cancel them.

Having said this, I renounce all contact with anything occult or satanic. If I have any "contact objects" (such as rings or necklaces or cards—any physical thing used in a ritual), I commit myself to destroy them. I cancel all satan's claims against me.

Lord, I repent for all of this and anything unspoken. Where there are unspoken or unrepented sins, I ask Your Holy Spirit to utter them now and shine a light on that dark place in me and in my generation. Please forgive me and us. Release me and my family (my wife/husband, children, and children's children) from the consequences of any and all of my and my ancestors' sins. By and through and because of the blood of Jesus, I bind every spirit empowered by these curses and command you all to leave me and my family now in the name of Jesus.

Having asked You to forgive me, I forgive all who have harmed me or wronged me—just as I want God to forgive me. In particular, I forgive (name the person). I also forgive myself.

Lord Jesus, I believe that on the cross, You were made a curse with every curse that was due to me that I might be redeemed from the curse and enter into the blessing. That means, You took on Yourself every curse that could ever come upon me. So I now release myself from every curse, every evil influence, and every dark shadow over me and my family. In Your name, by Your blood, and because of Your cross, Lord Jesus Christ, I break every curse and release myself from the consequences. I release myself from every evil inheritance from my ancestors. You have redeemed me from the curse of the law, and I have passed out from underneath the curse and entered into the blessing of Abraham—whom You blessed in all things.

By faith, I now receive my release, and I thank You for it.

- I thank You, Lord, that you have heard my prayer and that on the cross every curse over my life has been cancelled.

- *I thank You, Lord, that through the cross I have been delivered out of the domain of darkness and carried into the kingdom of Your love.*
- *I thank You, Lord, that because of the cross, satan has no more claims against me or my family or anything else that You have committed to me.*
- *Lord, my desire is to walk in obedience. Please help me do that. Having now been brought out from beneath the curse, let Your blessings come upon and overtake me.*

I pray this in the name of "Jesus Christ, the faithful witness, the firstborn of the dead, and the ruler of the kings of the earth. To Him who loves us and released us from our sins by His blood—and He has made us to be a kingdom, priests to His God and Father."⁵

If you prayed this by faith married with belief, then just as Jesus spoke to the paralytic lowered through the roof—and because of, by, and through His cross, and because He told us we could—I declare over you that your sins are forgiven, and that the curse over you and your family's life is broken (John 20:23). In agreement with God's Word, I decree and declare that, "Blessed are those whose lawless deeds are forgiven, and whose sins are covered; blessed is the man to whom the LORD does not impute sin" (Rom. 4:7–8; Ps. 32:1–2, NASB).

Personal note: In my experience, much like the sexual sin prayer, breaking curses can have layers. Sometimes one. Sometimes many. They, too, can be more like an onion than banana. Often, breaking one will reveal another. Don't get frustrated. And don't be afraid to go through this a few times. It doesn't mean there's something wrong with you. It means the enemy is entrenched and wants you in slavery. I've prayed this prayer with my wife and kids multiple times, and my children will tell you that when we've prayed it, they have felt stuff lift off of them.

Most days—before my feet hit the floor—I pray a very simple prayer. When I do, I am reminded of Job who rose early and made sacrifice for his family in the event that one of them might have sinned (Job 1:5). I pray: "Lord, forgive me of my sin and of my forefathers' sins. For any place in our lives where any of us have sinned against You. I'm sorry, Lord. I repent. Please forgive us. I plead Your blood over us." Along with that, I will read and pray through the scriptures I've included in the appendices. Doing so inclines my heart toward His. They remind me of what is true. Doing this helps me walk in the fear of the Lord. I believe this "blessing and curse" message may well be one of the most important messages to the individual believer and the corporate church following salvation.

Lastly, there is a thing that happens in this whole blessing-curse arena. People begin chasing blessing to the exclusion of a relationship with the One who blesses. Don't. Chase obedience and allow God to bless you in what follows. Chase the voice of God. Focus on intimacy with the Father, holiness, confession, repentance, worship, obedience, and His very presence. Climb up in His lap. Find Him while He may be found. Let these be the goal. Do that and you may find yourself covered up in and overtaken by blessing.

I realize this entire teaching can be misinterpreted as a prosperity gospel through a simple if-then statement: "If you break the curse, then you will walk in blessing." I do not believe that, nor am I saying that. There is no guaranteed formula, and it is God alone who blesses.

I'll leave you with Moses's words speaking to the people of God:

> I call heaven and earth to witness against you today, that I have set before you life and death, the blessing and the curse. So choose life in order that you may live, you and your descendants, by loving the LORD your God, by obeying His voice, and by holding fast to Him; for this is your life and the length of your days, that you may live in the land which the LORD swore to your fathers, to Abraham, Isaac, and Jacob, to give them. (Deut. 30:19–20, NASB)

I pray you choose life.

CHAPTER 9

You Will Be Hated by All

I t's been a full two days. Jesus cleansed a leper, healed the centurion's servant, healed Peter's mother-in-law, and when evening came, He cast demons out of many and healed all who were sick. The following day, needing rest and a break from the crowd, He climbed into a boat with the Twelve and took a nap only to be awakened by one of them telling Him how they were all about to die. He rebuked the wind and waves, and all of them for their lack of faith, and then exited the boat in the Gadarenes where He cast the legion of demons out of the crazed man. With the man now clothed, seated, and in his right mind, Jesus again loads into the boat and crosses back over to His own city where they brought Him a paralytic. Jesus forgave his sins, healed him, and the man rose and walked home.

Jesus then called Matthew the tax collector—one of the most hated people in all of society because he'd sold out to Rome—and He ate dinner with other tax-gatherers and sinners. Somewhere in all this commotion, one of the synagogue officials comes and tells Jesus that his daughter "lies at the point of death. Come and lay Your hands on her, that she may be healed, and she will live."[1] Jesus turns that direction but slows in the street to allow a broken and bleeding woman to touch the hem of His garment. When she does, He turns and calls her "Daughter." With the little girl's father tugging on His arm, Jesus arrives at his house to find the girl dead and people wailing loudly. Unphased, Jesus raises the little girl from the dead, and then heals two blind men on His way out of town. While the blind men are still dancing and screaming in the street, Jesus heals another demon-possessed man, and the people begin scratching their heads, "It was never seen like this in Israel!"[2]

And they're right.

The Twelve are watching this with rapt attention. Their heads on swivels.

Until now, the disciples had some context for the miracles Jesus had performed, as miracles were not entirely uncommon in the history of Israel: the dead had been raised to life, leprosy healed, the sun traveled backward, Daniel in the lions' den, Jonah in the belly of the whale, the plagues in Egypt, the Red Sea parting, water from the rock. . . .

But there was one miracle for which they had no context: the casting out of demons.

And not only was it new, but it was becoming commonplace in Jesus' ministry.

It's tough to determine if this is just a few days or weeks summarized in Matthew's Gospel, but regardless, in their minds, they are beginning to think that Jesus can defeat Rome. Usher in a new kingdom right here and now. Stop the oppression. Overturn the tyrant. That He possesses a power that they do not. But before the disciples can wrap their heads around what they are seeing with their own two eyes, Jesus calls the Twelve together. He is about to do something amazing:

> And when He had called His twelve disciples to Him, He gave them power over unclean spirits, to cast them out, and to heal all kinds of sickness and all kinds of disease. . . .
> And as you go, preach, saying, "The kingdom of heaven is at hand." Heal the sick, cleanse the lepers, raise the dead, cast out demons. Freely you have received, freely give.[3]

The disciples are giddy. Jesus has just done something no king has ever done. He gave them His power. Their minds are racing with possibilities.

Unable to contain their excitement, they whisper among themselves. But before they can get too far ahead of themselves, Jesus taps them on the shoulder, brings them in closer, a huddle of sorts, and speaks softly. Saying something they aren't expecting:

> Behold, I send you out as sheep in the midst of wolves. Therefore be wise as serpents and harmless as doves. But beware of men, for they will deliver you up to councils and scourge you in their synagogues. You will be brought before governors and kings for My sake, as a testimony to them and to the Gentiles. . . .
>
> And you will be hated by all for My name's sake. But he who endures to the end will be saved. . . .
>
> And do not fear those who kill the body but cannot kill the soul. But rather fear Him who is able to destroy both soul and body in hell.[4]

Luke picks up the narrative at this point. "So they departed and went through the towns, preaching the gospel and healing everywhere."[5]

So successful are they in their demon-casting-out-and-healing-all-sickness-and-disease campaign that Herod the Tetrarch feels threatened. He even starts talking to himself. Questioning himself. "But, I beheaded John. Right?" Many thought John the Baptist or Elijah had risen from the dead. The works the disciples are doing are on the level of the greatest ever to carry the name of God.

The disciples return with eyes the size of Oreos. Even they are amazed. They can't believe it. Jesus pulls them away secretly to Bethsaida for a debriefing, but the crowds hear of His presence and start amassing in large numbers. Seeing that it's late, the disciples tell Jesus He'd better send the crowd away. They have a long journey ahead. Jesus, who'd given them all authority and power, says, "You give them something to eat."

A quick inventory reveals five loaves and two fish. A quick headcount reveals five thousand men. Which may have been something like twenty thousand people including wives and children.

To their amazement, Jesus feeds the crowd and they collect twelve baskets of leftover food fragments.

In the days that follow, Peter confesses Jesus as the Christ, Jesus predicts His death and resurrection, and He tells them all that if any wish to follow Him, they must take up their cross. Given that the people haven't yet seen Him crucified, this is a bit of a mystery. It certainly has them puzzled when Jesus is transfigured bright as the sun alongside Moses and Elijah before their very eyes. Not to mention God's very voice echoes out of the crowd, "This is My beloved Son. Hear Him!"[6] The following day, a father implores Jesus to heal his son who is constantly thrown into the fire by a demon. Jesus rebukes the demon, heals the child, and hands the boy to his father.

This is the whirlwind in which the disciples find themselves. Luke speaks with an understated sense of humor when he says, "And they were all amazed at the majesty of God."[7]

Amazed? These men are out of their minds. They can't believe what they are seeing. Heaven has come to earth. The kingdom of God is at hand.

But look at how their mindsets change, as shown by what they do next:

- They start arguing over who's the greatest.
- They get jealous when they see other people casting out demons in the name of Jesus.
- When they enter a town of the Samaritans, the town does not receive Jesus. So James and John survey the situation and in their infinite wisdom, they say, "Lord, do You want us to command fire to come down from heaven and consume them, just as Elijah did?"[8]

Call down fire? Consume them?

Jesus turns and rebukes them, saying, "'You do not know what manner of spirit you are of. For the Son of Man did not come to destroy men's lives but to save them.' And they went to another village."[9]

The dichotomy is striking. Consuming fire versus salvation.

If only the disciples knew the power given to them. And what to do with it.

If only we did.

Eventually, their numbers grow to seventy. Rather than horde His power, solidify His position, and grind people beneath His thumb, Jesus shares it—a second time—and empowers others to do the same. Creating coheirs rather than slaves.

Speaking to the seventy, Jesus says, "Go your way; behold, I send you out as lambs among wolves." And after they'd gone and done what He'd told them to do:

> Then the seventy returned with joy, saying, "Lord, even the demons are subject to us in Your name."
>
> And He said to them, "I saw satan fall like lightning from heaven. Behold, I give you the authority to trample on serpents and scorpions, and over all the power of the enemy, and nothing shall by any means hurt you. Nevertheless do not rejoice in this, that the spirits are subject to you, but rather rejoice because your names are written in heaven."[10]

This is not Jesus the sandal-wearing carpenter speaking. This is Jesus the Bright Morning Star, crown on His head, ring on His finger. He is describing the most awesome battle ever, anywhere. Good versus evil, and good not only drove the enemy back but kicked them out. A complete rout.

Many of the disciples look at their hands, turning them over and back. For in their hands, they now hold that very same power. That casting-satan-down power. Think of the gleam on their faces. The fist pumps. The minds racing with possibilities. This is the first huddle before the first play when they are going to run up the score and hand an irrevocable defeat to the enemy.

Forever.

Then comes the cross. Where they stand powerless.

The Power to Live and Die

Did the disciples stare at the lifeless body of Jesus and think to themselves, *I guess we don't have all authority after all?* Did Jesus' words echo, "If anyone desires to come after Me, let him deny himself, and take up his cross daily, and follow me" (Luke 9:23)? Only after the cross did they come to understand what He put into their hands. And it was not the power to overthrow Rome. Jesus gave them, and us, the power to live His life and die His death. Period.

He reminded them of this after He was resurrected and before He ascended to His Father. Look at how similar His word choices are:

> Then they will deliver you up to tribulation and kill you, and you will be hated by all nations for My name's sake. And then many will be offended, will betray one another, and will hate one another. Then many false prophets will rise up and deceive many. And because lawlessness will abound, the love of many will grow cold. But he who endures to the end shall be saved. And this gospel of the kingdom will be preached in all the world as a witness to all the nations, and then the end will come. (Matt. 24:9–14)

These are the words of Jesus, and yet we don't hear them preached very much.

When Jesus restored Peter on the beach following His resurrection, He said this: "'Most assuredly, I say to you, when you were younger, you girded yourself and walked where you wished; but when you are old, you will stretch out our hands, and another will gird you and carry you where you do not wish.' This He spoke, signifying by what death he would glorify God" (John 21:18–19).

Late in his life, Peter was executed through a crucifixion in which he was hung upside down.

I am not making the case that Jesus was unkind to Peter. Far from it.

In my mind, this exchange occurs shoulder to shoulder, with Jesus' arm wrapped around Peter, in a whisper just inches from Peter's ear. Given the heartbreak of his denial, I think this exchange with Jesus was an encouragement to Peter. His heart needed to know and hear that his best friend, Jesus, knew that he, Peter, would in fact lay down his life for the truth of the gospel.

Jesus did not give them the power to escape hardship or suffering. He gave them the power to live His life and die His death. Listen when I say this: I believe with my whole heart that Jesus has, in fact, given us the keys to His kingdom, and with that comes authority and power. But having been given that gift does *not* mean we have escaped suffering on this earth. It does not. Not anymore than it did for Him or those who followed Him. This is Jesus speaking to the Pharisees, the hypocrites, the brood of vipers: "Therefore, indeed, I send you prophets, wise men, and scribes: some of them you will kill and crucify, and some of them you will scourge in your synagogues and persecute from city to city" (Matt. 23:34).

If you read that slowly, you'll see that Jesus sends believers like you and me, willingly, into places where He knows beforehand that we will be killed, crucified, scourged, and persecuted.

A Painful Conversation

Let's put a bookmark here. I want to walk you through a conversation I had with Jesus. This is not any kind of new revelation. In my mind, this conversation is no different than C. S. Lewis speaking through the voice of Aslan or writing *The Screwtape Letters*. So, I offer it in that vein.

Several months prior to this conversation, Christy, the boys, and I had suffered a prolonged injustice and deception, complete with prolonged pain. To counter it, I'd been on my knees. Been praying the Word. Been proclaiming it over my family. Been holding fast the confession of my faith without wavering. Been trying to encourage my kids when I was anything but encouraged. I knew then and know now what the Lord says about vengeance and, despite that, I was on the verge of assisting Him in carrying it out.

I also knew what He'd said about forgiveness, and I wanted nothing to do with it.

With this as the backdrop . . .

I was sitting in my driveway with my arms wrapped around my gut. My bottom lip sticking out. Not looking in His direction. I felt a tap on my shoulder, "You going to give Me that?"

I didn't even look at Him. "Give You what?"

He said nothing. He just poked at the raw wound in me that had started to scab over. When He pushed on it, pus oozed out. And it stunk.

Lying to Him would get me nowhere. I didn't feel like talking. "That hurts."

His response was calm. Almost amused. "I see that."

Doubled over, I winced and caught my breath. "Well, why don't You do something about it!?"

"I am."

I was not in a good place. Breathing shallow breaths around shrapnel of the heart. Huddled over the stone in my belly. I continued: "Does that include impaling our enemies' heads on stakes outside the city walls?"

A pause. His voice sounded amused. "You finished?"

I shook my head. "Not really."

He was quiet. Content to let me vent.

"Can't You see what's going on here? You healed the blind but seem blind to us."

His voice was closer. "Look up."

"What!?"

"Look up."

I was sitting outside so I did.

He asked, "Did you do that?"

"No."

"Well, for the sake of argument, will you concede that My view of you is slightly different than yours?"

"That does little to ease my pain."

"Charles?"

I shook my head. No answer.

"Charles."

"Yes."

"Do you trust Me?"

*In four words He'd gotten to the nugget. Where the rubber meets the road. This was **the** question. Problem was, my enemy was using my circumstances to suggest He was no longer trustworthy. And in my pain, I was listening more to the whispers of my enemy than Him. When I responded, I was bubbling in self-pity. "I did."*

"And it didn't pan out the way you thought it should, did it?"

I shook my head.

"Do you trust Me now?" I was about to open my mouth and ask Him what had changed when He said, "Think before you answer."

This was no small question.

A month or so prior, my family's pain had increased—a lot. The situation had worsened, and I'd reached my limit. When we thought things couldn't get any worse, they had. In the hours following, Christy and the boys and I found ourselves in our car, parked in the Tractor Supply store parking lot. We'd just exited a breakfast drive-thru, and I was so angry and hurt that I knew better than to drive. The last twenty-four hours had been excruciating. I was beyond angry and close to rage. I knew I'd better press Pause. Sip my coffee and take a deep breath. I was either going to remove someone's head from their shoulders and drive a stake through their collective chest, or I was going to yield and find a way to love someone(s) I had every reason to hate.

I wasn't the only one. As I looked in the rearview at my kids spread about the car, we all hurt. Pain was pasted across their faces. I had watched helplessly as one of my sons had sobbed so hard his shoulders shook—and I could do nothing to ease his pain. Every one of us was dinged and bruised and carried the scars of months of unrelenting ache. I sat in that car sweating, mind racing, barely holding it together.

My mind was firing a thousand thoughts a second but below all that, below my anger, I knew we needed to pray. I knew if I kept that stuff bottled up in me, that it'd eat me alive and that my doing so would open up doors in my children that would require a long time to close. I also knew I could not defend me and I could not defend them. I was absolutely powerless to effect any change in a really crappy situation.

I stood on the precipice. I was either going to erupt and scream a string of four-letter epithets followed by a course of action that included the infliction of pain, or I was going to be reduced to a puddle in the front seat. Probably a puddle because option A got me nowhere. And I don't mind Christy and the kids seeing me cry, that's not the point; they have on several occasions. But I did not want them to see me react in anger. I didn't want to drill those seeds of anger into my kids' hearts. We'd already lost enough. That reaction was not and is not the heart of Jesus. Life was foggy, the walls were pressing in, but I knew enough to know that.

So, I slid my hand beneath Christy's, opened up my mouth and squeaked out one word: "Lord."

That was it. That was all I could manage. Silence followed.

Let's leave that car a minute. Back to the driveway where the Lord had picked at the same scab. Weeks had passed from that front seat to this conversation with Him, and nothing had changed. If anything, conditions had worsened. I was raw. So, I side-stepped the question.

"Could we please talk about something else?"

He did not sound impressed. "We were talking about trust."

I spoke softly. "Trusting You with this is . . . difficult."

"Your emotions are lying to you."

I knew He was right. I was too tired to argue.

He sat next to me. "Do you know what it means to 'hope against hope'?"

I knew this phrase had been used to describe Abraham and the whole Isaac situation. "I think it means to hope even when you have none and no reason to."

He nodded. "Why do you think Abraham did that?"

"Don't know."

"He did it because I give life to the dead and call those things which do not exist as though they did."[11]

"I'm not sure I can wrap my head around that."

"It means I'm not limited by what you can see."

In the days and weeks and months prior to the parking lot fiasco, I had not sat idly by, swimming in my misery. I had actively searched the Word for the remedy. Anything. Any nugget to hold onto that spoke of our healing, deliverance, and redemption. I did find scriptures of blessing and prosperity. Of the Lord's deliverance. Yes, absolutely. Memorized them. And yes, God does desire our blessing. He promises it. Look at Psalm 1: "Whatever he does, he prospers" (v. 3, NASB). The Lord wants to open the floodgates and pour "exceedingly abundant" blessings into your and my lap (Eph. 3:20). He delights in it. Loves to give good gifts to His children (Luke 11:13). Made us alive together with Christ and lavished great love on us (Eph. 2:4–5). Calls us children (1 John 3:1). And His will toward us is good.[12] His promises are "Yes" and "Amen" (2 Cor. 1:20).

But as I unpacked the Word, what impressed me was not God's desire for our blessing, but our promised affliction. Our promised tribulation. Promised suffering. The testing of our faith.[13]

What I learned in those umpteen hours of study and crying out is that a gospel of Jesus Christ that includes blessing without suffering is a false gospel. It's a lie from the pit of hell, and those who propagate it are false prophets. I knew that Scripture says Jesus learned obedience through suffering and that did not bode well for me (Heb. 5:8). So, as this conversation rolled out, I knew what was coming. And I was not looking forward to it.

I am sitting here now writing this several years past that experience and as I type, I am staring at the screen through tears. The pain was real then. The memory of it is real now. I say that to show you the depth of the wound. But hold on—He didn't leave me there then and He isn't now.

He sat next to me. Shoulder to shoulder. "Did I test Abraham?"[14]

I knew that after a twenty-five-year wait and then thirteen years of living with his only son, Isaac, God told Abraham to kill him. The son of his love. God told him to slit his throat and let the blood drain down across the altar. Then, after He told him that, God let Abram travel three days and let it sink in while Isaac played along the path. My voice cracked. "Yes."

"Did I deliver My people Israel out of Egypt?"

I nodded but didn't look up.

"And did they cross the Red Sea on dry ground?"

Through miracles and wonders, the likes of which the world had never seen, the nation of Israel was delivered from the horrors of Egypt. From four hundred years of slavery and bondage. Walked out of Egypt carrying Egyptian gold. Straight into a desert. Three days later, they were parched. Thirsty. Children screaming. No water in sight. Then they came upon this spring. And the water was bitter. Bad. Couldn't drink it.[15] "Yes, but why did You lead them to a source of water that no one could drink?"

"I was transforming a nation of slaves."

"Into what?"

"A kingdom of priests."[16]

"Sort of backfired on You, didn't it?"

"How so?"

"Three million people grumbled and one man prayed."

He looked at me out of the corner of His eye. "A familiar reaction." A pause. "You remember what I used to heal the water?"

"A tree."[17]

He smiled and let that sink in.

I made the connection. "You know, they also make Louisville Sluggers out of trees."

He laughed then rerouted us. "Did I choose and anoint Saul as king?"[18]

"Yes."

"And when he departed from Me, did I send a distressing spirit to him? To afflict him?"[19]

"You did."

"Why?"

"To make room for David."

"And what was Job doing when satan came and asked Me for his life?"

I was afraid to answer. He picked up on it. "Go ahead, you can say it."

"Minding his own business."

"You're right. He was. And, was any man more righteous than Job?"

"No. He woke every morning and made sacrifice for his family."[20]

"You remember what he told his wife when she told him to curse Me?"

The picture of Job appeared on the backs of my eyelids. He was covered in pus and boils. Family dead. Fortunes gone. Scraping his skin with a potsherd. "'Shall we indeed accept good from God, and shall we not accept adversity?' In all this Job did not sin with his lips."[21]

"Do you see that I gave satan permission to inflict harm upon an obedient, righteous man?"

I swallowed. "Yes."

"What'd Jeremiah say about Me?"

"You test the righteous."[22]

"Tell me about Joseph."

"He was a dreamer, literally. Also, minding his own business. His older brothers got tired of his mouth so they sold him for twenty shekels of silver to the Ishmaelites and faked his death to their father. David described it in Psalm 105:16–19: "Moreover He [You] called for a famine in the land; He [You] destroyed all the provision of bread. He [You] sent a man before them—Joseph—who was sold as a slave. They hurt his feet with fetters, He was laid in irons. Until the time that his word came to pass, the word of the LORD tested him."

"How long was he like that?"

"Fourteen years."

"Can you see the bronze wrapped around his ankles?"

It didn't take long for the picture to appear. "Yes."

"Don't you think I could have released him from prison earlier?"

"Yes."

"And yet, I didn't."

I nodded my head in agreement.

"What did Paul tell the Romans?"

"We also glory in tribulations, knowing that tribulation (the testing of our faith) *produces perseverance."*[23]

"When was the last time you 'gloried in your tribulation'?"

"Never."

"What'd he tell the Corinthians?"

"We are hard-pressed on every side, yet not crushed; we are perplexed, but not in despair; persecuted, but not forsaken; struck down, but not destroyed"[24]

"And Timothy?"

"He told him to mix some wine with his water."

He chuckled in my ear.

I continued, "Share with me in the sufferings for the gospel according to the power of God."[25]

Knowing there was more, He waited.

"Endure hardship as a good soldier of Jesus Christ."[26]

"Keep going."

"All who desire to live godly in Christ Jesus will suffer persecution."[27] I scratched my head. "When do we get to the part where You, the God of angel armies, the God of battle-axe and spear, send a lightning bolt to my enemy's chest?"

I could hear pages flipping, being turned. He said, "I want to read you something out of Hebrews."

"While we're on the subject, who wrote Hebrews?"

He smiled. "Others were tortured, not accepting deliverance, that they might obtain a better resurrection. Still others had trial of mockings and scourgings, yes, and of chains and imprisonment. They were stoned, they were sawn in two, were tempted, were slain with the sword. They wandered about in sheepskins and goatskins, being destitute, afflicted, tormented—of whom the world was not worthy. They wandered in deserts and mountains, in dens and caves of the earth."[28] I could hear Him scratching His beard. "Have you been stoned?"

"No."

"Sawn in two?"

"No."

I heard more pages flipping. "For I consider that the sufferings of this present time are not worthy to be compared with the glory which shall be revealed in us."[29]

"I'm a long way from that perspective right now."

The pages flipped. "Love suffers long and is kind; love does not envy; love does not parade itself, is not puffed up."[30]

"That one too."

"For to you it has been granted on behalf of Me, not only to believe in Me, but also to suffer for My sake."[31]

This was a hard word. My eyes were watering.

He thumbed away the tear. "You okay?"

"I have a speck."

"Did Paul desire to know Me and the power of My resurrection, and the fellowship of My sufferings, being conformed to My death?"[32]

"He did."

He tapped Himself in the chest, "Let's turn the lens on Me a minute."

This would be painful. I waited.

"Did My Father bruise Me?"

"Yes."

"Crush Me?"

"Yes."

"Put Me to grief?"[33]

"He did."

"Did My Father do to Me what He spared Abraham?"

"Yes."

"Did I not taste death for everyone? Was I, the captain of your salvation, made perfect through suffering? Was I tempted so that I might aid those who are tempted?"[34]

I knew the verse. "Though You were a Son, yet You learned obedience by the things which You suffered."[35]

"Charles, if I learned obedience through suffering, what's that say about you?"

"It says my goose is cooked."

"And you will be hated by all for My name's sake. But he who endures to the end will be saved."[36]

"That one's always troubled me."

"Did I say anything in there about rescuing you in the midst of your stuff?"

"No."

"What two words catch your eyes?"

"'Hate' and 'endure.'"

"Did I tell My disciples, 'If anyone desires to come after Me, let him deny himself, and take up his cross, and follow Me; And he who does not take his cross and follow after Me is not worthy of Me'?"[37]

"Lord . . ."

He prodded me. "Is My Word true?"

"Yes."

"Tell Me."

"[It is] life to those who find them, and health to all their flesh."[38]

"Is My Word true?"

"I have treasured the words of Your mouth more than my necessary food."[39]

"And?"

"Your words were found, and I ate them, and Your word was to me the joy and rejoicing of my heart."[40]

"Don't stop now."

"'Is not My word like a fire?' says the LORD, 'And like a hammer that breaks the rock in pieces?'"[41]

"That all you got?"

"Your word I have hidden in my heart, that I might not sin against You."[42]

He paused, leaned in, and smiled. "Maybe you should bury it deeper."

I held up two stop-sign hands. "I know I'm being little, I realize my reaction is petty, I am tripping over my bottom lip, ripe with bitterness. But I am in pain."

He continued, "I know how to be abased, and I know how to abound. Everywhere and in all things I have learned both to be full and to be hungry, both to abound and to suffer need."[43]

"I'm not there yet."

"Do you thank Me, with all sincerity, for the times that you are full? When you are abounding?"

"No."

"Why not?"

"Honestly?"

He chuckled. "I'd prefer that."

"'Cause I'm spoiled. I think I'm entitled."

He nodded in agreement.

"Okay . . . that's my bad."

This time I didn't hear the pages flipping, which meant He was speaking it the same way He spoke it to Paul. "I now rejoice in my sufferings for you, and fill up in my flesh what is lacking in the afflictions of Christ, for the sake of His body."[44]

I laughed out loud.

"Something funny?"

"'Rejoicing in sufferings?' Seriously? When do I get to murmur and complain? 'Filling up my flesh in the afflictions of Christ'?'" I shook my head. "That's a tough word."

"Yes, it is, and it's coming from My son Paul who's been there, done that, and got the T-shirt to prove it. His rejoicing and filling up honored Me."

I rubbed the sore spot above my heart and offered no response.

He continued. "We told you before when we were with you that we would suffer tribulation, just as it happened, and you know."[45]

"Yes, You did that."

"And you didn't believe Me, did you?"

"It's not so much that I didn't believe You as I skipped over that one."

"So, you're Scripture picking."

"Pretty much."

"But, I thought you told Christy and your boys and all those guys in your Bible study that you don't get to do that. I think you used the words, 'accepting the whole counsel of God.'"

He was right. I had. "Lord, I know I'm a hypocrite. The evidence speaks for itself. I'm guilty. My righteousness is as filthy rags."[46]

"Yes, and all who desire to live godly in Christ Jesus will suffer persecution."[47]

"I ignored that one too."

"Do you desire to live godly in Me?"

"Sometimes."

"Not all the time?"

"Not when it hurts like this."

"Did Moses choose rather to suffer affliction with the people of God than to enjoy the passing pleasures of sin, esteeming My reproach of greater riches than the treasures in Egypt; for he [Moses] looked to the reward?"[48]

"Okay, Lord, seriously. We're talking about Moses."

"Don't 'seriously' Me. Nothing has tempted you except what is common to man. I will not allow you to be tempted beyond what you are able, but with the temptation will also make the way of escape, that you may be able to bear it."[49]

I rubbed my eyes. "You're killing me, Smalls."

He laughed. "So now your quoting movies?"

"Sorry. That's probably irreverent. But I'm still putting Moses on a pedestal. He spoke with You face to face!"

A pause. "What's this?"

"We're having this conversation in my mind. I'm not looking at Your face and hearing Your voice. I'm hearing my voice of Your voice."

"Read My Word and you'll see My face and hear My voice."

"I'm learning that."

"Is anyone among you suffering? Let him pray. Is anyone cheerful? Let him sing psalms."[50]

This time I laughed out loud. "Psalms? Are you kidding me? How about, 'Lock and Load! Fire in the hole. Incoming!'"?

"For to this you were called, because I also suffered for you, leaving you an example, that you should follow My steps. . . . But even if you should suffer for righteousness' sake, you are blessed. And do not be afraid of their threats, nor be troubled . . . For it is better, if it is the will of God, to suffer for doing good than for doing evil. . . . Therefore, since I suffered for you in the flesh, arm yourselves also with the same mind, for he who has suffered in the flesh has ceased from sin. . . . Yet if anyone suffers as a Christian, let him not be ashamed, but let him glorify Me in this matter. . . . But may I, the God of all grace, who called you to My eternal glory, after you have suffered a while, perfect, establish, strengthen, and settle you."[51]

"I don't think I can take any more of this."

He sat back, "Okay—in the infamous words of Inigo Montoya, let Me sum up."

"Did you just quote **The Princess Bride**?"

"Charles, I do have a sense of humor. I invented it."

"Okay, I'll give you that."

"Remember when Paul said—"

I knew where He was going. I held up a stop-sign hand. "Please don't quote that one. It makes me nauseated every time I hear it."

That had no effect. He continued, "From the Jews five times I received forty stripes minus one. Three times I was beaten with rods; once I was stoned; three times I was shipwrecked; a night and a day I have been in the deep; in journeys often, in perils of waters, in perils of robbers, in perils of my own countrymen, in perils of the Gentiles, in perils in the city, in perils in the wilderness, in perils in the sea, in perils among false brethren; in weariness and toil, in sleeplessness often, in hunger and thirst, in fastings often, in cold and nakedness. . . . If I must boast, I will boast in the things which concern my infirmity."[52]

"I think I'm going to throw up."

"Do you think for one second that I wasn't standing there every time that rod tore the skin off his back?"

"I'm trying not to think about it."

"Does not the potter have a right over the clay, to make from the same lump one vessel for honorable use and another for common use?"[53]

"Please don't quote what comes next. I don't think I can take it . . ."

"What if I, although willing to demonstrate My wrath and to make My power known, endured with much patience vessels of wrath prepared for destruction? And I did it so to make known the riches of My glory upon vessels of mercy, which I prepared beforehand for glory."[54]

"Yeah, I don't even know what to do with that."

"Think about this: my friend Peter was crucified upside down. My brother James was stoned. Eleven of my twelve apostles were killed. Some were burned at the stake. Some were skinned alive. Boiled in oil. Stephen was stoned. Paul was beheaded in a Roman prison."

I raised a finger to protest. "I'd like to keep my head where it is."

"I was betrayed by one of My closest friends, whipped with a Roman scourge while My best friends watched. I was rendered 'unrecognizable as a man,' then crucified while those around Me mocked Me and spat on Me and drove a spear through My chest."

My ears hurt. I hung my head in my hands, pressing out the tears.

He spoke over me. "When do you think Joseph understood My purposes?"

I wiped my nose on my shirt sleeve. "About the time his brothers walked in asking for grain."

"So what do you think that process required of him?"

I knew the answer. I just didn't want to speak it.

He prodded. "Go ahead."

"Trust."

He opened my Bible to John 16:33. The words in red popped off the page. "These things I have spoken to you, that in Me you may have peace. In the world you will have tribulation; but be of good cheer, I have overcome the world." He pointed to the word "tribulation." You see that?"

"Yes, Lord."

*"The Greek is **thlipsis**. It means, 'pressure, oppression, stress, anguish, tribulation, adversity, affliction, crushing, squashing, squeezing, distress.' It's what happens when you crush grapes or olives in a press." He paused. I knew it before He asked it. He leaned in closer. "Where was I arrested?"*

"In the garden—where they pressed the olives."

"You starting to get the picture?"

"Yes." I exhaled deeply and spoke slowly. It wasn't so much a defense as a venting. "Okay, I get it. In this life, I will suffer. I got it. You've proven Your point. So, can the suffering end? Because right now I am still in pain!"

When I looked down we were in Psalm 34. His fingers pointed at the words as He read. His hands were calloused. Weathered. Both fisherman and carpenter. But it was the hole that caught my attention. "I sought the LORD, and He heard me, and delivered me from all my fears. . . . This poor man cried out, and the LORD heard him, and saved him out of all his troubles. . . . The righteous cry out, and the LORD hears, and delivers them out of all their troubles. . . . Many are the afflictions of the righteous, but the LORD delivers him out of them all."[55]

I was about to offer an objection as to how He had not done that for us, when He pointed again. "You see that word 'all.'" He looked at me, nodding. "It means just that. 'All.'"

He turned the page. "The Spirit Himself bears witness with our spirit that we are children of God, and if children, then heirs—heirs of God and joint heirs with

Christ, if indeed we suffer with Him, that we may also be glorified together. For
I consider that the sufferings of this present time are not worthy to be compared
with the glory which shall be revealed in us."[56]

"I'm ready for the glory."

Another turn of the page. "And we know that all things work together
for good to those who love God, to those who are the called according to His
purpose. . . . What then shall we say to these things? If God is for us, who can be
against us? . . . Who shall separate us from the love of Christ? Shall tribulation,
or distress, or persecution, or famine, or nakedness, or peril, or sword? As it is
written: 'For Your sake we are killed all day long; we are accounted as sheep for
the slaughter.' Yet in all these things we are more than conquerors through Him
who loved us. For I am persuaded that neither death nor life, nor angels nor
principalities nor powers, nor things present nor things to come, nor height nor
depth, nor any other created thing, shall be able to separate us from the love of
God which is in Christ Jesus our Lord."[57]

He paused and whispered four words for effect. "Sheep for the slaughter"?

I knew what He was getting at. I nodded.

"Charles, when I say, 'I feel your pain,' I'm not kidding. I'm the Lamb who
was slain."

Tears streamed down my face.

I flipped over to Romans 16:20: "And the God of peace will crush satan under
your feet shortly." I tapped the words, waiting. "What about this one? What about
a good ol' fashioned butt kicking?"

He flipped me back to 1 Peter 1:6–9. "Like Peter, I am refining your faith. By
fire. To do that, I have to burn some stuff away. It can be painful but it makes the
gold more pure. The higher the heat, the more pure the gold."

"And the greater the pain," I quipped.

He nodded knowingly.

I turned slowly back to the Old Testament where Job was in the midst of his
trial and still had twenty-three chapters of suffering to go before his life is made
right. My fingers touched the words. "I know that my Redeemer lives, and He
shall stand at last on the earth; and after my skin is destroyed, this I know, that in
my flesh I shall see God."[58] My finger landed on the words "my Redeemer lives." I

leaned into Him. I said, "Lord, I know I'm a mess right now, but I really do want to be like this. In the midst of all this, I want to declare across the darkness that wants to blanket me that You live, and that I will see You."

"You will. You are."

Words wouldn't come, so I flipped to the end of Job and just tapped the words on the page. "I know that You can do everything, and that no purpose of Yours can be withheld from You. . . . I have heard of You by the hearing of the ear, but now my eye sees You. Therefore I abhor myself, and repent in dust and ashes."[59]

He whispered in my ear. "Take a look around."

I did.

"You see where you are? This place?"

"Yes."

"It's right where I want you."

"You did this on purpose?"

"I allowed it."

"Everything?"

"Everything that ever happens to you has been sifted by My sovereign hand."

"That's difficult for me."

"I know."

"And You want me to trust You?"

"Completely."

"You're not making it any easier."

"I will never leave you nor forsake you."[60]

"It doesn't feel like it sometimes."

"Are you going to listen to your feelings or Me?"

"Lord, I feel like my stomach has been sliced open, my guts have spilled out on the ground, and people are stomping on my insides."

"I'm near to the brokenhearted and save those who are crushed in spirit."[61]

I tried to say something untrue, and He cut me off. "Many are the afflictions of the righteous. But I, the Lord, deliver him—that is, you—out of them all."[62]

"But what about the feel-good prosperity gospel? Media is full of Bible-thumpers talking about my prosperity and how I can make my life better."

"Not all of them know Me."

"But don't You want us to prosper? I mean, Lord, we are getting our lunch handed to us down here."

"Blessed is the man who walks not in the counsel of the ungodly, nor stands in the path of sinners, nor sits in the seat of the scornful; but his delight is in the law of the LORD, and in His law he meditates day and night. He shall be like a tree planted by the rivers of water, that brings forth its fruit in its season, whose leaf also shall not wither; and whatever he does shall prosper."[63]

I pounded the pages, "Exactly! Whatever he does—"

He interrupted me. "What does that word **prosper** mean?"

"Well, I would imagine it is the opposite of me right now."

"Look it up."

I started flipping through the books on my shelf. While I did this I could hear Him muttering over my shoulder, "Buy you books, send you to school, and all you do is chew on the covers."

"My dad used to say that to me."

"Where do you think he got it?"

I found the definition. "To prosper is like a military commander returning from a battle campaign, having successfully accomplished his orders."

"Keep going."

"During that campaign, he probably slept on the ground, fought and lost, suffered wounding, knew temporary defeat, but afterward, when he came to the end of his campaign, he returned to his commander, complete with scars and a limp, having accomplished his orders."

"Charles, that's prosperity. To accomplish your orders. Blessing flows out of that. Out of hearing and obeying My voice. Period. You align yourself with My Word, My orders. Don't twist it and make it fit your circumstances. Or run to it only when you've made such a big mess that you feel yourself swirling around the bowl."

I offered no response. Didn't even attempt to look up.

He continued, "Remember My servant Abraham?"

"Yes."

"Remember when he sent his servant to find a wife for Isaac?"

"Yes."

"How did the servant describe his own journey?"

"He said You 'led me to the house.' And later, You 'led me in the way of truth.'"[64]

"See that word 'led'?"

I nodded.

"See how he followed?"

Another nod.

"To be led by Me is prosperity. To follow Me is blessing."

"Even if it leads to affliction?"

He nodded, "Even if."

"But Lord, we did follow You. It's what got us in this mess in the first place."

"I am not on your time schedule."

"I know."

He continued, "Do I give strength to the weary?"[65]

"Yes, they run and don't grow weary."[66]

"Have I armed you with strength?"[67]

"You have trained my hands for war and my fingers for battle."[68]

"Have I met all your needs?"[69]

"I would have lost heart unless I had believed that I would see the goodness of the LORD in the land of the living."[70]

"Am I your comfort?"[71]

"You prepare a table before me in the presence of my enemies."[72]

"Did you hear what you just said?"

I shook my head. "You just totally broke our rhythm. We were on a roll. I said one, then You said one, and then You had to go and mess it up."

He laughed. "Am I your hope?"

"The anchor of my soul."[73]

"Your salvation?"[74]

"And glory and honor and power belong to You."[75]

"Then what's your problem?"

"You make Your people experience hardship?"[76] I scratched my head. "The NKJV reads, 'You have shown Your people hard things."

He flipped to Hebrews 11 and tapped the page, never taking His eyes off me. He didn't need to say anything. I got the picture.

"Well, when You put it that way . . ."

"Charles, I've never 'put' it any other way."

"Okay, so I have a tendency to forget."

"But . . ."

He didn't let me finish. *"You trust Me with your whole heart?"*[77]

"You're my refuge and my fortress. In You I will trust."[78]

"You sure you wouldn't rather be someplace else?"

"A day in your courts is better than a thousand outside."[79]

"Then do it. In deed. Not just in thought."[80]

The enormity of life pressed in on me. I waved my hands across it. *"You sure You got this?"*

"I uphold all things by the word of My power."[81]

"Including this?"

"I am not pacing the halls of heaven popping antacids over your situation."

I was quiet a minute. *"What about my pain?"*

"Declaring the end from the beginning, and from ancient times things which have not been done, saying, 'My purpose will be established, and I will accomplish all My good pleasure.'"[82]

I stood up, opened my arms and unloaded it on Him. *"Take it."*

With the precision of a heart surgeon, He lifted the shrapnel.

I turned to go, but He tapped me on the shoulder. Another poke. *"All of it."*

I had given Him most of it, the stuff on the surface, but I'd shrouded the one thing I was holding onto. The one thing I was not about to give Him. I folded my arms. *"But Lord, if I let go of that, then I can't be angry."*

"I know."

"Then how are those people going to get what they've got coming?"

"I thought you said vengeance was Mine."

"It is, but—"

"Why all of a sudden are you getting into the vengeance game?"

I mumbled something.

"What's that? I didn't hear you."

"I said, 'cause You're not moving fast enough."

"We've already covered that. You really want to go back there?"

"Not really."

Another poke. Brush strokes appeared before my eyes as He painted a mental picture that He had painted several times. Two hands appeared, holding a red can, pouring gasoline into a Styrofoam cup. A picture worth a hundred thousand words.

I held up a stop-sign hand. "Don't. I don't think I can handle any more."

He poked the deeper shrapnel in the same way we fish for splinters. "Just so you'll know, I'll let you keep it. I'll never take from you what you don't give Me."

"Great. So I can rot from the inside out."

He beckoned with His hand. "I'm waiting."[83]

"Okay, say I do. Say I give you that too. Other than a raw, bloody, gaping hole, just what am I left with?"

I could hear Him moving toward me. His arms wrapped around me. I felt His breath on my face. My Father held me. "You're left with Me."[84]

So I opened up and gave Him the last piece. My anger. My bitterness. My unforgiveness. My judgment. My right to be vindicated.

Again.

For the umpteenth time.

His voice was soft. "Let's go back to the car. The parking lot. You remember?"

I did. It was tender to me. "Yes, Lord."

"Mind if I replay the video?"

"I'd like that."

The video opened on the steam rising off my coffee. I tried to pray, but I could only get a single word out of my mouth. Just, "Lord. . . ."

We sat in the Tractor Supply parking lot in awkward silence until my youngest son, Rives, eleven, opened his mouth and began to pray. For me. There in that car, eleven years old did what forty-five could not. What's more, my eleven-year-old warrior stood and fought the thing that was killing me. And he prayed the most honest, tender, forgiving prayer I think I've ever heard. And when he openly forgave the people causing our pain, something in me broke.

When Rives finished, John T, fifteen, prayed. And he did the same: openly, verbally, by name, forgiving those who'd hurt us. Followed by Charlie, seventeen. And then Christy.

I sat in the front seat of that car while the prayers of my wife and children stripped my anger away. Their words peeled it off in layers. In Buick-sized chunks. And there, in that naked place, I began to "see" and "know" with something deeper than my pain, that the promises of God are and were true. I can't explain that. I just knew it. On a DNA level. There and then, God made the truth of His truth true to me. Along with this came a desire and willingness to forgive. And trust me, that desire didn't come from me. Still doesn't.

"Yes Lord, You were in the car."

He prodded me. "But, what?"

I turned slightly in shame. "That feeling in me lasted only a few days."

"What changed?"

"Me."

"So?"

"So, knowing that, I can't promise you that we won't be right back here tomorrow."

"You mean, like yesterday?"

I shrugged. "That doesn't bother You?"

"Nothing about you bothers Me."[85]

"Are we looking at the same me?"

"You're perfect."[86]

"But don't You get tired of this?"

"Why would I get tired of this?"

"Same stuff, different day."

"You and I have just spent the last hour and a half talking. Hanging out. With some pretty deep honesty on your part. And, you let Me take from you some stuff that wants to kill you."

"And don't You get tired of that?"

"You don't bore Me. And I never tire of you."[87]

"You have an answer for everything."

"I invented the questions."[88]

"I'm just telling You right now that I'll see You tomorrow."

"Charles?"

"Lord."

"I'll be waiting."

"Your ways are higher."[89]

"And My love is deeper.[90] *Speaking of deep—"* He poked at my wound. *"How's that feeling?"*

No pus this time. *"Better."*

"You trust Me?"

I was hesitant. *"Yes, I do."*

"But, what?"

"Why do You ask me questions like this if You already know what I'm thinking?

"To give you the chance to tell Me the truth."

"Why?"

"Because doing so makes you free."[91]

"Free of this would be good."

He nodded in agreement. *"Keep going."*

"I will need some help continuing to trust You once we quit talking."

"I work in you both to will and to do according to My good pleasure."[92]

"Paul said that to the Philippians."

"And now I'm saying it to you."

"What's it mean?"

"It means, I've got this. I've got you. And, I've got those you love."

"And tomorrow?"

"My grace is sufficient."[93]

"Even if I show up in this same crummy state?"

"My strength is made perfect in your weakness."[94]

"You already said that one."

"Wanted to make sure you were paying attention."

"What if I'm worse than today?"

"I'll arm you with strength for the battle. You'll run and not be weary. You'll run against a troop. Leap over a wall."[95]

I sat in silence while He read my thoughts and doubts, and then answered them before I uttered an objection.

"I will go before you and make the crooked places straight; I will break in pieces the gates of bronze and cut the bars of iron."[96]

"I like that one."

"The horse is prepared for the day of battle, but deliverance is of the LORD.*"*[97]

"That one too."

"I tested you at the waters of Meribah."[98]

"Not too crazy about that one."

"If you should suffer for righteousness' sake, you are blessed."[99]

Silence.

"Do not be surprised at the fiery ordeal among you, which comes upon you for your testing, as though some strange thing were happening to you . . . If you are reviled for My name, you are blessed . . . If anyone suffers as a Christian, he is not to be ashamed, but is to glorify God."[100]

I looked at Him, "We could do this all day couldn't we? Can I ask You one more question?"

A beautiful smile. "Always."

"What about . . ." I couldn't complete the sentence.

He leaned in closer. "Victory?"

I nodded.

He turned my attention back to the cross. A picture I'd studied ten thousand times. The slide show played across my mind's eye. To His body, broken, battered, unrecognizable as a man. Then He took me to the tomb. Empty. Stone rolled away. Two angels sitting, smiling, at either end of empty burial clothes. Neatly folded. Lastly, He showed me His current position. His chair. The throne next to the Father. His crown. Sword strapped about His thigh. Keys dangling from His belt. And for the rest I don't have words. He didn't need to say anymore.

His fingers touched my chin, turning my face toward His. "Charles, I a shield for you, your glory and the One who lifts up your head."[101]

Somewhere in there, I caught a glimpse of His face.

Choose to Trust Him

Like the believers in Acts, we—through many trials—must enter the kingdom of God (Acts 14:22). We won't always experience instant victory. Yes,

He has given us all power and authority, and yet we suffer too. Sometimes at His hand. God didn't promise me or you a life without struggle. For reasons I can't always understand, His dominion does not preempt my suffering. That day is coming but it's not here yet.

Despite this, He rules in the midst of His enemies. They are His footstool. I experience His victory through my battle, and His triumph through my trial. That's tough for me to stomach but no less true. Daniel was thrown into a lions' den to prove his faith. His three friends into a furnace.

Paul told the believers in Rome, "But I know that when I come to you, I shall come in the fullness of the blessing of the gospel of Christ" (Rom. 15:29). And yet we know in the natural world this didn't happen. Paul was attacked, bound, declared a "plague" by his own people, and left in prison without cause for two years (Acts 24:5, 27). Then, as a wrongly-accused Roman citizen, Paul appealed to Caesar. Journeying to Rome in shackles, he was placed aboard a ship that encountered what sounded like a hurricane: "Now when neither sun nor stars appeared for many days, and no small tempest beat on us, all hope that we would be saved was finally given up" (27:20). After fourteen days, the ship ran aground on the island of Malta where it was crushed by the waves. All 276 persons made it ashore safely, but the entire ship and its cargo was lost (27:27–44). Once ashore, Paul gathered sticks to make a fire and was bitten by a viper, which fastened to his hand. Three months later they sailed to Rome where Paul lived in house-arrest for two years—writing the letters to the Ephesians, Colossians, and Philippians. Years later, following his second arrest, he was beheaded.

Let me back up to the beginning of Romans. Listen to what Paul said before all of this happened: "For God is my witness, whom I serve with my spirit in the gospel of His Son, that without ceasing I make mention of you always in my prayers, making request if, by some means, now at last I may find a way in the will of God to come to you" (Rom. 1:9–10). The King James Version says it this way, which might be more correct: "if by any means now at length I may have a prosperous journey by the will of God, to come unto you."

Does that sound like a prosperous journey to you?

Paul described his walk with the Lord this way:

From the Jews five times I received forty stripes minus one. Three times I was beaten with rods; once I was stoned; three times I was shipwrecked; a night and a day I have been in the deep; in journeys often, in perils of waters, in perils of robbers, in perils of my own countrymen, in perils of the Gentiles, in perils in the city, in perils in the wilderness, in perils in the sea, in perils among false brethren; in weariness and toil, in sleeplessness often, in hunger and thirst, in fastings often, in cold and nakedness. (2 Cor. 11:24–27)

As Saul of Tarsus became the Paul we know and love, he was blinded on the Damascus road and went three days without food or water. He was praying for help when the Lord told Ananias, "Go, for he [Paul] is a chosen vessel of Mine to bear My name before Gentiles, kings, and the children of Israel. For I will show him how many things he must suffer for My name's sake" (Acts 9:15–16). This is God talking about His chosen vessel and what He will do to Him. That word *suffer* means to experience something evil, the opposite of free action, and to experience a sensation or impression. To be vexed. Jesus used the same word to describe what will happen to Him in Mark 9:12. And yet what came of Paul's suffering, imprisonment, and execution? About two-thirds of all the quotations I'm using in this book to encourage you.

God's ways are higher than ours.

My circumstances do not dictate the truth of my reality. God does. His Word does. The tough part of learning this lesson is the painful migration of the information traveling from my head to my heart. That can take a while. It's one thing to convince my mind; it's another to persuade my heart.

Truth is, we do and will suffer. I'm not telling you to like it. I'm not telling you to wish for it. I'm just trying to encourage you that when you're in the midst of it, don't let the enemy fill your mind with questions about God's goodness, His faithfulness, or His unfathomable love for you.

My problem is that I am a sinner, and I like to grovel in my own self-pity because being a victim is easier than trusting Him. Being a victim takes no faith. Trusting Him takes all that I have.

I want to counter the false gospel that we are the captains of our own prosperity. We are not. He is. Notice, I've said nothing about victory. Our victory is established. We, through Christ, and like Christ, are victorious. Might not look like it at the moment, but that day is coming. I'm simply holding up the idea that He defines victory differently than we do—that is, the cross. Jesus was and is victorious on the cross, and that victory provided us the power to live His life and die His death and reign with Him as children and coheirs.

Here, on this side of the cross, for the refining of our faith, we, at times, live in and are *sent by Him* into both a den and furnace. Why? I don't know. I'm a sheep, and sheep are dumb, but it has something to do with faith. And because without faith it's impossible to please Him (Heb. 11:6). I am neither invulnerable nor immune to suffering, and I live in the middle between the promise of suffering and the promise of deliverance. I can't explain that, but I know it's true. And in that middle place, I have a choice: I can throw in the towel, rot from the inside out, or I can stand, hold fast, and declare—with equal vigor—that He is good even when my circumstances are not and even if they don't pan out the way I hope. This does not mean that I don't hope and dream and desire. It means I choose to trust Him. Regardless and whatever my lot.

And therein lies the nugget. It's a choice. What will you choose?

Lord, I'm a mess. I'm in pain. I'm hurting. Some of which I brought on myself and some I had nothing to do with. I'm groveling in self-pity, and at the moment I'm playing the victim because it's easier to wrap myself in misery than trust You. I'm sorry for that. Please forgive me. I don't want to be this way. I'm sorry for my whining. My complaining. Seems like I've done a lot of it, but I figure You're big enough to handle the messy depths of me. You were right when You said I have an enemy that has come to kill, steal, and destroy. He has, and to some extent I've let him. He's also pillaged some of my hopes and dreams. My wife's and kids' hopes and dreams.

But Lord, You came to give us life to the full. I know that. I also know that "life to the full" does not mean it will work out the way I hope. It might, I sincerely hope it does, but that's not the point. The point is this: my circumstances do not dictate Your nature or Your love for me. Period. You speak that which is not as though it is. I need to say that again for my benefit—my God speaks that which is not as though it is. And, for the record—my Redeemer lives.

I know that You can do all things and that no purpose of Yours can be withheld from You. That Your will toward me and us is good, and look at what great love You have lavished on us that You would call us children of God for that is what we are. Your mercies are new every morning. And though we sow in tears, we will reap in joy. Jesus, You are faithful. Holy. True. The brightness of the Father's glory. The exact representation of His glory. You uphold all things by the word of Your power. You are King of kings. The Ruler of the kings of this earth. Your sword is girded on Your thigh. You are the Lion of Judah. Lamb upon the throne. You alone hold the keys to death and Hades. You defeated everything that wants my head on a platter, and when You said, "It is finished," You weren't kidding.

Lord, I have complained. A lot. I have thought unkindly toward others. Been unforgiving. Bitter. Angry. I've thought horrible things about other people who are your children. I'm sorry for all that. Forgive me. Please. Really. I don't want to carry this stuff anymore. Take it. It's Yours. All of it. I forgive those who have wronged me. Outright and completely. I tear up the IOU. I release them from my judgment. And in obedience to Your Word, I pray for them. I bless them in the name of Jesus. We have come through and, to a very great extent, are still in, a period of trial. Of tribulation. Of suffering. I'm not saying this to poke Your pity. I'm saying it in the same way David said it to You—where else would I take this thing in me? Who else is big enough to handle this? No one. Hebrews speaks of those who heard the Word, but it did not profit them because it was not united with faith. With belief. I don't want to be one of them. I want Your Word to sink deep roots in me. So in desert times, like this, I can produce fruit rather than pus. So I reflect Your glory and not my junk. So Your name is made known to generations.

Please unite Your Word in me with faith, for I know that You promise me that Your Word will not return void, and it will accomplish the purposes for which You sent it. Lord, I trust You. I trust You with today. With tomorrow. With the outcome. And what may come. Please help me to trust You. Forgive me when I don't. I can't do it on my own. You are faithful. Lord, I invite You, by the power of Your Holy Spirit, to speak to me. Out loud. Audibly. However my spirit can hear Yours. I invite You to silence my enemy who whispers lies about You.

In the name of Jesus, I rebuke, bind, and cast down the whisperer of lies and tell him to shut up! satan, you are liar and a defeated punk, and you will be muzzled and not speak lies about my King who rules and reigns over all—and that includes you. you may not live rent free in my mind, you may not offer arguments that exalt themselves against the knowledge of God, and you may not speak anything contrary to the promises of God as etched in His Word. Period.

Lastly, Lord, there is this wound in me. You know the one. My enemy would like to use that wounded place to purchase. To grab ahold of me. But if You heal that wound, he can't hold on. So Lord, come now. Holy Spirit come heal me. I breathe in You and breathe out pain and infirmity. Be my balm of Gilead. Be my Jehovah-Rapha. My healer. Jesus, I thank You that You have done, are doing, and will continue to do this.

Lastly, Lord, let Your word take deep root in me so that when I need You, Your words will bubble up in me and we can have conversations like this.

In Jesus' Name, amen.

CHAPTER 10

No Gone Is Too Far Gone

I imagine he stunk. Clothes tattered. Hair matted. Beard stained. One shoe missing a sole. The other worn through. Personal hygiene out the window. Chin, once high, now drags his chest. His eyes scan the ground, afraid to make eye contact lest he bump into a creditor. One front tooth is missing. Another is cracked. The chest full of gold chains is gone. Sold. Gambled. Or stolen. The ring his father once gave him was pawned weeks ago. He is now skinny, ribs showing. Hungry. And he's not just mildly entertaining the idea of what might be in the fridge. He is nauseated and can think of little else. The once lofty air has left the building.

This silent ending had a boisterous beginning. Not uncommon. It sounded like this: "I want what I want, when I want it, because I want it, and I want it right now." His friends poured gasoline on the fire and pretty soon he was spitting flames. Angry, spiteful, full of himself, he went to his father. Stared down his nose. Disdain spread across his lips. He spouted: "I want my share. Now." Given the culture, his demand was unconscionable. Sort of like saying, "You are dead to me. I want nothing more to do with you and your silly, pathetic life. I'll take what's mine. From this moment, you're no longer my father and don't ever speak to me again."

Pockets full, he turned his back and, surrounded by a fair-weather posse, walked away. Laughing. Skipping. Slapping backs. Sucking courage from a brown bag. Glorious sin on the horizon.

Behind him, the father stood on the porch, a piercing pain in his chest.

The distance increased. Time passed. A poor fund manager and unwise in pretty much every way, his prodigal living was short-lived. High life led to low life. The boy lived it up. Drunk whatever. Smoked whatever. Bought whatever. Slept with whomever. Whenever. Wherever. He was a man with no control over his spirit. Like a city broken down without walls.[1]

To make matters worse, famine entered the story. The writing on the wall became clear. Once the sugar daddy had been picked clean, the posse stampeded.

Broke, hungry, alone, and ashamed—but not quite humbled—he "joined himself" to another.[2] Said another way, he sold himself as a slave. Don't miss this: he's a Jewish boy going to work for a Gentile farmer raising pigs. This is apostasy. He could not have been any more unclean. There were laws about this, and he had broken all of them.

Standing in that pen, surrounded by manure and swarming flies, holding the slop bucket, he stands just one final rung from the bottom.

We pick up the story as he is staring into the bucket with a raised eyebrow, watering mouth, and thinking, *That's not so bad. I could probably get that down.* The translation speaks of carob pods—sort of a bean-looking thing with the consistency of shoe leather. One of the only fruit-producing plants to actually produce fruit in that area during times of famine. It's a last resort—even for the pigs.

Can you see him scratching his head? Deliberating? Staring around to see who might be watching? This is where he steps off the ladder. Feet on the bottom—of the bottom. He has attempted to pull fire into his bosom, and it is here that we see the third-degree burns.[3] Not only has he sinned and fallen short, gone his own way, astray, he has missed the target entirely. His righteousness is "like filthy rags."[4] By "rags," Isaiah means used menstrual cloths. Let me spell this out. Left to our own devices, like our prodigal, the best we can produce absent a right relationship with the

Father is no better than a bunch of used feminine products. That may offend you, but that's the point. Everything about the prodigal is offensive, and he is paying the price of his offense.

But notice what finds him. There in that muck and mire and sour stench and poor choices and sin piled high, something swims past the reasonable filter of his mind and into the still-tender, yet-to-be-calloused places of his heart. And it's not condemnation and finger-pointing shame. It's the memory of his dad. The love of the father.

Of all places for love to find him. (If you could see me, I am fist pumping.)

Someone once asked me, "When is gone too far gone?" Here's my answer in a nutshell: there is no place on planet Earth that the love of the Father or the blood of Jesus can't reach. His arm is not so short that it cannot save (Isa. 59:1). That means, this side of the grave, no one—and I don't care who they are or what sin or sins they have or are committing—is too far gone. There's yet hope. The blood of Jesus cries out to us and speaks a better word than that of Abel (Heb. 12:24).

"But . . ." You raise a finger and shake your head in protest. "You don't know what I've done." Or, you're pointing now, the anger rising. Spit forming in the corner of your mouth. "You don't know what they've done! To me." You're right. I don't. What I do know is that "while we were still sinners, Christ died for us" (Rom. 5:8). That means at our worst, our most offensive, while suffering the consequences of our own shame and defiant choices, and a long way from home—Jesus "poured out His soul unto death" (Isa. 53:12). Why? Ask Him yourself. I won't spoil it for you. This is the mystery and wonder and majesty of the cross.

Scripture doesn't say it, but I think our prodigal ate the pods. A guess, yes, but it may well be an educated guess because Scripture does say, "When he came to himself" (Luke 15:17). What better than the bitter, nasty aftertaste of the pod to shake some sense into him. Something akin to a two-by-four to the mule's head.

I love what happens next. He turns around.[5] Note: he is turning his back toward his sin, and setting his face toward his father. Isaiah talked about this too. He calls it setting his "face like a flint."[6] Look up "repentance" in the dictionary, and you will see a picture of this. A hesitant jog at first. Then a chin-raising trot. Lungs taking in air. When he reaches the hill a mile out from the farm, he is sprinting. Arms flinging sweat, a trail of dust in his wake. If you listen closely, you can hear the beginning of a sound emitting from his belly. Low. Guttural. It is the sound of pain leaving his body.

And here's the best part. My favorite picture in this story. It's the father. Still standing on the porch. Yet to leave his post. One hand shading his eyes. Scanning the horizon. Searching for any sign of movement.

Something atop the hill catches his eye. He squints. Leans. "Can't be. Too skinny." A shake of the head. "No swagger," he thinks to himself. "But . . ." Then a deeper glance as the figure gets closer. Doesn't take long for that signature body language to register. The father exits the porch as if shot out of a canon. Having closed the distance, the son falls at his father's feet. He is groveling. Face to toes. Snot mixing with tears. "Father, I have sinned."[7]

The father will have none of this. He lifts him, falls on his neck, and kisses him. Pause here: I need that picture. The father kissing the son of squalor who willfully betrayed him. How many times have I done this? I cannot count.

The son protests, arm's length, he has yet to make eye contact, "But Dad, I'm not worthy. . . ."

The father waves him off, orders his servants, "Clothe my son! Bring me a ring! Carve the steaks! Raise the tent!" Servants scatter. The son stands in disbelief. Tattered and shattered. "But, Dad. . . ." The son has come undone. "You don't know what all I've done. I'm unclean. Please forgive—"

The father gently places his index finger under his son's chin and lifts it. Eye-to-eye. He thumbs away a tear. His eyes speak the words the son has needed to hear since he turned his back. The father pushes matted hair out of his eyes. "You, my son, are my son. Once dead, now alive. All is forgiven."[8]

Nothing Is Excluded. No Exceptions.

If you're the parent or loved one of a prodigal, let me bolster your hope with this: the Father has yet to leave His post. Eyes scanning the horizon. He sees the child. No darkness, no matter how dark, can hide him. Job says it this way: "For He [the Father] looks to the ends of the earth, and sees under the whole heavens" (Job 28:24). This hasn't all of a sudden changed because we're two thousand years on this side of the cross. It's not like God's eyesight has grown dim.

And despite the son's total and complete depravity, the father is not interested in making him or her a slave. Even though that's his right. He is about total restoration. A complete returning to sonship. An heir with all the rights and privileges thereof.

If you're a prodigal, with nothing but bad choices, poor decisions, and carnage in your rearview, and you're now surrounded by pigs and manure and staring at the pods, let me say this to you: I don't care what you've done, where you've gone, where you are, or who you've become; the truth is this—the sanctifying, redeeming, justifying, snatching-back-out-of-the-hand-of-the-devil-blood-of-Jesus reaches to the far ends of the earth (1 John 1:7). Meaning? You can always come home. This side of the grave, no mess is too big. No gone is too far gone. To think otherwise is to make a mockery of the sacrifice of Jesus.

Don't believe me? Don't take my word for it. This is Paul, speaking to the Romans. Like us, they'd ventured a long way from God. Paul called them "haters of God" (Rom. 1:30). He said, "What then shall we say to these things? If God is for us, who can be against us? . . . Who shall bring a charge against God's elect? It is God who justifies. Who is he who condemns? It is Christ who died, and furthermore is also risen, who is even at the right hand of God, who also makes intercession for us" (Rom. 8:31, 33–34). I can see Paul shaking his head. Think about it, Christ Himself, our High Priest, seated at the right hand of God with the earth as His footstool, is interceding for us. For you. For me. He has His Father's ear.

Paul continues, "Who shall separate us from the love of Christ? Shall tribulation, or distress, or persecution, or famine, or nakedness, or peril, or sword? . . . Yet in all these things we are more than conquerors through Him who loved us" (Rom. 8:35, 37).

Here's the good part. Actually, it's all good. This is just especially good. "For I am persuaded that neither death nor life, nor angels nor principalities nor powers, nor things present nor things to come, nor height nor depth, nor any other created thing, shall be able to separate us from the love of God which is in Christ Jesus our Lord" (Rom. 8:38–39).

If you unpack this, nothing is excluded from this list. No exceptions.

Isaiah says this: "I will say to the north, 'Give them up!' And to the south, 'Do not keep them back!' Bring My sons from afar, and My daughters from the ends of the earth" (43:6).

He Finds Us

Let me end with this. And I've already said it, but it's one of my favorites and can't be repeated enough. When we say this, we should stand on our rooftops and shout at the tops of our lungs: "I am persuaded that neither death nor life, nor angels nor principalities nor powers, nor things present nor things to come, nor height nor depth, nor any other created thing, shall be able to separate us from the love of God which is in Christ Jesus our Lord" (Rom. 8:38–39).

Don't think I'm letting you or me off the hook. I'm not. To receive such unmerited grace, we are required to do one thing. But, it's pretty simple and everyone can do it.

Turn. That's it. Just turn back.

Don't shake me off. First step is always the toughest. Try it. Stand up, pitch your pride, if you have any left, and put one foot in front of the other. Then another. The writer of Hebrews put it this way: "Therefore, since we have so great a cloud of witnesses surrounding us, let us also lay aside every encumbrance and the sin which so easily entangles us, and let us run with endurance the race that is set before us, fixing our eyes on Jesus" (12:1–2, NASB). Think about it, there is a host in heaven cheering you on. Pulling for you. Rooting for your return. You have your own cheering section. And see that word *fixing?* That's key.

I don't care what the shameful voices in your head tell you, the lies that the memories whisper, here is the truth about you and me: even in a far off country, wasted life, stripped bare, smeared, squandered, nothing but scar tissue and shameful old self-inflicted wounds, the love of the Father finds the son.

He finds us.

"God demonstrates His own love toward us, in that while we were still sinners, Christ died for us" (Rom. 5:8). Let that sink in. It ought to rattle your head. No mess is too big. No shame too deep. No sin too horrible. And don't worry about what you'll say. When you return and stand face-to-face, you can't tell Him anything He doesn't already know. Nothing separates you from His love.

"So Charles," you ask with a finger in the air, "Are you telling me there is no place I can go that's too far gone?" That's exactly what I'm telling you. No gone is too far gone.

Lord Jesus, I'm a prodigal. I'm guilty of all of the above. I've lived for me. And me alone. I've done everything You told me not to do and as a result, I'm a wreck. Surrounded by the slop of my own mess. If I started right now and had ten lifetimes, I couldn't clean up this mess. I'm sorry. That doesn't seem to even begin or get at it, but Lord, I'm sorry. I repent. I repent for every wrong word, wrong deed, wrong thought. I admit I caused this mess. I am to blame.

But Lord, You tell me that I can always come home. That there's no place where Your blood can't snatch me back. So Lord, I need Your blood to reach down, snatch me out, and cleanse me. Wash me white as snow because I'm anything but. Father, for all those people that I hurt or betrayed or rejected or lied to or stole from or hurt physically or emotionally, I'm so sorry. Please bless them. Return to them everything I wrongly stole from them. Return the pieces of them that I selfishly kept. Make them whole again.

And Lord, while You're at it, make me whole. I don't want to be a slave anymore. I want to come home. To be Your child. To dwell in Your shelter and rest in Your shadow. To be wrapped in Your wings—the Sun of Righteousness with healing in Your wings. Heal me. Take this broken thing I call "me," and don't just sew me back together, but make me new, for You tell us that You and You alone make all things new. So, make me new.

And Father, while I can't erase my past, would You please enter my memory and heal the pain those memories bring. Let me know Your love, Your forgiveness, Your grace despite my complete and total depravity. Father, in Your name and by Your blood, in the undefeated and magnificent name of Jesus, I rebuke, bind, and cast down the enemy who would seek to use my past or those memories to keep me from turning out of this pen of pigs and slop and running for home. Jesus, because You told me that I can and have every right to, I place Your cross between me and any scheme of the enemy to bring me back here or remind me of who I used to be.

Lord, I have been crucified with You, and it's no longer I who live but You who live in and through me. And the life I now live, I live by faith in You who gave Yourself for me. Lord, while I was still a sinner, I mean right here, You gave Yourself for me. I can't even begin to wrap my head around it, but I'm taking Your Word for what it says because I'm at my end.

Lastly, I know that Your Father made You who knew no sin to be sin for me that I might become the righteousness of God in you. I know I don't deserve that, but You, in Your mercy, gave me what I didn't deserve and withheld from me what I did. Lord, I'm Yours. This day. The next. Every day. Take all of me. Father, I'm turning now. Walking away from all this. Leaving this bucket right here. I'm not looking back. Would You please let me ask one thing? When I crest this hill, and I see my home in the distance, please let me see You standing on the porch. Please give me a vision of You.

In Jesus' Name, amen.

I wrote this prayer in tears, knowing some of you were in that place and needed walking out. My heart is both pierced and full. I don't know who it is, may never know, but somebody, somewhere, just left a really bad place. Let me be the first to tell you, you're free. No longer a slave. For the rest of you, having prayed this prayer is awesome, but if you really are a prodigal, you need to turn. So, don't wait. Turn. Run back. Don't stop. Don't look back. Don't let your past whisper in your ear. Haul butt. Kick up the dust.

For, even now, right this second, the Father is launching Himself off the porch.

Here He is now. His breath on your face. Covering your face in kisses. He is screaming with joy at the top of His lungs.

CHAPTER 11

The Deepest Wound of
the Human Soul

t's the ninth hour. Jesus hangs from the nails. He's struggling to breathe.
Drowning in His own lung fluid. Too tired to pull or push Himself
back up. The holes in His hands and feet are stretched. His shoulders, and
probably several of His ribs are "out of joint."[1] Dislocated. He has been
punched in the face, His beard has been plucked out, He's been beaten by
rods, and three-inch acacia thorns have been shoved into His skull. The
skin, muscle, and sinews of Jesus' back, sides, and face have been ripped
off by a Roman scourge. Blood drips off His toes. When Isaiah says His
"visage was marred more than any man,"[2] or He was unrecognizable as a
man, this is that moment. He's also naked. Completely.

As an aside, you might be thinking, *I thought we were beyond the cross.*
As in, we've already talked about that, been there and done that, and
you're asking, "Why do we have to go back there? Haven't we already
talked about that a lot? It hurt a lot the first time." Yes, but I get in trouble
when I travel beyond the shadow, and protection, of the cross. Moses said,
"He who dwells in the secret place of the Most High shall abide under the
shadow of the Almighty" (Ps. 91:1). Paul said, "For I determined not to
know anything among you except Jesus Christ and Him crucified" (1 Cor.
2:2). And, "But God forbid that I should boast except in the cross of our

Lord Jesus Christ, by whom the world has been crucified to me, and I to the world" (Gal. 6:14).

Earlier in that same letter, Paul reamed out the church in Galatia for losing their vision of the cross: "Foolish Galatians, who has bewitched you, before whose eyes Jesus Christ was publicly portrayed as crucified?" (Gal. 3:1, NASB). They had begun looking for wisdom elsewhere and took their eyes off Christ. As a result, the church went far astray. It is the desire of our enemy to take our eyes off the cross.

Truth is, I know me, and I need the constant reminder. Hence, we return to the cross.

Here hangs the righteous, sinless, spotless, obedient Son of the Most High God. The one who knew no sin, who became sin for us.[3] Who "has borne our griefs and carried our sorrows."[4] Despised, smitten, stricken, afflicted, pierced, crushed, scourged, oppressed, cut off from the land of the living, assigned a grave with wicked men, crushed by His very own Father, sent here for this very purpose. Intentionally put to grief. Knowing anguish. Pouring out His soul to death. Bearing the ages on His shoulders.

Until now, He hasn't opened His mouth. Silent as a lamb led to slaughter. But somewhere in here, Jesus cries out. Screams at the top of His lungs. Just a couple of words, but if you listen carefully, the words betray the emotion. The wound. Jesus the man is talking. "My God! My God!" Another lift. A shallow inhale. A frantic look. Until now, perfect, He and the Father had known unhindered communion. The two had been one. But now they are not. He screams. "Why have You forsaken Me?"[5]

Think about it. Jesus, had never done a single thing wrong. Ever. He was totally obedient. In all things. And for some reason, this same Jesus has just been rejected by the Father. For the first time in His life, He is alone.

Don't miss that.

Let me give you a battlefield analogy. You're in the military. Part of a unit. That unit is shot up, captured, and your men are being tortured. The enemy sends you videos of your people screaming. You mount a rescue operation. Drop in through cover of night. Storm the prison. There's a fight. You're wounded multiple times. It's bad. You've placed high ordinance explosives on every prison door. Blow them off the hinges. Sprung from their cages, you carry each prisoner to the evac zone. Not one man is left behind. You lay down cover fire while the helicopter loads the wounded. When they lift to safety, you get on the radio to contact your ride out. Mission accomplished. The pilot's voice cracks through the static, "ETA fifteen seconds." You can hear the chopper blades whipping through the air. The pilot sees you, he hovers fifteen feet above the grass where you lie bleeding. The enemy is closing. You can hear their shouts. See the moonlight glisten off their bayonets. You won't last another five minutes. The pilot gives you the thumbs up and yells, "Good job!" Then he pulls back on the stick and disappears into the clouds while the enemy slips out of the grass.

In the ninth hour, that is exactly what is happening to Jesus.

We know that in this moment, when He was most obedient, when He laid down His life, when He was staring death in the face, Isaiah tells us God the Father has "forsaken you. . . . With a little wrath, I hid My face from you" (Is 54:7–8). In the ninth hour, all the weight of the world's sin, the billions of us on this planet, all our black-hearted stuff, has been dumped on the carpenter's shoulders. And for some reason God looked away. And when He did, Jesus cried out, "Dad, why have you forsaken/ rejected Me?!"

I don't know the entirety of the reason, but I don't think the reason had to do with what He was seeing. With so much sin. I think God can handle the sight of our sin. He's been looking at it a long time. I think the reason is deeper. I think there's more at work. Much more.

The point is this—Jesus *knew* rejection. Deeper and more painful than any of us have ever known or experienced. And we need to lose the argument that Jesus' divinity somehow prevented or saved Him from experiencing (or that it somehow made it easier) the wound to His Spirit that occurred with complete and total rejection by both man and God. Because the fact that Jesus knew rejection both at a depth and to a degree never before or since known by man is what allows Him—and

Him alone—to minister to and heal every one of us who have ever known rejection at any level. The cross of Jesus Christ is *the* place where we give Him all the bad that has come upon us, and He exchanges it for all the good that was due Him.

Look at that moment through the eyes of Jesus: "Jesus cried out with a loud voice, saying, '*Eli Eli, lama sabachthani*,' that is, 'My God, My God, why have You forsaken Me?'" (Matt. 27:46). One word tells us all we need to know. "Forsaken." When Jesus needed His Father most, the Majesty on High was nowhere to be found. Jesus' one phrase is a verbatim quote of the beginning of Psalm 22. In the Hebrew culture, an oral culture, when someone quoted the first line of a poem or song, they were expecting the listener to fill in the rest. In that culture, saying the first line and repeating the whole thing were essentially the same thing.

Everyone standing around Him knew what He was saying: "Dad, I'm crying out but You don't answer. I'm a worm. Not even a man. I'm a reproach. Despised. People are sneering at Me. Bulls have surrounded Me. Their mouths are open like a ravenous and roaring lion. I don't have much left. I'm poured out like water. All My sockets are dislocated. My heart is melting. My strength is gone. My mouth is dry. My tongue sticks to the roof of My mouth. Dogs circle Me. They've pierced Me. They're gambling for My clothes. I won't last another five minutes!"

This is the Son of Man crying out to the Father.

Look at Psalm 69, another messianic psalm:

> Reproach has broken my heart,
> And I am full of heaviness;
> I looked for someone to take pity, but there was none;
> And for comforters, but I found none.
> They also gave me gall for my food,
> And for my thirst they gave me vinegar to drink. (Ps. 69:20–21)

Until this moment, Jesus and God the Father had known unhindered union. Perfect intimacy. The sinless Son had done everything asked of

Him. As these words leave His mouth, the Lamb of God is currently carrying away the sins of the world. He is our propitiation. Pouring out His soul. Here, in this very moment, Jesus has become sin (2 Cor. 5:21). If ever there was a moment in human history when a father was proud of a son, it was here in this moment. And yet, here in this moment, the Father is silent. Offering no response.

Here, for the first time, Jesus knows something He's never known. And it is this "knowing" that kills Jesus. Yes, the crucifixion would have eventually done the job, but Roman crucifixions were routinely known to last twelve hours or more. It's why the soldiers broke the legs of the other two criminals hanging alongside Jesus.

Jesus, Savior of the world, died with a broken heart. A shattered soul. And the autopsy shows that the King died of the deepest, most painful wound of the human soul.

Rejection.

Total and complete. Jesus was rejected by His friends, brothers, enemies, and lastly and most importantly, by the Father.

All of us have known this sickening emotion. Further, we know without ever being taught that the absolute worst thing you can do is leave someone behind. Especially someone who is worth rescuing. This begs the question, "Why did God do this?" Put a bookmark here. I'll come back to it.

A Different Kind of Wound

As I look at my life and ministry as a writer, teacher, athlete, friend, and so on, rejection is my greatest hurdle. Most of the time rejection is done to us. Meaning, we're innocent. Which makes it a different kind of wound. A slice in your soul. Death by a thousand cuts. I've also learned I'm not alone in this.

When we are rejected, we find ourselves alone, powerless, no control, no authority, no strength, no value, no power, no voice. No nothing.

Rejection is a wound and attaches to our DNA. It festers. Fills with pus. Scabs over. Scar tissue. It becomes like the soft side of Velcro. And because we have an enemy that prowls around like a roaring lion wanting to rip our heads off and post them on stakes outside the city wall, he walks by, spots our leaking wounds, and says, "I think I'll throw a dart right there." Then he dips the dart in gasoline, sets it on fire, and launches it at our chests.

For many, the wound of rejection is our jugular. It's like hobbling a warhorse. You don't have to kill it to make it ineffective. Just tie up one leg, and it's useless.

But why is this? And how is satan such an expert? Let me explain.

The being we know as satan or lucifer is described with some detail in Daniel, Isaiah, Ezekiel, and Revelation. Isaiah wrote:

> Your pomp is brought down to Sheol . . .
> And worms cover you.
> How you are fallen from heaven, O lucifer . . .
> Cut down to the ground. . . .
> For you have said in your heart:
> 'I will ascend into heaven,
> I will exalt my throne above the stars of God;
> I will also sit on the mount of the congregation. . . .
> I will ascend above the heights of the clouds,
> I will be like the Most High.' (14:11–14)

Then in verse 19 it says, "But you are cast out of your grave like an abominable branch." Notice the words "cast out."

Daniel 8:11 says he, lucifer, "exalted himself as high as the Prince of the host; and by him the daily sacrifices were taken away, and the place of His sanctuary was cast down."

This is a stark demotion for the being who in Ezekiel 28:12–13 is described as "full of wisdom and perfect in beauty." He had been "in Eden, the garden of God." He was covered with "every precious stone . . .

sardius, topaz, and diamond, beryl, onyx, and jasper, sapphire, turquoise, and emerald with gold." And here we learn something peculiar about lucifer. "The workmanship of your timbrels and pipes was prepared for you on the day you were created" (v. 13). Let me dissect this.

First, lucifer was created. Remember that. It'll change the way you wage war. Second, notice the timbrels and pipes. Another translation says "tambourines and flutes." Both make melodious sounds. Why did God Most High give lucifer noise-making capabilities unless He wanted him to make a joyful noise? Like you and me, lucifer was created to worship. To make worship. But why, where, and to whom? I think we find out in the next sentence: "You were the anointed cherub that covers" (28:14).

"Anointed" means set apart for a purpose. If we look at the ark of the covenant, the "covering cherubs" physically covered the mercy seat. "And over it the cherubims of glory shadowing the mercyseat" (Heb. 9:5, KJV). The Greek word for "mercy seat" is *hilasterion*. It refers to the lid of the ark. The place of atonement. And it is the place where, once a year, the high priest sprinkled the blood of the spotless lamb to make atonement for the people. Paul tells the Romans, "God hath set forth [Jesus] to be a propitiation through faith in his blood" (Rom. 3:25, KJV). John tells us, "Herein is love, not that we loved God, but that He loved us, and sent his Son to be the propitiation for our sins" (1 John 4:10, KJV).

The connection I'm trying to make is this: Jesus both makes propitiation for us and He is our propitiation. He is the only High Priest to ever do so. In this role, He is constantly covered by an anointed cherub. Ezekiel goes on to say lucifer was "on the holy mountain of God . . . walked back and forth in the midst of fiery stones . . . perfect in your ways . . . till iniquity [or rebellion] was found in you" (Ezek. 28:14–15).

I know people who think otherwise, but I believe lucifer was one of three archangels in heaven, and that his sole purpose was to tend to Jesus. God the Father has an archangel, the Holy Spirit has an archangel, and Jesus has one. Remember where it said in Isaiah 14:12, "How you are fallen from heaven, O lucifer [Day Star], son of the morning [Dawn]"? We know from Revelation 22:16 that Jesus is the "Bright Morning Star." I think it was lucifer's job to daily announce the Son. And I believe that given his particular set of gifts, he was in charge of worship in heaven and responsible to bring it about. That's why he was given the pipes. But somewhere in here iniquity, or rebellion, was found in him.

I think that after seeing all the adoration laid down at Jesus' feet for so long, lucifer grew jealous. That's why in Isaiah he tried to reach up and grab or exalt himself five times. Contrast that with Jesus, who, "although He existed in the form of God, did not regard equality with God a thing to be grasped, but emptied Himself, taking the form of a bond-servant, and being made in the likeness of men. Being found in the appearance as a man, He humbled Himself by becoming obedient to the point of death, even death on a cross" (Phil. 2:6–8, NASB).

Five times, lucifer tried to reach up and grasp something that wasn't his. Resulting in his fall. On the other side, Jesus stooped down, and God raised Him up.

So, this perfect, wise, created being who walked among the fire in the throne room—who could sing like a lark, bring the stars out of hiding to reflect the Son's glory, who reflected light like a disco ball on steroids—got a big head and started whispering among the other angels. "You could do better. Really. You're underappreciated." Since lucifer is described as a talebearer, it would make sense in all his commerce or trade that he would spread lies (Ezek. 28:16).

God the Father caught wind, lucifer's rebellion was exposed, and he was "cast out . . . an abominable branch" (Isa. 14:19). Which is an interesting juxtaposition when you consider that Jesus is referred to as the branch of David (Isa. 11:1).

So, lucifer was cast out. Flung headlong from heaven. Remember what Jesus told His apostles? "I saw satan fall like lightning" (Luke 10:18). Jesus was there. In the throne room. A member in the transaction. Once I understood this, it changed the way I viewed Jesus' testing in the wilderness—He and satan knew each other really well. In John, Jesus said, "The ruler of this world will be cast out. And I, if I am lifted up from the earth, will draw all peoples to Myself" (John 12:31–32).

Notice that nearly every time Scripture talks about satan in this context, it describes him as cast out. "Cast out" means rejected or made or considered a horror. To cast out means to eject, drive out, expel, pluck out, to throw with violence. It's also related to dung or manure. Meaning to fling, or deliberately hurl. Revelation 12:4 (KJV) says God "*cast* them [those who joined lucifer] to the earth." The text continues: "the great dragon was *cast out*" (12:9), "the accuser of our brethren is *cast down*" (12:10), "And when the dragon saw that he was *cast* unto the earth, he persecuted the woman" (12:13, emphasis mine).

The point I'm trying to make is this: being cast out is now part of satan's very nature. It's in his DNA. he didn't get what he wanted, and what he had was taken away. He's not happy about that.

So, he's been flung to earth. Now what does he do? Makes war with the children of Eve (Rev. 12:13, 17). Okay, I get it, but what's he looking for? I think he shows his cards in Matthew 4:9 when he told Jesus, "All these things I will give You if You will fall down and worship me." It was a lie. he couldn't give Jesus anything. Ultimately, it was not his to give. But look at that one word: "worship." There's the nugget. That's what he wants. Adoration. Praise. To be looked at the way all of us look at Jesus.

Note this: you live in a world where both Jesus and satan are looking for worshipers.

These are the only two options. As the story plays out in Revelation 13:4, we see him get some of what he wants. "So they worshiped the dragon." Yes, satan wants your worship. His primary weapon to accomplish this is to cause you to think that he knows how you feel and convince you that you've been rejected or cast out just like he was. It's a lie, but since the garden he's been more cunning than any beast which the Lord God made. The words he uses are part of the same "Has God indeed said . . ." lie he told Eve in Genesis 3:1.

Speaking of the word *cast*, rarely in Scripture does it carry a positive connotation. You can be cast into prison, cast into hell, cast out of the temple, cast into the sea, cast into outer darkness where there is weeping and gnashing of teeth, cast into a lake of fire where they are tormented day and night, or others can even cast lots for your clothes. The only really positive use is in Revelation 4:10 when the elders around the throne of God cast their crowns at His feet.*

After satan was cast down, God crafted His most perfect and intimate creation. Molded him from the dust, and pressed His lips and nostrils, took a deep breath, and emptying His lungs, He breathed into our lungs the very *ruach* or breath of God—making you and me living souls.

As if that weren't enough, in Matthew 10:1, Jesus gives us the power to cast out satan and anyone working with him. "He gave them power over unclean spirits, to cast them out, and to heal all kinds of sickness and all kinds of disease."† So, the same power that booted satan out of heaven has been placed in our mouths. You think satan likes us for that? Not only that, but when we exercise that authority, when we cast out, it's a reminder to satan that the kingdom of God has come. Matthew 12:28 (NASB) says: "If I cast out demons by the Spirit of God, then the kingdom of God has come upon you."

What's this got to do with you and me? You and I walk through an imperfect world leading imperfect and singular lives, and, whether due to no fault of our own or our own stuff, we are rejected and suffer the pain of rejection. When this happens, the slice in our souls that occurs is a very real wound. Don't discount this. Your very soul has been sliced.

That slice festers, fills with pus, scabs over, and scars. The enemy sees it because he knows what to look for, and he says, "Oh, there's a wound of rejection. I'll target that. I'll use it to turn his or her heart cold. To convince him or her that so and so doesn't and never did love them. That he or she is alone." If we are not careful and we don't capture every thought and bring it to the captivity of Jesus (2 Cor. 10:5), either consciously or unconsciously, then we may find ourselves agreeing with those lies.

Targeting and opening that wound is not the enemy's only focus. He likes to crawl inside and live there. Like a spiritual squatter. It's the

---

* Please, Lord, include me in that number.

† There are scholars who believe that power died with the apostles and did not pass to you and me. I am not in that camp.

place from which he likes to spew his lies. Lies such as, "You deserve better"; "God doesn't have your best interest at heart"; "Those people don't really . . ."; "She doesn't really love you"; "See! I told you. You can't trust Him."

If satan can get you to believe what he believes, you—by your actions—will spiral down and rescind your worship of Jesus. To satan, we represent the same authority that cast him down. If satan can get you mired in the pit of rejection, then you'll have a really tough time accepting the love of the Father. This opens us up like Velcro to a spirit of rejection.

Here's what I mean. Ephesians 6 tells us our struggles are not against flesh and blood, but against the rulers and principalities of this dark world. And though we walk in the flesh, we don't war there (2 Cor. 10:3–5). Our job is to destroy the speculations and every high thing that exalts itself against the knowledge of God. That means, those things we can't see like to grab ahold of our wounds and then build strongholds in our minds. The spirit of rejection becomes one of the lenses through which we see life. It's like water to a fish. Most of us have no idea we are seeing through it because it's our lens.

If you have trouble expressing love, trusting others, or opening up, chances are good that somewhere you might have a wound of rejection standing in the way. Blocking the floodwaters. If we're being honest, we all do.

When we live out of that wound, allowing it to dictate and/or influence our emotional responses to situations and relationships—especially close ones—we can spiral into stuff like self-pity, bitterness, and a sullen brooding. We can also become arrogant. Saying stuff like: "I deserve better"; "I'll take what's mine because it was withheld from me in the first place"; "I was passed over, so I'm justified." In my experience, arrogance is a self-protection thing.

Bear with me. It gets worse. When this is who we become, when we live out of this place, out of this spirit of rejection, we gravitate toward some other power, something that makes us feel powerful. For guys, it can look like a porn addiction. Sexual immorality. Infidelity. Other outlets look like some form of medication. Alcohol. Drugs. Prescription or otherwise. Then there are the medications we approve in society, such as performance and food. For some of us, we feel as though we've been robbed of authority so we assume or exercise illegitimate authority. Meaning, we assume leadership not bestowed. Not earned. Not given to us by a higher authority. Doing so is a protection mechanism. And if we can exercise some form of power, we can mitigate our own rejection. We can also become attracted to people with power, or people who are lifted up on a pedestal. A spotlight. I can't explain this, but there is something in us that just likes being near powerful people because it makes us feel powerful.

Lastly, and this is my default, we become indifferent. We say to ourselves, "If I don't let you in, you can't hurt me." It's a lie. It's also *not* the heart of Jesus.

The Remedy

A few pages ago, I asked you to put a bookmark at the question: "Why did God do this?" Meaning, why did He reject Jesus?

Let's go back to the cross. "About the ninth hour" (Matt. 27:46). Here, for the first time in His life, Jesus knew rejection. He knew the soul-deep pain of being forsaken. And God the Father does this on purpose. Why? Because, the last thing Jesus did on the cross was to take every wound of rejection from all of humanity, and after He had done so, He uttered this: "It is finished" (John 19:30). Then He gave up His spirit.

But notice, it was only finished after Jesus had been rejected.

After He gave up His spirit, He climbed down off the cross, walked into hell, dumped every single wound at the feet of satan, and said, "These are My children. I've accepted them all. Not a single one is rejected. You're defeated. Again. I'll take those keys. I'm going back home to throw a party. Put a robe on each of their shoulders, give each a ring, and add a room onto My house. My children are coming home to live with Me."

God the Father rejected and forsook His Son, and when He did this, when He intentionally wounded His Son, Jesus was then—and only then—able to take your wound of rejection from you. He did this for you and me so that He could stand with us in the deepest, darkest, most hurt places of our souls.

If you're one of those people who can't understand what the shed blood of a Man two thousand years ago has to do with you here, today, let me say this: "Christ died for the ungodly. . . . While we were still sinners, Christ died for us" (Rom. 5:6,8). You and I have been sanctified through the offering of the body of Jesus Christ once and for all (Heb. 9:28; 10:10). And if you think two millennia makes a difference, it doesn't. "Jesus Christ is the same yesterday, today, and forever" (Heb. 13:8).

The wound of rejection is something done to us. And unlike lucifer, we usually experience it after we've done something right. Which makes it all the more poignantly painful. Don't believe me? Rewind the tape. Twenty-four hours prior to the crucifixion. The Last Supper. Jesus stood and disrobed to His underwear. Bore a basin of water. Scooted along the ground washing each of His disciples' feet. He untied the sandals. Washed off the dirt, mud, and manure. Tenderly holding each foot—these feet which He fashioned from the dust of the earth. Each was muscled. Strong. Calloused. Showing three years of miles traveled. Together. They belonged to those He loves. His most trusted friends and brothers. He dried each, soaped another, rinsed and rubbed with fragrant oil. Halfway through He looked up and stared—into the eyes of Judas.

Could you wash the feet of your betrayer?

Turn this inward. Toward yourself. Close your eyes. Where have you been rejected? If you know what I'm talking about, it shouldn't take long for the images to flash before your eyes. All those pus-filled places.

If you are a follower of Jesus, I can promise you this has happened or it will happen. Jesus said so: "You will be hated by all for My name's sake" (Mark 13:13). That word *hate* means to "reject, detest." It implies the moral decision made by someone else to value themselves above you. If you thought that they think they're better than you, you're right. They did. It's why they rejected you. John adds this in his Gospel: "If they persecuted Me, they will also persecute you" (John 15:20). How about this one? "Therefore Jesus also, that He might sanctify the people with His own blood, suffered outside the gate. Therefore let us go forth to Him, outside the camp, bearing His reproach" (Heb. 13:12–13).

When was the last time you suffered outside the gate and willfully bore Jesus' reproach?

Okay, so great, Charles, you've just picked the scab off the most crappy place in my life. So, what now?

What is the remedy?

The cross. On the cross, Jesus took all the bad and gave us all the good. It's the point of the cross. This means, at His invitation, we take Jesus our wound, our rejection, our pus-filled, maggot-encrusted scabs, and hand them to Him on the cross. We walk up and let Him pull them out by the handle. In exchange, He wraps us in a robe of His acceptance. This is part of the mystery and beauty of the cross. We give Him our wounds. He gives us His acceptance. He adopts us as His children. He heals us from the inside out.

This is the magnificent exchange.

Don't believe me? "But as many as received Him, to [us] He gave the right to become children of God, to those [of us] who believe in His name: who were born, not of blood, nor of the will of the flesh, nor of the will of man, but of God" (John 1:12–13).

When I pray for folks wrestling with this wound, I will speak the words of Paul over them: "He has delivered us from the power of darkness and conveyed [transferred] us into the kingdom of the Son of His love" (Col. 1:13).

The difficult aspect of this healing, this remedy, is that it's conditional. Actually, there are two conditions. Maybe this strikes you the wrong way. You raise a finger. A fist even. "But, Charles, what about unmerited grace? I don't think I can handle any more conditions. I thought I didn't have to work for this Jesus stuff." This is grace. Poured out for you.

The first condition is this: Expose your wound to the light and offer it to Him. Stand in front of the cross, bare your chest, point out the wound, and say, "Jesus, this is killing me. I can't carry it anymore. Please take it. Will You take it?" And because of what He did two thousand years ago, He alone is qualified to lift it out and heal.

But here's the second condition, and this is where the rubber really meets the road. Just like Jesus said, we are commanded to forgive those who've wounded us. Rejected us. Not only to forgive, but to bless and not curse. "Father, forgive them" (Luke 23:34). This is where we carry the cross. I've already spent an entire chapter talking about forgiveness, so I won't rehash it here, but let me summarize because I, too, tend to forget: forgiveness is *not* an emotion. Or a feeling. Forgiveness is a willful decision of our gut. If you want healing here—if you want to be rid of this festering wound of rejection—these two are required. Five times in the New Testament we are told that if we do not forgive, our heavenly Father will not forgive us. Let that sink in.

If you want healing and forgiveness, you have to offer it. Unconditionally.

Some of you are looking at your wound, and you're shaking your head. "Too deep." "Been here too long." "You don't understand." "Ask me anything but that."

Let me point you to the Son of Man who hung on the tree. Right now, this second, Jesus is asking if you will let Him have it.

This is the beauty and mystery of the cross: it works both *for* us and *in* us. The cross is both the guarantee of our salvation and the instrument by which the Lord heals and delivers us here while on this earth. It's the sword with which He cuts our present-day chains.

In Revelation 12:11, we are told that we, you and I, overcome him, satan, through the blood of the Lamb and the word of our testimony. To overcome rejection, we must walk into the Holy of Holies, the presence of God, with the blood in one hand and a right confession on our tongues. As I understand it, that word *testimony* means "a right confession." Literally, it means "to say the same thing as." That means we have adopted the right testimony when we say the same thing that Jesus has already said of us. When we agree with Him. This means the remedy is not rocket science.

It's actually quite simple and can be understood and practiced by simple folk like me. The practice of overcoming is speaking what is true from His Word in an attitude of reverence and worship. And in so doing, allowing the Holy Spirit to supernaturally heal the wounds that have festered in darkness for so long.

The last thing satan wants you to do is remind him what Jesus has said about you and me. It makes his ears burn and he can't stand it. he has to flee.

Note: this is not the new age practice of speaking positive thoughts. The power of this transaction has nothing to do with you and me. The only credit we get in this deal is whether or not we are obedient to speak it. The power comes and the exchange occurs when we agree in faith with what the God of the universe has spoken and declared to be true about you and me.

This is what I mean:

Father—Lord Almighty,

You are faithful. You are trustworthy. I can and do trust You. Your plans toward me are good. All things—all things—work together for my good, and that includes those times in this life when I have been rejected. Knowing that, I forgive those who have rejected me. My mother, father, siblings, friends, coaches, bosses, anyone in authority who has ever rejected me, I forgive. Having forgiven them, as Your Word directs, I pray for them and I bless them by name in the name of Jesus.

Having blessed them, I bring to You, Jesus, all the wounded places in me. Every one. I hold them up before You and give You permission to heal. I ask You to heal me. I ask You to take from me every influence of every spirit of rejection. Here and now, in the magnificent, matchless, and undefeated name of Jesus, I rebuke and cast down the spirit of rejection in my own life. Today and forever. You are a liar. And a deceiver. And I call you out by name. Spirit of rejection, come out. You are cast down. You are ejected. You are expelled.

Father, I thank and praise You for my salvation. My deliverance. My healing. My sanctification. I trust You with my soul. With the deepest places in me. With my heart. With every place that I know emotion. And I give You those places. I entrust them and me to You. Holy Spirit, finger of God, I invite you into those places vacated by the spirit of rejection and ask that You heal every wound. Starting right now. I ask You to surround those places in me, baptize those places in me, let rivers of living water flow up and out of those places that have sat stagnant so long. Father, I cast my crown down at Your feet. I worship You and You alone.

Father, I surrender and yield entirely, completely, and only to You and ask that You stand guard at the entrance to my soul, that You command Your angels concerning me, to prevent any spirit of rejection, after it has roamed dry and arid places, from returning and seeking to reinhabit the places in me that it has just been cast out of. I ask, Father, that there be no vacancy in me. That when that spirit returns he finds my house swept clean and inhabited by You and You alone. I overcome him, satan, by Your blood and my agreement with Your testimony.

So, I agree:

- *That while I am persecuted, I am not forsaken (2 Cor. 4:8–9).*
- *That You will never leave me nor forsake me (Heb. 13:5).*
- *That You are the One who goes with me perpetually, that You are and will be with me forever, and that You will never leave me nor forsake me (Deut. 31:6, 8).*
- *That as You were with Moses, so You will be with me. That You, Lord God, are with me wherever I go, and that You will never leave me nor forsake me (Josh. 1:5, 9).*
- *That You stood with me and strengthened me, that You will deliver me from every evil work and preserve me for Your kingdom (2 Tim. 4:17–18).*
- *That You will not leave my soul in hell, nor will You allow Your Holy One to see corruption (Ps. 16:10).*
- *That You will and have redeemed my soul from the power of the grave (Ps. 49:15).*

- *That I have never seen the righteous forsaken (Ps. 37:25).*
- *That You have inscribed me on the palms of Your hands and that You contended with him who contends with me (Isa. 49:16, 25).*
- *That, like Jesus, for a mere moment You have forsaken us, but with great mercies You will gather us, and with a little wrath You hid Your face from us for a moment, but with everlasting kindness You will have mercy on us (Isa. 54:7–8).*
- *That I shall be called by a new name which You, Lord, by Your mouth will name, and that I shall be a crown of glory in Your hand. That I am not forsaken, that my land is not desolate, because My Lord delights in me, My God rejoices over me (Isa. 62:2–5).*
- *That Your thoughts toward me are of peace and not evil, that You will give me a future and a hope, that when I call upon You and pray to You, that You—the God of the universe—listen to me, and that when I seek You, I find You (Jer. 29:11–14).*
- *That You have blessed me with every spiritual blessing in the heavenly places in Christ, that You chose me before the foundation of the world, that I would be holy and without blame before You in love, that You predestined me to adoption as your son in Christ Jesus to Himself, and that You have made me accepted in the Beloved. That in You, I have obtained an inheritance, and that I have been sealed with the Holy Spirit who is the guarantor of my inheritance (Eph. 1:3–6, 11, 13–14).*
- *That You have given me a spirit of wisdom and revelation in You and that the eyes of my understanding have been enlightened, so that I may know that I am called and that I may know what is the hope of that calling, and what is the exceeding greatness of Your power toward me who believes (Eph. 1:17–19).*
- *That I who was once far off have been brought near by the blood of Jesus Christ (Eph. 2:13).*
- *That You, my Father, have bestowed love upon me, and that You call me Your child (1 John 3:1).*

- *That You, the Son of God, were manifested so that You might destroy the works of the devil. That every spirit that confesses that Jesus Christ has come into the world is of God Your Father, and that I, Your child, through my confession in agreement with You, have overcome that spirit of the Antichrist, that greater are You who is in me than he that it in the world (1 John 3:8; 4:2–4).*
- *That You, Jesus, are the Son of God, that God abides in You, and that You abide in God, and that I get to dwell in Your shelter and rest in Your shadow (1 John 4:15; Ps 91:1).*
- *That there is no fear in love because Your perfect love has cast any and all fear out of me. I have been made perfect in love (1 John 4:18).*
- *That I am of God, that I know You, that I hear You, and that by this I know the spirit of truth and the spirit of error (1 John 4:6).*
- *That I have been crucified with You, Jesus, that it is no longer I who live but You who live in and through me, and that I know Your Father accepted You and so He accepts me (Gal. 2:20).*
- *That I have not received a spirit of bondage again to fear, but I have received the Spirit of adoption; that I am Your child, a joint heir; that I know every single thing that happens to me is for Your good; that You are for me and therefore none can stand against me; that You are at the right hand of God making intercession for me; and that nothing, not one single thing, can ever separate me from You. That I am more than a conqueror through You who loves me. That nothing—not death nor life, angels nor demons, things present nor things to come, height nor depth, nor any other created thing, can separate me from Your love (Rom. 8:15–16, 28, 31, 34, 37–39).*
- *That You made Him who knew no sin to become sin for us that we might become the righteousness of God (2 Cor. 5:21).*

And these last few are my favorites:

- *That by one offering You have perfected for all time those of us who are being sanctified (Heb. 10:14).*
- *And because of all this, I will rejoice greatly in the Lord, my soul will exult in my God, for He has clothed me with garments of salvation, He has wrapped me with a robe of righteousness. (Isa. 61:10).*
- *But as many as received Him, to us He gave the right to become children of God, to those of us who believe in His name: who were born, not of blood, nor of the will of the flesh, nor of the will of man, but of God (John 1:12–13).*
- *You will not leave us orphans; You will come to us (John 14:18).*
- *That You have delivered me from the power of darkness and transferred (conveyed) me into the kingdom of the Son of Your love (Col. 1:13).*

Father I thank You that because You cried out, "My God, My God, why have You forsaken Me?" we can proclaim, "He has done this," and "It is finished" (Ps. 22:1; John 19:30).

In Jesus' Name, amen.

Let me encourage you not to speed past this. Don't just turn the page. Linger here. What are the words He is speaking to you that tell your heart, in the words your heart needs to hear, that you are His child? That He loves you more than you can know. Some of you need to read Song of Solomon. Others need to read Ruth. Somebody needs to read the story of Joseph. Somebody else needs to read John 21:15, where Jesus restored Peter on the beach. Psalm 63. Psalm 107.

His Word is a love story. The greatest ever told. What are the words His heart is speaking to yours?

CHAPTER 12

The Peg on Which
Everything Hangs

The sun is down. Darkness blankets Jerusalem. They are reclining at supper. Celebrating the Feast of the Passover. Normally a joyous time. Prior to dinner, Jesus stands and takes off His outer garments. Doing the very thing He did when He left heaven.

> Christ Jesus, who, being in the form of God, did not consider it robbery to be equal with God, but made Himself of no reputation, taking the form of a bondservant, and coming in the likeness of men. And being found in appearance as a man, He humbled Himself and became obedient to the point of death, even the death of the cross.[1]

Jesus ties on the apron of a bondservant—representing a servant by choice and not conquering—and kneels before His friends. I can't read this without hearing the echo of Jesus' response to the mother of the sons of Zebedee: "Whoever desires to become great among you, let him be your servant. And whoever desires to be first among you, let him be your slave—just as the Son of Man did not come to be served, but to serve, and to give His life a ransom for many."[2] The only sound in the room is that of water spilling over dirty feet then returning to a basin. One by one, Jesus washes their feet.

This includes Judas.

Jesus scoots over to Peter's feet, and Peter recoils. "You're not washing me, Lord." Jesus continues to disciple His disciple, "For I have given you an example, that you should do as I have done to you. . . . A servant is not greater than his master."[3] These words will be important in a few minutes.

John, writing after the event, said it this way: "Now before the Feast of the Passover, when Jesus knew that His hour had come that He should depart from this world to the Father, having loved His own who were in the world, He loved them to the end."[4]

This right here, this Last Supper, this moment when their feet are drying—this is the beginning of the end.

He dries their feet, and they recline at the table, but Jesus' heart is heavy, and they pick up on it. Jesus scans His friends, "I do not speak of all of you. I know the ones I have chosen; but it is that the Scripture may be fulfilled, 'He who eats My bread has lifted up his heel against Me.'"[5] Jesus becomes troubled in His Spirit. His face shows it, and He speaks the source of His pain, "One of you will betray Me."[6] The disciples whisper among themselves. They are confused. Peter motions to John who is leaning against Jesus' shoulder. Peter asks quietly, "You're closest—who's He talking about?"

John shrugs. He turns to Jesus. "Lord, who is it?"[7]

Jesus replies, "It is he to whom I shall give a piece of bread when I have dipped it." He then dips the morsel and gives it to Judas Iscariot. The Bread of Life willingly giving His body to the one who would betray Him. Forgiveness before the sin. Then, gently and firmly, Jesus gives Judas permission, "What you do, do quickly."[8] At the time, only Judas understood. The rest would in a few hours.

Now, alone with the remaining faithful eleven, in the last few hours they have together, Jesus captures their attention and says, "A new commandment I give to you."[9]

The word "new" rattles around in their minds.

The Pharisees: A Pack of Hyenas

This whole idea of a new commandment started years prior during the Sermon on the Mount. Jesus is speaking:

> You have heard that it was said, "An eye for an eye and a tooth for a tooth." But I tell you not to resist an evil person. But whoever slaps you on your right cheek, turn the other to him also. If anyone wants to sue you and take away your tunic, let him have your cloak also. And whoever compels you to go one mile, go with him two. Give to him who asks you, and from him who wants to borrow from you do not turn away.[10]

This new instruction turns the judgment and wrath of the Old Testament law on its head. Those listening have no framework for this. Nor for what comes next.

Jesus continues: "You have heard that it was said, 'You shall love your neighbor and hate your enemy.' But I say to you, love your enemies, bless those who curse you, do good to those who hate you, and pray for those who spitefully use you and persecute you. . . . Be perfect, just as your Father in heaven is perfect."[11]

This command to love your enemies and bless those who curse you is met with raised eyebrows by the religious leaders because it's a measuring stick none of them measure up to. Ever since, they have been trying to trap Jesus. To trip Him up. He has raised the bar to an even more uncomfortable level than Moses did. Their distaste for Jesus and His teaching grows as the religious rulers continue to scheme and tag team in an effort to get rid of Him.

A year or two passes, and the Pharisees are sick of Jesus. And His words. They've had enough. They can't take any more. Jesus is a threat to their power, their way of life, and they want Him gone. So they whisper behind closed doors. Every question to Him is a baiting. Every interaction a test.

Jesus is not blind to this. In one exchange, speaking in a parable to anyone who would listen, He tells them how the kingdom of heaven is like a certain king who held a wedding feast for his son. He sent out servants to invite guests, but they were not willing to attend. In this very moment, Jesus is inviting guests. None accept.

The Pharisees miss the warning and continue their scheming. Hoping to increase their influence, they join forces with the Herodians, a Jewish sect loyal to Herod. These are the sell-outs. Their words are ripe with cynicism. With entangling. They said, "Teacher, we know that You are true, and teach the way of God in truth; nor do You care about anyone, for You do not regard the person of men."

Nothing could be further from the truth. Their words betray them and show just how far they are from the heart of Jesus.

They continue, "Tell us, therefore, what do You think? Is it lawful to pay taxes to Caesar, or not?"

Jesus shakes His head. "'Why do you test Me, you hypocrites? Show Me the tax money.' So they brought Him a denarius. And He said to them, 'Whose image and inscription is this?' They said to Him, 'Caesar's.' And He said to them, 'Render therefore to Caesar the things that are Caesar's, and to God the things that are God's.'"[12]

Standing just feet apart, the Salvation of the whole world is speaking directly to them, but their hearts are cold and they don't get it. Blind to the Son, they render nothing.

Later in the day, the Sadducees, who did not believe in a bodily resurrection, come and ask Him this convoluted question about a man who died and left his wife to his brother. That brother died, as did the next, all the way down the line to the seventh brother. The Sadducees want to know whose wife she is in heaven—even though they categorically deny an afterlife. This is useless theological wrangling. Head games rooted in deception.

Jesus is losing His patience. "You are mistaken, not knowing the Scriptures nor the power of God. For in the resurrection they neither marry nor are given in marriage, but are like angels of God in heaven." After answering their question, notice what Jesus does next. He addresses the heart of the matter. Their unbelief. "But concerning the resurrection of the dead, have you not read what was spoken to you by God, saying, 'I am the God of Abraham, the God of Isaac, and the God of Jacob'? God is not the God of the dead, but of the living." And when the multitudes heard this, they were astonished at His teaching."[13]

The back and forth continues. Rising to a fever pitch. Finally, the Pharisees, hearing that Jesus has silenced the Sadducees, crowd around Him. A pack of hyenas and the pack is growing hungry. One of the scribes, a raised chin and enlightened air, asks Him, "Which is the first command-ment of all?" Jesus answers him, "The first of all the commandments is: 'Hear, O Israel, the LORD our God, the LORD is one. And you shall love the LORD your God with all your heart, with all your soul, with all your mind, and with all your strength.' This is the first commandment."[14]

This was not new to them.

The Covenantal Name of God

Let's back up. Briefly.

Moses and the nation of Israel had just experienced the greatest deliv-erance in the history of mankind. Three million slaves walked out of Egypt carrying Egyptian gold only to bump into a sea, which miraculously split allowing them to walk across on dry ground, only to watch the sea come crashing down on the enemy army of chariots chasing them. A few days later, Moses climbed a mountain to hear from God. While he was gone, the nation of slaves—who were fearful he might not return—fashioned and worshiped a golden calf, which they made from Egyptian gold. This spiritual adultery was akin to marrying your spouse and then sleeping with someone not your spouse on your wedding day.

Moses descended the mountain in a rage, broke the tablets, burned the golden calf, ground it to powder, and made the people drink it. He reamed out Aaron, commanded the Levites to kill anyone continuing in calf worship, and then he fasted forty days and forty nights—no food or water—hoping God would not kill the entire nation (Deut. 9:18). After his fast, he eyed the mountain and told the people, "You have committed a great sin. So now I will go up to the LORD; perhaps I can make atonement for your sin" (Ex. 32:30).

Moses hewed two new stone tablets and climbed the mountain. When he reached the summit, he found God waiting. No lightning bolt to the chest. No angel of death. No slow beheading. Moses is dumbfounded that he and the people of Israel are still alive, but he's also curious. What occurs is possibly one of the most intimate conversations ever recorded between man and God during which Moses makes an amazing and daring request: "Please, show me Your glory" (Ex. 33:18).

Moses, the greatest leader the world will ever know, having seen the greatest deliverance the world has ever known, having witnessed the greatest display of signs and wonders ever, and having spoken "face to face, as a man speaks to his friend," with I AM for months (Ex. 33:11), has finally garnered the gumption to ask the one question that heretofore he's been afraid to ask: "Can I see Your face?"

God stashed Moses behind a rock, covered him with His hand, and passed by—allowing Moses a never-before-seen glimpse of His glory. Not too much. Just enough. And as He was passing by He spoke His name, the name by which the nation of Israel and we are to forever know Him:

> And the LORD passed before him and proclaimed, "The LORD, the LORD God, merciful and gracious, longsuffering, and abounding in goodness and truth, keeping mercy for thousands, forgiving iniquity and transgression and sin, by no means clearing the guilty, visiting the iniquity of the fathers upon the children and the children's children to the third and the fourth generation." (Ex. 34:6–7)

All words matter, but some words matter more. And these matter a lot. This is one of the most significant statements ever made. This is the covenantal name of God. His forever name that never changes. In it, He defines Himself by character traits which He expresses toward us—such as mercy, grace, longsuffering, and unmerited forgiveness for the rebel and iniquitous. See that phrase "merciful and gracious"? The word *merciful* there has its roots in a word that means "womb." Or, "to be soft toward," as a mother would be toward a child. It references the same love Jesus expressed when, four times in the Gospels, the writers say Jesus was "moved with compassion" (Matt. 9:36; 14:14; Mark 1:41; 6:34). We see this same yearning as Jesus weeps over Jerusalem, "For I say to you, you shall see Me no more till you say, 'Blessed is He who comes in the name of the LORD!'" (Matt. 23:39).

See those words, "abounding in goodness"? The word *goodness* comes from the Hebrew word *hesed* (pronounced "hessid," or phonetically, "kheh'-sed"). *Hesed* has many meanings and is difficult to express in one word. In fact, it's not really fair to try to express it in one word. It's an all-encompassing word that means goodness, kindness, piety, beauty, favor, mercy, and pity all rolled into one. *Hesed* is God's faithful expression of covenant love of and for His people. Never-changing. Never-ending.

An argument can be made that this may be one of the more important words in Scripture, and we see a beautiful thread woven throughout the entirety of Scripture. Psalm 136 used *hesed* twenty-six times to describe how God's mercy endures forever. King David referred to God in 2 Samuel 22:26 (also Psalm 18:25) as, "with the merciful You will show Yourself merciful." *Hesed* is often translated as "lovingkindness" or "mercy." It's usually expressed within the bonds of a family. David showed *hesed* to Mephibosheth. Rahab expressed *hesed* to the spies. It is unmerited favor and is central to God's character. Solomon described it in Proverbs 16:6 (KJV): "By mercy and truth iniquity is purged." Jesus spoke of the same expression when He said, "I desire mercy and not sacrifice" (Matt. 9:13).

Hesed is a relational concept. The closest of bonds. Husband-and-wife kind of stuff. Intimacy. Vows. Tenderness. It's both an attitude and an action. It preserves and promotes life. It is the very content of covenant—or *berit*. David repeated this name in his prayer in Psalm 86:15–16 saying, "But You, O Lord, are a God full of compassion, and gracious, longsuffering and abundant in mercy and truth. Oh, turn to me, and have mercy on me!" These words speak of a God who is approachable, not horrible. He is a covenant keeper, despite the fact that those with whom He is in covenant don't keep their end.

In Proverbs 3:3, when Solomon was giving instruction to his son, he used the same word: "Let not mercy and truth forsake you; bind them around your neck, write them on the tablet of your heart." When Hezekiah proclaimed to all Israel and Judah a command to keep the Passover in 2 Chronicles 30:9, "for the LORD your God is gracious and merciful, and will not turn His face from you if you return to Him," Hezekiah was directly referring to Exodus 34 (and Deuteronomy 7). Lastly, the psalmist says the Lord crowns us with lovingkindness (103:4). He crowns us with *hesed*.

This continuing thread shows that the meaning and importance of *hesed* has never faded from the Hebrew mindset. If anything, it has remained at center stage. At the forefront of their minds.

Here is the best part. In Exodus 34, *hesed* is paired with "abundant." It is used to amplify the amount of goodness. Abundant, or *rab*, is derived from *rabab*. In Psalm 144, David used this same word to mean "a thousand times ten thousand." So, "abounding in goodness" is mercy times ten thousand times a thousand. Or, as we see in Exodus 34, mercy ten million times over.

Forty years after God named Himself on the mountain, Moses returned to this word when he reviewed the law, the Ten Commandments, with the nation of Israel before they walked into the promised land. Moses was reminding the people of the nature of God: "For I, the LORD your God, am a jealous God, visiting the iniquity of the fathers upon the children to the third and fourth generations of those who hate Me, but showing mercy to thousands, to those who love Me and keep My commandments" (Deut. 5:9–10).

"Mercy to thousands" is *hesed* to His people.

This understanding of *hesed* was foundational in the Hebrew mindset of the self-existent and eternal Jehovah. Here in Deuteronomy 5, Moses was reminding them of God's mercy in Exodus 34. And this reminder becomes the bedrock upon which he speaks Deuteronomy 6—the *Shema*. The greatest commandment.

The Greatest Commandment

Now back to Jesus and his response to the pack of hyenas. The greatest commandment. "Hear, Oh Israel. . . ." We call this verse the *Shema* (pronounced "SHE-ma"). The word means "hear," which is obviously the first word of the verse. I've heard it said that a truer translation of that word might be "listen listening," which means to listen with both ears and your heart—your whole person. To let the words sink down through your ears and into your heart where they take root.

The *Shema* is one of two prayers specifically commanded in the Torah, it's one of the oldest daily prayers among Jews, and has been recited morning and night since Moses spoke it. Everyone listening to Jesus knew what He was saying by heart, and it is arguable that everyone within earshot had prayed these very words several thousand times. Ironically, those listening are not "listen listening," which is proven by the fact that they are trying to trap Jesus.

In the listeners' minds, Jesus is quoting Moses as he gave the law to the nation of Israel. But remember, Jesus—the tabernacle of God,[15] the Word become flesh[16]—is the One who gave this very word to Moses on the mountain. He's the One who named Himself as His Glory passed by. All of this started with Him, and He spoke it first. So, while He's quoting Moses for their benefit, He's actually just repeating what He said fifteen hundred years prior on the mountain, which was then repeated through the mouth of Moses:

> Therefore hear, O Israel, and be careful to observe it, that it may be well with you, and that you may multiply greatly as the LORD God of your fathers has promised you—"a land flowing with milk and honey."
>
> Hear, O Israel: The LORD our God, the LORD is one! You shall love the LORD your God with all your heart, with all your soul, and with all your strength.
>
> And these words which I command you today shall be in your heart. You shall teach them diligently to your children, and shall talk

of them when you sit in your house, when you walk by the way, when you lie down, and when you rise up. You shall bind them as a sign on your hand, and they shall be as frontlets between your eyes. You shall write them on the doorposts of your house and on your gates. (Deut. 6:3–9)

Jesus doesn't need to quote the whole chapter. Everyone listening can recite it by heart.

When these faithful eleven listen to Jesus, and He reminds them to love the Lord their God, their minds immediately focus on the *hesed* love of God. Traits of mercy. Grace. Longsuffering. Forgiveness to the idolatrous, stiff-necked rebels who rejected God at Sinai and betrayed Him. In their mind, these are the unmerited expressions of God's love.

Jesus continues. "And the second, like it, is this: 'You shall love your neighbor as yourself.' There is no other commandment greater than these" (Mark 12:31).

Here Jesus quotes Leviticus: "You shall not take vengeance, nor bear any grudge against the children of your people, but you shall love your neighbor as yourself: I am the LORD" (19:18).

This, too, is spoken into a context. As His teaching has spread, Jesus has also been challenging the listeners with this whole business about "who is my neighbor?" Those testing Him are looking for a legal loophole. A way out. There are conditions to entering the kingdom of heaven, and they know full well that they don't meet them. In a similar exchange, a lawyer asks Him, "What shall I do to inherit eternal life?" (Luke 10:25). Jesus answers with a question. "What is written in the law?" The lawyer answers Deuteronomy 6:5 and Leviticus 19:18. Jesus nods. "You have answered rightly." But knowing he either hadn't or couldn't do this, the lawyer gets testy. "And who is my neighbor?" (Luke 10:29). His body posture asks the unspoken question, *How far do I have to take this?*

Jesus then tells the crowd what you and I have come to know as the parable of the Good Samaritan. A certain man went down from Jerusalem to Jericho. Thieves wound him. Strip him. Leave him for dead. As he's lying there in a puddle of his own blood, a priest sees him, crosses to the opposite side of the street and walks on by. Everyone listening to Jesus knows the restrictions in the law governing the touching of someone in this man's condition. It was forbidden in Leviticus 21:1–4. So their smug internal reaction is that the priest was justified in doing nothing. Same with the Levite who also crossed on the other side of the road. But then came the Samaritan. A half-breed. An idolater. Not welcome nor able to set foot in the temple. And for some reason, he had compassion. Got the man to a hospital. Paid his medical bills. Checked on him. Provided for his future care.

Jesus is not only defining their neighbor, but He's dropping the gauntlet on this idea of mercy. The same idea He has been breathing down their necks since He called Matthew the tax collector and was then criticized for eating with him and other sinners. At the time, Jesus had responded by quoting from the book of Hosea, which is akin to Him saying, "Come on guys, you should know this." Jesus says, "I desire mercy and not sacrifice" (Matt 9:13). Here in the story of the Samaritan, Jesus is once again reinforcing this idea of unmerited mercy.

And they hate Him for it.

The New Commandment

This was the cauldron of testing that led to the Last Supper. The disciples have grown used to it. So in this quiet moment at their last meal together, Jesus looks at them and says, "A new commandment I give to you." With emphasis on "new." Jesus—the lawgiver, the Word, the Alpha and Omega—is speaking with His friends. Each of the eleven men in that room is listening with rapt attention because something new is about to be spoken. Something which hasn't been spoken since Moses disappeared into the cloud and came back shining brilliantly carrying two stones. The disciples know that these words supersede everything spoken before. As difficult as it is for them to believe it, this new law is more important than and weightier than Moses.

This revelation is mind-blowing. How can this be?

They lean in. Waiting. Pin drop. The mystery of the universe, the secret of the ages, is to be revealed here. Jesus whispers, "Love one another. . . ." He pauses, knowing they will remember this moment for years to come. Then He says quietly, "as I have loved you. . . . By this all will know that you are My disciples, if you have love for one another."[17]

I imagine several of them scratched their heads and asked, "By this what?" Maybe they thought back through the last three years reminding themselves of the nature of Jesus: He preached, healed the sick, cast out demons, raised the dead, performed miracles. And while these events are awesome, I'm not sure they changed their understanding of the expressed love of God. Maybe those events served to change their understanding of His power, but I'm not sure they saw anything different than what they'd expected regarding the love of God.

Now, fast forward twenty-four hours as they stare in horror at Jesus' blood dripping down His lifeless body and staining the grooves of the cross. Staring at the limp body of Jesus, I believe their understanding of the expressed love of God was shattered, and they understood exactly what Jesus meant when He said, "By this. . . ."

The expressed love and nature of God, which was first defined in Exodus and reaffirmed in Deuteronomy, Jesus finished on the cross. The love of God for mankind is now rooted in something that until now, had not really crossed their minds. In fact, they had probably thought they were exempt from it—by the law. Prior to now, the *hesed* love of God as they understood it had been rooted in mercy and longsuffering and forgiveness. Everything told to them in Exodus 34 and Deuteronomy 5. Which they willingly accepted. But now, in Jesus, love is rooted in self-sacrifice.

The laying down of a life. Me for you.

This blew their minds.

There in the upper room, Jesus knows what's coming. He knows what they are about to see. He knows the disciples are going to be gutted. Their hearts shredded. They are simply not going to be able to wrap their heads around the next seventy-two hours. So after dinner, wanting to make sure they heard Him the first time, He says it again: "These things I have spoken to you, that My joy may remain in you, and that your joy may be full. This is My commandment, that you love one another as I have loved you. Greater love has no one than this, than to lay down one's life for his friends."[18]

I wonder as they stared at the cross from a distance, as they listened to Jesus writhe in pain and pour out His soul unto death and forgive all of us, if these words echoed: "As I have loved you . . ." and "Lay down his life for his friends."

For the disciples, watching Jesus die was the beginning of the paradigm shift of what it means to love God and your neighbor.

Late in his life, the apostle John would write, "He who says, 'I know Him,' and does not keep His commandments, is a liar, and the truth is not in him." I wonder if John wrote this from experience, from having seen those who once believed turn away when times were difficult. He continued, "But whoever keeps His word, truly the love of God is perfected in him" (1 John 2:4–5).

When John says, "keep His word," he means to lay down his life. Only in sacrifice is the love of God perfected in him.

Even in older age, John never lost sight of the message and kept it rather simple:

> For this is the message that you heard from the beginning, that we should love one another. . . . And this is His commandment: that we should believe on the name of His Son Jesus Christ and love one another, as He gave us commandment. . . . In this is love, not that we loved God, but that He loved us and sent His Son to be the propitiation for our sins. Beloved, if God so loved us, we also ought to love one another. (1 John 3:11, 23; 4:10–11)

I wonder how many times the disciples looked back upon the Last Supper and played the mental video of Jesus washing Judas's feet.

So, let me ask a gut-wrenching question: *Could you wash Judas's feet?*

Jesus allowed Himself to be led like a lamb to the slaughter. He willingly gave Himself up. He is the full expression of "as I have loved you."

Are we?

We Are Conduits, Not Generators

As the model and love of Jesus spread throughout the writers of the New Testament, it began to take shape in their words. We've all heard this before, but listen to Paul:

> Though I speak with the tongues of men and of angels, but have not love, I have become sounding brass or a clanging cymbal. And though I have the gift of prophecy, and understand all mysteries and all knowledge, and though I have all faith, so that I could remove mountains, but have not love, I am nothing. And though I bestow all my goods to feed the poor, and though I give my body to be burned, but have not love, it profits me nothing.
>
> Love suffers long and is kind; love does not envy; love does not parade itself, is not puffed up; does not behave rudely, does not seek its own, is not provoked, thinks no evil; does not rejoice in iniquity, but rejoices in the truth; bears all things, believes all things, hopes all things, endures all things.
>
> Love never fails. But whether there are prophecies, they will fail; whether there are tongues, they will cease; whether there is knowledge, it will vanish away....
>
> And now abide faith, hope, love, these three; but the greatest of these is love" (1 Cor. 13:1–8, 13).

Suffers long. Kind. Doesn't envy. Doesn't parade itself. Not puffed up. Isn't rude. Doesn't seek its own. Not provoked. Doesn't think evil. Doesn't rejoice in sin. Rejoices in the truth. Bears all. Believes all. Hopes all. Endures all. That looks a whole lot like the name God gives Himself on the mountain. The covenant love of God has never changed.

If I'm being honest, every time I hear that scripture quoted at a wedding, I tend to zone out. Brush it off. *I mean, are you kidding me? I'm expected to do that? Nobody does that.*

Save one Man. And He said if we love Him, we'll do the same.

Paul worked so many miracles and to such an extent that people were asking him to touch their handkerchiefs. He knew power. He walked in it. And he exercised the power of God. But having seen wonders and signs and miracles, look at what he tells his spiritual son: "Now the purpose of the commandment is love from a pure heart, from a good conscience, and from sincere faith." The NASB says, "The goal of our instruction is love from a pure heart" (1 Tim. 1:5).

Paul did not say *a* goal or *one* goal, but *the* goal.

There is only one thing in this universe or any other that is stronger than death. Love. The events at Calvary proved this. Love can't be quenched or drowned, and it never fails (Song 8:7; 1 Cor. 13). And, in one of my favorite verses, Paul tells us that nothing—not one single thing ever in this universe or any other, that has ever existed or will—can separate us from that love (Rom. 8:37–39).

Now, if you, like me, are sitting there shaking your head—don't. I have good news. The Spirit helps in our weaknesses (Rom. 8:26). And remember what Jesus said to the father battling unbelief, "All things are possible to him who believes" (Mark 9:23).

Let's look one more time at Jesus' resurrection. The disciples were meeting behind closed doors for fear of the Jews. They were whispering. Crying. Cussing. Maybe Peter was sharpening his sword. Then to their great surprise, Jesus walked through a wall, showed them His holes, ate food, and said this: "As the Father has sent Me, I also send you" (John 20:21). Then He breathed on them. And in my mind, because this is Jesus who fashioned us from the dust and pressed His lips to ours—the mound of clay—and breathed a whole breath into our lungs, I think He did the same here. Somehow, Jesus got in their business, filled up His chest with air, exhaled on them and in them, and said, "Receive Holy Breath." Or, "Receive the Holy Spirit" (John 20:22).

And the Spirit He was giving them was a resurrected, death-conquering, loving-your-enemies, sacrificing, me-for-you Spirit. Then He said, "If you forgive the sins of any, they are forgiven them; if you retain the sins of any, they are retained" (John 20:23). In short, "I am sending you out to love as I do. And if you do, others will know it. And if you don't, they'll know that too."

While the carnal, fleshly side of us is going to look at this as an impossible task, Jesus knows this. So, before He returned heavenward from the Mount of Olives taking the sunset with Him, in the company of a hundred million angels welcoming Him home, Jesus said, "Behold, I send the Promise of My Father upon you; but tarry in the city of Jerusalem until you are endued with power from on high" (Luke 24:49).

What's the promise?

I can't encapsulate the whole promise, but I do know this: Jesus promised to send us a part of Himself, which, when we received Him, would help us live and love as He did.

This should take some pressure off of us.

Paul told the Romans, "The love of God has been poured out into our hearts by the Holy Spirit who was given to us" (Rom. 5:5). That means it doesn't start with me. I just open up and receive it.

We're conduits. Not generators.

Three verses later, Paul told them God demonstrated that love "in that while we were still sinners, Christ died for us" (Rom. 5:8). What kind of a God would die for the sinful people He created? Why not just zap them from the earth? Why put up with us? Would you die for sinful you? My questions betray how little of His love I understand. An understanding equal to one grain of salt in the ocean. Or one star in the night sky.

Listen to Peter. "And above all things. . . ." Stop right there. He just said, "above all things." That means we should take him seriously and do this one thing above everything else. He continued, "have fervent love for one another, for 'love will cover a multitude of sins'" (1 Peter 4:8). Here Peter is, in part, quoting Proverbs 10:12, because Peter knew a thing or two about needing his sin covered. This word *fervent* is an interesting word choice on his part. It means "to stretch." It's the same word used in Matthew when Jesus stretched out His hand and healed both the leper and the man with the withered hand. It's also the same word used by Jesus when He told Peter by what death he will die. "When you grow old, you will stretch out your hands and someone else will gird you, and bring you where you do not wish to go" (John 21:18, NASB).

Here is John, the one whom Jesus loved: "There is no fear in love; but perfect love casts out fear, because fear involves torment. But he who fears has not been made perfect in love. We love Him because He first loved us" (1 John 4:18–19).

We love because He first loved us.

This is Paul admonishing the church in Galatia: "For you, brethren, have been called to liberty; only do not use liberty as an opportunity for the flesh, but through love serve one another. For all the law is fulfilled in one word, even in this: 'You shall love your neighbor as yourself'" (Gal. 5:13–14).

All the law is fulfilled in one word. Love.

He Loves Us Because He Loves Us

If we really believed in God's love the way we are intended to believe it, we wouldn't be fearful under pressure, wouldn't compete wrongly with others, wouldn't covet, wouldn't strive with other people, wouldn't fear their promotion over ours, wouldn't be jealous of another.

His love is unconditional. He just loves because He loves us. Scripture never gives us a reason why. We don't earn it. Don't deserve it. It can be apprehended only by revelation of the Holy Spirit. When Scripture records that "Jesus was moved with compassion," a truer translation might read, He was "moved in his bowels." The Greek word *splagchnizomai* means "the inward parts" or "seat of the affections" and has its roots in a word that means "womb." That's the same place we know and understand the love of God—in our gut. It's also the same place we make the decision to love like Jesus, down where our love lives. If you feel unlovable by something that you've done, let me let you in on another secret. You're ability to love and be loved has nothing to do with you. Or what you've done. If you can't earn it, then you can't unearn it.

He loves us because He loves us.

Also, if you're looking at your life and thinking ahead to judgment, or sitting in prison staring at a sentence this life will never serve, or staring in the rearview mirror of your life and all the carnage left in your wake, or remembering conversations or actions or—let me comfort you. If you are in Christ Jesus, you have been crucified with Him, and it's no longer you who live but Him who lives in and through you, by faith. This means when, at judgment, Jesus introduces you to His Father, He—the Father—sees His Son's (Jesus') righteousness wrapped around you like a blanket. Having washed you white as snow. Have you ever really looked into freshly fallen snow? So don't worry if you, like me, are a total failure here. The cross did for us what we could never do. That's what makes it so incredible.

Here's another secret—our enemy, satan, hates the fact that you know, experience, receive, and live in the love of the Father because he can't and never will. Our enemy lives in a loveless world. Devoid of. Absent of. Total vacuum. And because he can't change this fact, he is working overtime to assault the love you receive—and make you doubt that it exists in the first place. he has assigned his minions to assault and torment you to keep you where he is. If he can't change his own pain, he wants you to experience the same. Right this minute, the enemy is chipping away at your reservoir, at your desire to love, at your love of the Father and your belief in His love of you. The motive behind the "has God indeed said" lie, which started in the garden, is really just the vaguely masked statement, "He doesn't really love you—and never has."

Although God named Himself in Exodus 34 and Deuteronomy 5, He told us of His love for us much sooner. Way back in Genesis 3. He was mopping up the mess made by Adam and Eve. Speaking to the serpent, He said, "He [Jesus] shall bruise your head, and you shall bruise His heel" (Gen. 3:15). Three chapters in and God—looking way down the timeline at you and me and all of mankind—has already promised to send us the remedy we will need when we need it: the serpent crusher.

Now, look at Jesus as He is praying to His Father in the High Priestly Prayer. Jesus is talking with His Father, and we get to listen in. It's beyond amazing. God talking to God. Look at the very first word: "Father." This is the name which Jesus reveals to us about the One to whom He is talking. Until Jesus, God had been revealed as many things, but seldom Father. For the first-century Jew, this idea is wholly unbelievable. He says, "I have manifested Your name to the men whom You have given Me out of the world" (John 17:6). Then He says, "I have given them Your word; and the world has hated them because they are not of the world" (v. 14).

He ends the prayer with this: "Father . . . for You loved Me before the foundation of the world. O righteous Father! The world has not known You, but I have known You; and these have known that You sent Me. And I have declared to them Your name, and will declare it, that the love with which You loved Me may be in them, and I in them" (vv. 24–26).

First, God the Father loved the Son before the foundation of the world. Before time. And evidently, that love was and is so great and so unbelievable that Jesus came here, did all that He did and endured all that He endured, so that you and I might know the love with which the Father loved Him and is in Him. Remember when Jesus talked about the kingdom of heaven being like a man who found a great pearl in a field and sold all he had to buy the field? It makes a lot more sense when you view it through this lens.

The motivating factor for Jesus was, is, and remains the love of the Father—"that the love with which You loved Me may be in them." This is the secret of why Jesus did what He did. And it is His great desire that we know this same love and share in it. But, until we add sacrifice, we don't know it.

Jesus is "the way, the truth, and the life. No one comes to the Father except through" Him (John 14:6). There's a lot here but don't miss the obvious: Jesus is taking us somewhere, and that somewhere is to His Father. Why? It's like the sibling who shakes us awake, "Come see. You're never going to believe this." We have literally been delivered "from the power of darkness and conveyed [transferred] . . . into the kingdom of the Son of His love," and we did nothing to deserve that gift (Col. 1:13).

The Father's love for you and me is not reasonable. You'll never wrap your head around it. Understanding the sacrifice of a son for people who aren't worthy to untie the sandals of the one being sacrificed makes no sense. What kind of king would do such a thing? He's either the village idiot or His love for you and me is more than we can fathom. The only way we can get to some sort of understanding is revelation. The apostle John knew this: "Behold what manner of love the Father has bestowed [lavished] on us, that we should be called children of God!" (1 John 3:1). How do you take ungodly, rebellious sinners and call them children? It can only occur with some crazy kind of love.

In Psalm 63, David wrote from the wilderness of Judah. A desert. He said this: "Your lovingkindness is better than life. . . . In the shadow of your wings I will rejoice" (Ps. 63:3, 7). Like the woman who anointed Jesus' feet with her tears, David had been forgiven much and, as a result, knew much love. See those words, "lovingkindness is better than life"? A thousand years before the sacrifice of Jesus, David had received a revelation into the loving heart of God. He is offering us something that is more valuable than our very own lives—something, which, if we love Him, we will offer to others. Also, the word that David uses for "lovingkindness" is *hesed*. Maybe the reason all the disciples, save John, laid down their lives and died as martyrs is because they knew this. Knowing and living in the sacrificial love of God is better than life, which makes laying mine down a choice I'm willing to make. Freely.

Look one more time at the life of Jesus.

Jesus was seated at dinner with Simon, a Pharisee. As He was eating, an uninvited woman "who was a sinner" (the suggestion here is that she was an immoral woman, a prostitute), brought an alabaster flask of fragrant oil and stood at Jesus' feet, weeping. She didn't address Him and didn't speak. We know nothing else about her, but judging from her body language something in her life, some sin, was crushing her, and her only desire was to get clean. Not knowing what else to do, she knelt and began to wash Jesus' feet with her tears, kissing His feet and drying them with her hair. In that culture, a woman would never let her hair down in public. That was saved for intimacy with her husband. Doing so was like saying, "I am uncovered, and you are seeing the truth of me." Lastly, she anointed Jesus' feet with oil—a tool of her trade. The same scent she used to advertise her services.

The Pharisee watched all this with amusement and thought to himself, "This man, if He were a prophet, would know who and what manner of woman this is who is touching Him, for she is a sinner." (Luke 7:39). Jesus, knowing his thoughts, said, "Simon, I have something to say to you." The Pharisee responded, "Teacher, say it." Jesus continued:

> "There was a certain creditor who had two debtors. One owed five hundred denarii, and the other fifty. [A denarius was equal to one day's wage.] And when they had nothing with which to repay, he freely forgave them both. Tell Me, therefore, which of them will love him more?"
>
> Simon answered and said, "I suppose the one whom he forgave more."
>
> And He said to him, "You have rightly judged." Then He turned to the woman and said to Simon, "Do you see this woman? I entered your house; you gave Me no water for My feet, but she has washed My feet with her tears and wiped them with the hair of her head. You gave Me no kiss, but this woman has not ceased to kiss My feet since the time I came in. You did not anoint My head with oil, but this woman has anointed My feet with fragrant oil. Therefore I say to you, her sins, which are many, are forgiven, for she loved much. But to whom little is forgiven, the same loves little." Then He said to her, "Your sins are forgiven."

And those who sat at the table with Him began to say to themselves, "Who is this who even forgives sins?"

Then He said to the woman, "Your faith has saved you. Go in peace." (Luke 7:40–50).

David knew this love. The woman at Jesus' feet knew this love. It is Jesus' desire that you and I know it.

In both cases, they "loved much." Neither David's past sin, nor hers, had any ability to hinder their present ability to know, receive, and express love. So, take heart. No matter who you are or what you've done, you, too, can love just like Jesus.

Remember the woman caught in adultery? Dragged naked into the temple? She was expecting shame. Stones. Death. Jesus doodled in the dirt like a child. He loved her. The woman at the well. A Samaritan with five husbands. She expected to be treated less-than. Talked down to, if at all. Jesus looked her in the eyes. Interacted with her. Asked her for water. Revealed her secrets—without shame. He loved her. What about the tax gatherers and sinners? Jesus ate with them. Went to their homes. Loved them. Thief on the cross? Loved him—into paradise. Woman with the issue of blood? Stopped a crowd. Reached through. Lifted her up. Called her "daughter." Loved her. Bartimaeus at the gate? Called him forward. Touched his eyes. Healed his heart. One among many. Loved him. Peter, on the beach, after the denial, crucifixion, and resurrection. Jesus fixed him breakfast over a charcoal fire—the same type of fire over which Peter had denied Jesus— wrapped His arm around him and restored him to full sonship with all the rights and privileges thereof. Loved him. Charles Martin, sitting in his office, trying to write. Wondering to himself, *What in the world have I gotten myself into?* Forty-eight years of sin, baggage, and rebellion. And yet Jesus is here, sitting alongside. "Write this. Tell them about Me." I scratch my head, "Who am I that I should speak for You?"

He whispers, "My son."

He loves me. And yet I am wholly and completely unqualified.

Love First, Power Second

When Jesus sent His Spirit on Pentecost and entrusted the believers with all power and authority, it was because they had first settled the love issue. They loved Him. They'd proven it. It's the reason for their tears. The reason for their broken hearts. He knew He could trust them with gifts and power because they first knew love. Love came first. Then power.

I get this so backward sometimes.

When the apostles who were in Jerusalem heard that Samaria had received the word of God, they sent Peter and John (Acts 8:14). While there, they bumped into the local witch doctor. Simon the Sorcerer. He'd made a name for himself as someone who had power for "he had astonished them with his sorceries for a long time" (Acts 8:11). Peter and John traveled down to meet the new converts, and while they had already been baptized in water, the two apostles prayed that they might receive the Holy Spirit in the same way they had at Pentecost.

> And when Simon saw that through the laying on of the apostles' hands the Holy Spirit was given, he offered them money, saying, "Give me this power also, that anyone on whom I lay hands may receive the Holy Spirit."
>
> But Peter said to him, "Your money perish with you, because you thought that the gift of God could be purchased with money! You have neither part nor portion in this matter, for your heart is not right in the sight of God. Repent therefore of this your wickedness, and pray God if perhaps the thought of your heart may be forgiven you. For I see that you are poisoned by bitterness and bound by iniquity." (Acts 8:18–23)

Someone poisoned by bitterness and bound by iniquity is not motivated by love. Simon wanted power. Not relationship with the lover of his soul. You can exercise power and not be rooted in love.

Many of us in the church want power. We want to see miracles, healings, deliverance. And I'm in that camp. Bring it. Come, Lord Jesus. And I think Jesus does too. It's for freedom that He set us free. But—and this is a big "but"—the expression of power not rooted in me-for-you love has no place in the kingdom of God.

One last time, Jesus is speaking. "Hear, O Israel: The Lord our God, the Lord is One, You shall love—"

Stop right there.

We need go no further.

The commandment is love. Period. With all you've got. Heart, mind, soul, strength, everything. At all times. And at all costs.

The truth is we are commanded to do this, and if I'm being honest, I don't. Or, I do when it suits me or I know the cost—which isn't love. Paul, in his letter to the Romans, wrote: "Love is the fulfillment of the law" (Rom. 13:10). Think about that. The fulfillment of the whole law is love. This commandment is ridiculously simple. And yet, left to ourselves, it is massively impossible.

If We Love Him

So, how are you doing? How well are you loving as Jesus loved? Let me make it more specific. How about that person in the cubicle next to you? The one with the veil and the prayer rug or the bumper sticker they are continually ramming down your throat? How about your physical neighbor? The person next door who wrote an anonymous complaint to the HOA and cost you a few thousand? How about that guy you work with who talks behind your back, spreading lies? The one that got you demoted? How about the one that falsely accused you or sent Child Protective Services to your home and took your children from you? Want something closer to home? How about your spouse? That person you sleep with. Men, what would your marriage look like if you loved your wife sacrificially? Like Jesus loved the church (Eph. 5)? What if we loved our wives without expectation of what we got in return?

Most of us have no idea because we've never done it. Just being honest, without a daily, personal encounter with the Holy Spirit, I don't have a clue.

Want something tougher? How about your ex-wife or ex-husband? How about that business partner who stole the company you started? What if you've found yourself pregnant and you have no interest in being a parent? What would the sacrificial love of Jesus do?

I have no idea what horrible things have been done to you, but I'm looking at the cross and the words spoken by the One hanging there, and I'm asking myself, *What if all this is true?* What if He really meant what He said? What if my singular command is to love you more than I love me?

And if I understand Him, He's telling us that if we love Him, we will do just that. Love like He does. It's proof that we do. That bearing His name and calling ourselves His means loving like He does. That includes washing Judas's feet and laying down our lives for people who aren't worth it.

This is the reason for Pentecost—the reason we have His Spirit. He sent us His Comforter, His Helper, because He knew we couldn't do this alone. Yes, He sent us His Spirit so that we might live in the expression of His gifts in the same way He did, that we might exercise the power and authority He has absolutely given us—the keys to the kingdom—but don't miss the first requirement. Love. When the Holy Spirit fell on the apostles in the upper room and the building shook, Jesus was making good on His promise to send His Spirit (Acts 2:2). And the reason He was comfortable trusting them with His Spirit is because they had passed the do-you-love-Me test. Yes, they did. Love is the soil where the Spirit takes root. Without the sacrificial love of Jesus as the soil, there is no fruit of the Spirit.

We need His Spirit like we need air. This language may be loaded because of past abuse, but we need to be baptized in and filled with His Spirit. To be completely immersed in. We need to give His Spirit permission to rule and reign in us. To move in us. To be released in and through us. To make us like Him. And remember, because we tend to forget this, His Spirit was in Him on the cross. His Spirit got whipped too. His Spirit descended into hell and defeated the enemy. The Holy Spirit is not somehow separate from Jesus or His body. He is Jesus. And He's not somehow new to the scene. He was hovering over the surface of the waters at cre-ation. I believe that when God spoke, the Spirit carried out the orders of creation. Which means He is uniquely qualified to create whatever is needed in you so that you can love like Jesus.

When the Spirit is present and indwelling, the result is tangible: "But the fruit of the Spirit is love, joy, peace, longsuffering, kindness, good-ness, faithfulness, gentleness, self-control" (Gal. 5:22–23). Without love, the other eight don't exist.

The love of Jesus is many things, but at the end of the day it is ulti-mately sacrificial. And it is this sacrificial component that sets it apart from everything. If there is no sacrifice, then it's not Jesus' love. The bar that Jesus sets for us is to not only love, pray for, and bless our enemies, but to die for them.

The opposite of this love is pretty easy to spot. It looks like this:

> But know this, that in the last days perilous times will come: For men
> will be lovers of themselves, lovers of money, boasters, proud, blasphem-
> ers, disobedient to parents, unthankful, unholy, unloving, unforgiving,
> slanderers, without self-control, brutal, despisers of good, traitors, head-
> strong, haughty, lovers of pleasure rather than lovers of God, having a
> form of godliness but denying its power. And from such people turn
> away!" (2 Tim. 3:1–5)

See that word *unloving*? I'm guilty, but it's one of the following phrases that worries me a bit: "having a form of godliness but denying its power." I pray this is not me.

Last one. It's Paul to the Romans:

> And even as they did not like to retain God in their knowledge, God
> gave them over to a debased mind, to do those things which are not
> fitting; being filled with all unrighteousness, sexual immorality, wick-
> edness, covetousness, maliciousness; full of envy, murder, strife, deceit,
> evil-mindedness; they are whisperers, backbiters, haters of God, violent,

proud, boasters, inventors of evil things, disobedient to parents, undis-
cerning, untrustworthy, unloving, unforgiving, unmerciful; who,
knowing the righteous judgment of God, that those who practice such
things are deserving of death, not only do the same but also approve of
those who practice them. (Rom. 1:28–32)

The interesting thing to me about the scripture above is how accu-
rately it depicts the downward fall and trajectory of us as people when we
don't love God with all that we are.

I grew up in a rather charismatic church. Some of my earliest memories
are watching all the gifts in operation. As I've grown older, while I still
desperately desire the full expression of all the gifts, I am convinced that
without the sacrificial love of Jesus as the soil in which those gifts grow,
we are just a bunch of drum sets without a click track.

The love of Jesus is the peg on which everything else hangs. It is the
anchor line (Heb. 6:19). And, from God's heavenly perspective, a cross is
simply a peg driven into the face of the earth.

Love Them

Everything in this book has led to this moment. Jesus has washed our feet
and is seated with us at dinner. A cup in His hand. He looks at each of us.
He knows us by name. "I want to ask you to do something for Me." A tear
cascades down His cheek as He is "moved with compassion" at the sight of
a hurting and dying world. "Love them—as I have loved you."

Earlier in this book, I asked, "Do you really want to call yourself a
Christian? Forgive someone who doesn't deserve it." If you're going to forgive the unforgivable, you have to first love the unlovable. That type of
forgiveness flows out of this kind of love. And this kind of love comes only
from Him.

The Holy Spirit brings it from the throne room—a gift from our
Father—and pours it into our chests.

Before we pray, let me offer an invitation: if you haven't been water baptized, go do it. Jesus did. The apostles did. We should too. Don't wait. Call somebody. Go now. And baptism is not rocket science. It's a public profession of your faith in Jesus Christ as Lord and Savior expressed by being dunked in water. And don't get all caught in immersion versus nonimmersion versus sprinkling versus misting versus. . . . If you want a little bit of Jesus, then get a little bit of water. If you want all of Jesus, dive in. Take a bath. Swim to the bottom.

Go, do it. Pick some place you'll remember. Swimming pools work. So do oceans. Rivers. Make your faith known and in so doing, make His great name known to the nations.

Then, maybe even while you're soaking wet, come pray this. Like many of the prayers that have come before, I have to do this one from my knees. Or flat out and facedown.

Join me.

Lord Jesus . . . Father . . . help. I know, more than anything, that I need Your love. I want to love like You, but I know me and I know that left to myself I don't come close. Please, right here, right now, rain down Your Holy Spirit in me, on me, and through me. I give You permission to rule and reign in every molecule of every cell of every place in me. I completely and whole-heartedly yield to You. I surrender my heart to Yours. I am asking that You fill me in the same way You filled Your friends on the night of Pentecost. I'm not thinking about how this has been used or abused in the history of the church or how TV preachers have adulterated it or how late night talk shows have mocked it. I am talking about You filling me with You, and I don't care what that looks like or sounds like. I am not ashamed of the gospel, and I want all You have to offer.

Fill me. Overflow me. Rule and reign in me. Shake this building. Shake me. Shake my foundation. Do a new thing. Father, baptize me in the power, person, and love of Your Spirit. Change me forever. Jesus, I want to follow You, be like You, be known as Yours. Without Your love, I'm a sounding gong or clanging cymbal. Lord, when people meet me I want them to see Your reflection and hear Your tone of voice. To get a glimpse of You.

Please Jesus—rain down Your love in, on, and through me. Lord put Your hand on my shoulder. Give me eyes to see people the way You see them; give me Your love for others. For the unlovable. A tender heart is not enough. I need love. The real thing. The powerful, tenacious, merciful, longsuffering, keeps-no-record-of-wrongs, forgiving, sacrificial, me-for-you kind. Please allow me an encounter with You that simply explodes my heart with that kind of love. Let me walk away from here changed. Forever.

Because if I knew Your love, like really knew it so it was the deepest thing in my gut—like Your love for the woman caught in adultery, for Bartimaeus, for the woman with the issue of blood, for Peter on the beach, for the centurion's servant, for Lazarus, for the Canaanite woman, for Your friends, for me, like when You wept over Jerusalem—it would change everything about me. From the inside out. And I'd be more like You. And the people around me would see, feel, and experience Your unchanging, never-ending, sacrificial love. Your Father loved us and gave us You, His only Son, as the way to get back to Him. You obeyed, without protest, and came here on a rescue mission. A prisoner exchange. You for us. Love laid down. Love poured out. You walked into the slave market and said, "I'll buy them all." And when the market owner demanded payment, You poured out every drop of blood in Your body. You held nothing back. The life of the flesh is in the blood, and You gave it to us upon the altar to make atonement for our unloving souls.

Jesus, when I look at what You did for me, I am undone. Shredded. But in the deepest, truest part of me, as much as I know my own heart, I desire to love like that. Like You. Please do that in me. Give me that love so I can give it back to everyone I encounter.

In Jesus' Name, amen.

CHAPTER 13

Will You Bear His Name?

They call him "the Butcher." He has just returned from speaking with the high priest where, "breathing threats and murder against the disciples," he asked for letters authorizing his campaign of extinction.[1] Followers of Jesus have spread into Syria, and Saul is hunting them down, house to house, one by one. In his breast pocket, he is carrying those signed letters that he will use to drag followers of the Way out of their homes and return them to Jerusalem for trial.[2] If they resist, he will behead them or run them through with a sword in the streets.

His reputation precedes him—a reputation built on, among other events, the murder and stoning of a young convert named Stephen where Saul stood in smug, condescending agreement holding the coats of those throwing stones. He "was consenting to his death."[3] Now at his prime, his zeal is unmatched, as are his tactics and his thirst for violence. In truth, he is a terrorist. The worst of his kind. People live in abject terror because of him. He is singularly focused, a one-man killing machine. The high priest and council of elders will bear witness, Saul was on a mission to persecute the church of God beyond measure. To destroy it.[4]

By all accounts, including his own, Saul of Tarsus was a Jew of Jews, a model Pharisee. Writing to the people of Philippi some years later, he described himself this way: "Circumcised the eighth day, of the stock of Israel, of the tribe of Benjamin, a Hebrew of the Hebrews; concerning the law, a Pharisee; concerning zeal, persecuting the church; concerning the righteousness which is in the law, blameless."[5] Later in his life, when arrested in Jerusalem and dragged out of the very same temple from which he used to drag believers, he offered this defense: "I am indeed a Jew, born in Tarsus of Cilicia, but brought up in this city at the feet of Gamaliel, taught according to the strictness of our fathers' law, and was zealous toward God as you all are today."[6] His parents placed him under the instruction of one of the greatest teachers in the history of Israel—Gamaliel.

Saul, of keen intellect and gifted mind, excelled rapidly and by the age of twelve, had memorized the Torah. All five books. By heart. He then spent seven years studying and memorizing the prophets. "I advanced in Judaism beyond many of my contemporaries in my own nation, being more exceedingly zealous for the traditions of my fathers."[7] Also, in a sovereign twist of providence, he was born a Roman citizen.[8] This fact alone will radically alter the course of his life in the years ahead.

As a Pharisee of Pharisees, it is safe to say he knew the law of Moses as well as anyone of his day. This meant he knew the prophecies—more than six hundred—about the Messiah. That the Messiah would sit on David's throne. Isaiah 7. Isaiah 9. Psalm 132. Daniel 7. By other personal accounts, he was not overly attractive, and not an especially good speaker, but he was a serious law follower and he found value in his fanatical obedience. We're not exactly sure how old he was, but I tend to think he was either a contemporary of Jesus or slightly younger. In my book, he was younger.

Physically, he was probably short, and he spoke at least Hebrew, Aramaic, and Greek. By trade, he was a tentmaker. Some have suggested that meant he made clothing or some sort of covering to escape the desert heat, that is, a tent. At any rate, he worked with his hands and was used to working with canvas and heavy needles. Stitching. He knew how to take measurements which meant he must have known, understood, and could work in mathematics, which suggests a logical mind.

When John the Baptist spoke to the Pharisees and said, "You brood of vipers,"[9] he would have been aiming those words at people such as Saul. Saul would have been a viper. We don't know if he ever heard Jesus speak, and we don't know if he was one of the Pharisees to whom Jesus so often spoke, but if he was a witness to the ministry of Jesus, it is more likely that he was standing on the sidelines with his hands in his pockets. Disdain painted on his face. Whispering behind his back. Possibly a stone in his hand. When Caiaphas, the high priest, said, "It is expedient for you that one man die for the people, and that the whole nation not perish,"[10] Saul would have agreed wholeheartedly.

If he had been at the trial of Jesus, he would have been screaming, "Release Barabbas! Crucify Him!" And if he had been at the crucifixion, he would have been mocking Jesus, laughing, agreeing with those who said, "He saved others; He cannot save Himself. . . . Let this Christ, the King of Israel, now come down from the cross, so that we may see and believe!"[11]

Then came the Damascus road.

The Pharisee of Pharisees

Chin high, an arrogant air, the world at his feet, the Butcher of Tarsus is licking his chops. On the surface, today is an ordinary day and he is traveling an ordinary road. Dusty. Big rocks. Potholes. A trade route. Lots of people come this way. The road on which Saul finds himself is just an everyday stretch of well-traveled road.

But this is the day, and this is the road, on which God—once again—forever changes the course of human history. Following today, the world will never be the same.

Saul turns a corner and without warning, without prelude, without introduction, God Most High has moved the sun from ninety million miles away to just a few feet in front of Saul's face. Blinded and disoriented, Saul falls to his knees. The definition of shock and awe. Struggling to breathe, Saul hears a voice say: "Saul, Saul, why are you persecuting Me?"

Groveling, Saul manages a response: "Who are You, Lord?" Interestingly, this is much the same question Moses asked God after he returned with Him up the mountain following the children of Israel's worship of the golden calf.

The Bright Morning Star, the One who upholds all things by the word of His power, responds with gentle kindness and abounding mercy: "I am Jesus whom you are persecuting."[12] Then Jesus says the most peculiar thing—a statement which suggests a history of interaction between Jesus and Saul to which we are not privy. Only Saul knows the truth. Whatever the case, it speaks of "the kindness of God [that] leads [us] to repentance."[13] The statement is unexpected and it's almost as if Jesus pauses and ambles up alongside Saul, leaning over, whispering in his ear. A knowing tone in His voice. "It is hard for you to kick against the goads."[14]

A goad was a sharp stick held by farmers leading a team of oxen down a row as they plow. To steer the beast, the farmer pushes the stick into the rump of the ox and holds it there. They don't poke. They hold it. It's a sustained pain, not a flash. The stubborn ox either turns, obeying the pain in its rump, or it kicks against it—whereby the farmer only pushes harder and deeper. Point being, no amount of kicking will escape the goad.

Jesus has been sticking Saul for some time. Only Saul knows how long. Saul knew the Word of God as well as anyone of his day. Is it possible when Jesus said this that Saul remembered the psalmist's words, "In faithfulness You have afflicted me."[15]

Saul stumbles off the road and spends three days without sight. No food. No water. His life, as he knows it, is over. The word of Saul's blindness spreads like wildfire and brings shouts of jubilation from the disciples and other followers of the Way.

Elsewhere in the town of Damascus there was "a certain disciple . . . named Ananias." All we really know about him is that when Jesus spoke to him, he, like Samuel as a boy in the temple, said, "Here I am, Lord."[16] Chances are quite good that he was a bit surprised when God tapped him on the shoulder:

> So the Lord said to him, "Arise and go to the street called Straight, and inquire at the house of Judas for one called Saul of Tarsus, for behold, he is praying. And in a vision he has seen a man named Ananias coming in and putting his hand on him, so that he might receive his sight."

Then Ananias answered, "Lord, I have heard from many about this man, how much harm he has done to Your saints in Jerusalem. And here he has authority from the chief priests to bind all who call on Your name."

But the Lord said to him, "Go, for he is a chosen vessel of Mine to bear My name before Gentiles, kings, and the children of Israel. For I will show him how many things he must suffer for My name's sake."[17]

If you were God and wanted to communicate *the* message through which you were to save the entire human race, would you entrust it to someone who'd spent his life trying to eradicate the carriers of that message?

His ways are higher than mine.

Ananias scratches his head. "Ummm. . . . Lord, did you say Saul?"

"Yes."

"Of Tarsus?"

"Yup."

Long pause. "Are we talking about the same guy? I mean, the prisons and cemeteries are full of people he put there. Many don't have their heads. I'd like to keep mine where it is. Wouldn't it be better to just let him. . . ."

The Lord repeats himself, "Go. For he is a chosen vessel of Mine to bear My name before Gentiles, kings, and the children of Israel."

Hear that? "Chosen vessel." How about this one? "Bear My name." I love that. I see Paul wrapping himself in a banner with Jesus' name on it like Rocky did after he knocked out the Russian.

We've already talked about this, but don't let your eyes skip over it simply because you don't like what it says: "For I will show him how many things he must suffer for My name's sake."

Ananias rose, walked in obedience, laid hands on the blind Butcher, and said, "'Brother Saul, the Lord Jesus, who appeared to you on the road as you came, has sent me that you may receive your sight and be filled with the Holy Spirit.' Immediately, there fell from his eyes something like scales, and he received his sight at once; and he arose and was baptized."[18]

Scales.

Ever wondered how long they'd been there? I think they'd been there a while. All the way back. When Saul sat in the synagogue. Read the law of Moses. Listened to Jesus—if he listened to Jesus. Stared at the cross. Scorned Stephen. As he dragged children from their homes. Saul had been blind his whole life. But it wasn't until that dusty stretch of road that he was able to see his own blindness.

It's what happened after the scales fell off that interests me.

After Damascus, Saul spent a few years in Arabia.[19] Then he returned to Jerusalem where he presented himself to James and the other leaders of the church. And then a decade or more passes. His first letters—that we know of—were written to the Thessalonians in AD 50 or 51. Some sixteen years after Jesus' ascension. All total, he wrote at least thirteen of the twenty-seven books of the New Testament.*

Allow me an aside. Is it just me, or does it strike anyone else as ironic that, on the one hand, Saul requested letters of condemnation with which he imprisoned and executed, and on the other, while imprisoned and awaiting execution, he (now called Paul) wrote letters of proclamation and freedom? "It was for freedom that Christ has set us free" (Gal. 5:1, NASB). The sovereign hand of God leaves me shaking my head but gives me great hope. In His economy, nothing is wasted. Not even the worst and most blind among us.

And that should give you and me immeasurable hope.

What happened to Paul after the Damascus road? Here's how Paul described his life:

We are hard-pressed on every side, yet not crushed; we are perplexed, but not in despair; persecuted, but not forsaken; struck down, but not destroyed—always carrying about in the body the dying of the Lord Jesus, that the life of Jesus also may be manifested in our body. For we who live are always delivered to death for Jesus' sake, that the life of Jesus also may be manifested in our mortal flesh. So then death is working in us, but life in you. (2 Cor. 4:8–12)

---

* Officially, the church ascribes Hebrews to him, but I don't think he wrote it. To me, it doesn't sound like him, but I'm giving you my opinion as a writer and not a Bible scholar.

Later he added:

> I speak as a fool—I am more: in labors more abundant, in stripes above measure, in prisons more frequently, in deaths often. From the Jews five times I received forty stripes minus one. Three times I was beaten with rods; once I was stoned; three times I was shipwrecked; a night and a day I have been in the deep; in journeys often, in perils of waters, in perils of robbers, in perils of my own countrymen, in perils of the Gentiles, in perils in the city, in perils in the wilderness, in perils in the sea, in perils among false brethren; in weariness and toil, in sleeplessness often, in hunger and thirst, in fastings often, in cold and nakedness. (2 Cor. 11:23–27)

Paul knew a thing or two about suffering.

Many of us want the Damascus road experience. How many want what follows?

And see that part about "always delivered to death for Jesus' sake"? The sufferings of Paul were preordained by God Most High. Everything that happened to Saul had been sifted through the sovereign hand of God. While Paul walked in faith, worked miracles, and saw the dead raised to life, his external circumstances did not necessarily improve once the scales fell off. The gospel did not become a magic wand for comfort and self-gratification.

One of the things that changed the most for Saul was his picture of himself. While giving proof of Jesus' resurrection, Paul lists Jesus' reappearance to Peter (Cephas), the twelve, more than five hundred brethren, James, all the apostles, then he mentions himself: "Last of all He was seen by me also, as by one born out of due time" (1 Cor. 15:8). That phrase, "one born out of due time," is a graphic term in which Paul describes himself at the time of the call of the other apostles as an undeveloped, aborted fetus incapable of sustaining life.

When he writes Timothy, he's become rather self-aware.

> Although I was formerly a blasphemer, a persecutor, and an insolent man; but I obtained mercy because I did it ignorantly in unbelief. And

the grace of our Lord was exceedingly abundant, with faith and love which are in Christ Jesus. This is a faithful saying and worthy of all acceptance, that Christ Jesus came into the world to save sinners, of whom I am chief. (1 Tim. 1:13–15)

Gone is the arrogant Butcher.

And see that phrase, "sinners, of whom I am chief"? Think back—he's remembering dragging people out, executing them, purging the church. He can still hear their cries for mercy. Feel the stickiness of their dried blood on his hands. Paul's heart is broken with the rearview memory of his own life. It's one of the many things he suffered.

Lastly, we know that Paul died in a Roman prison. Probably in his mid-sixties and probably by beheading—because they were tired of his mouth. But while they silenced his tongue, they couldn't quiet his pen. Which is still speaking today. Loud and clear.

I cannot pretend to encapsulate the entire life of Paul here, but I'm comfortable saying this—the turning point for Saul was that stretch of road toward Damascus. God met him, blinded him, and broke him, and only then was he any good to the kingdom. And in terms of kingdom work, it's safe to say that Paul carried his weight. He got the Word out. And it got out to you and me. Paul became that writer that David talks about in Psalm 45, which as a good Jew, he'd have known: "My heart is overflowing with a good theme; I recite my composition concerning the King; my tongue is the pen of a ready writer. . . . I will make Your name to be remembered in all generations" (Ps. 45:1,17).

What About Us?

The story of Saul's life and Paul's later ministry and death begs a few questions.

First, as a follower of Jesus, a member of the Way, would Saul have enough evidence to drag me out of my house? Or would he pass by only to drag my neighbors out by their pajamas? Teddy bear in tow. Leaving me standing in my front yard holding the remote control. I flag him down, "What about me?"

He waves me off. A dismissive shake of his head. "No. You're good."

No, I'm not good.

Second, what are my scales? What am I blind to? This is like asking a fish to describe water. He can't conceive of either its presence or its absence because it's always been there, but I'd be willing to bet that if I asked the Lord to pop off my scales, and then gave Him access to my eyes—and heart—He would, and my perspective of that clear liquidy stuff I've been swimming in would change.

And I'd be willing to bet I'm not alone in this.

Don't think Saul is alone in his blindness. He's an archetype. Jesus says this: "For the hearts of this people have grown dull. Their ears are hard of hearing, and their eyes they have closed, lest they should see with their eyes and hear with their ears, lest they should understand with their hearts and turn, so that I should heal them" (Matt. 13:15).

He's talking about us. Absent Jesus, we're blind as bats.

Third, let's look at Paul's words. At great expense—even his life—Paul spoke the truth. He held fast, stood firm, threw off everything that hindered, finished the race. And here's the really cool thing: while he's dead and gone, and somewhere his bones lie dusty, his words are still speaking. Today, right this second, someone is reading his words. Then and now people were, are, and will be cut free from the stuff that enslaves them. Those precious, magnificent, priceless, life-giving words continue to lead people to the bleeding feet of Jesus hanging eye-level on a cross, the dirty linen of an empty tomb, a risen Savior. Paul's words made known a name not his own. And made it known for all time. Words do that. They matter. They cut people free.

Jesus said, "By your words you will be justified, and by your words you will be condemned" (Matt. 12:37). So, just getting gut-level honest, what's the effect of your words? At the end of your life, whose name will be remembered? Is there enough evidence before the judge to convict you?

There are people in our lives whom we see as just downright evil. Beyond redemption. Blind as bats. We don't want anything to do with them and hope they burn in hell. And you probably have good cause to think that. Some of them have hurt you and me deeply. Without cause. They're just jerks, and deep down we don't care if they rot. But, if the whole counsel of God is true—and it is—then no one is beyond redemption. "The LORD's hand is not shortened, that it cannot save" (Isa. 59:1). What if that miserable, scum-sucking sinner that you're thinking of right this moment is God's chosen vessel, and He's calling you to be Ananias? I mean, really?

What if this is true for me and you?

What if Ananias had told the Lord, "I'll pass. That joker can melt into the prison floor for all I care." If you are a believer, an argument can be made that you have Ananias to thank.

I'm not saying this is easy. But it is worth thinking about. Might also take some forgiveness on our parts. Or a lot. And my roadmap for much of the cleanup has been Paul's words.

The roadmap exists because Ananias did what he was told to do. Right when he was told to do it. Without question. Without knowing the outcome. Without prejudice. Just like Abram who rose early. Maybe Ananias is the lost hero of this story. Sort of like the guy who told Billy Graham about a Savior named Jesus. Is the Lord goading you? Is He using this to do it? Are you kicking? How's that working out for you?

Saul was cruising down the Damascus road. Skipping along. A man with a plan. Had it all figured it out. Letters of death stuffed in his coat pocket. Many of us are waiting for a Damascus road experience. Blinding light. A voice out of the darkness. But, what if you've already had it? What if it's sitting between two dusty covers somewhere in your house? What if it's staring at you now? What about your scales? Are you blind? Are you kicking against something that pains you? Won't go away?

Now jump across to the other side. The scales are popped off. Are you ready for what follows? Have you underlined, circled, and highlighted that word *suffer* in your Bible? Do you count it all joy when you do? Are you, like Paul, willing to bear on your body the marks of Jesus? (Gal. 6:17). What's your view of yourself? Chief among sinners? Born out of due time? Is your heart broken with the rearview picture of yourself? How about your words? Do they matter to you the way they matter to the Lord? If Ananias walked in right this second and laid hands on you, would you recoil or relax? Are you willing to receive the Holy Spirit? Are you open to a permanent course correction? Lastly, are you Ananias? Scratching your head. Deliberating.

Don't doubt it—you have a role in this story. You, too, are a chosen vessel.

Saul knew where he was going. Had it all planned out. Letters in his pocket. First stop was an everyday stretch of road. Dusty. Well-traveled. Rocky. Potholes. A trade route.

Just like the one you're on right this second. The one that's currently staring you in the face.

The road to Damascus was the turning point in Paul's life, and it is the turning point in yours. And mine. Paul met Jesus in the flesh. John gives us powerful description of that same resurrected Jesus when he later meets Him on the island of Patmos:

> I was in the Spirit on the Lord's Day, and I heard behind me a loud voice, as of a trumpet, saying, "I am the Alpha and the Omega, the First and the Last," and, "What you see, write in a book and send it to the seven churches which are in Asia: to Ephesus, to Smyrna, to Pergamos, to Thyatira, to Sardis, to Philadelphia, and to Laodicea."
>
> Then I turned to see the voice that spoke with me. And having turned I saw seven golden lampstands, and in the midst of the seven lampstands One like the Son of Man, clothed with a garment down to the feet and girded about the chest with a golden band. His head and hair were white like wool, as white as snow, and His eyes like a flame of fire; His feet were like fine brass, as if refined in a furnace, and His voice as the sound of many waters; He had in His right hand seven stars, out of His mouth went a sharp two-edged sword, and His countenance was

like the sun shining in its strength. And when I saw Him, I fell at His feet as dead. But He laid His right hand on me, saying to me, "Do not be afraid; I am the First and the Last. I am He who lives, and was dead, and behold, I am alive forevermore. Amen. And I have the keys of Hades and of Death. Write the things which you have seen, and the things which are, and the things which will take place after this." (Rev. 1:10–19)

I love those words: "alive forevermore."

Imagine a trumpet blasting behind your head right now—louder than any rock concert. And a voice coming out of the blast. You turn around where you are met by the sun, and you see the One described above. John says he fell at His feet as though dead. What other response is there?

This is Jesus.

This is resurrected, living, breathing, speaking, talking, walking, calling, conquering, undefeated, magnificent, redeeming, sanctifying, justifying, ransoming, snatching-us-back-out-of-the-hand-of-the-devil Jesus. He met with Paul. He met with John.

And He wants to meet with you.

Here.

Now.

Will You?

I started this book describing how, in my limited imagination, Jesus left His throne in heaven to be born here. He willingly gave up His crown there for our humanity here. After His resurrection, He walked back into heaven where God the Father launched Himself off His throne, covered His face in kisses, and all the host of heaven welcomed home the Bright Morning Star. I believe the joy of that day will only be equaled when Jesus returns to bring all of us home with Him.

John's picture of Jesus is this picture. The same picture Stephen pointed to just before they stoned him: "But he, being full of the Holy

Spirit, gazed into heaven and saw the glory of God, and Jesus standing at the right hand of God, and said, 'Look! I see the heavens opened and the Son of Man standing at the right hand of God!'" (Acts 7:55–56).

This picture is Jesus ascended. Clothed in kingly and priestly garb. Seated on a throne at the right hand of God Most High where He has been for two thousand years since returning. Right this second, this Jesus is interceding for you. For me. In perfect union with the Father. Knowing the same love which He knew before the worlds were formed. Before time began (John 17:24).

Most of this book has been concerned with getting cleaned up. Cut free. Letting the Word cleanse us from all the stuff we carry about. But here at the end—or the beginning—and we are starting to look beyond the mirror. Outside of ourselves. Like Paul, you are His chosen vessel. The road from this day forward stretches out before you. And right this second, a trumpet blasts. Ear-splitting. You turn. You are standing face-to-face with the Son.

All of your life, every road you've ever traveled, has led to this one. Despite what the enemy whispers in your ear, you are a chosen vessel.

Will you bear His name? Even if it means suffering?

I was about to write a prayer for us—I've actually written and deleted it twice—but felt that's not what the Lord wants. I think He wants me to step aside, to move out from between you two and let you write your own. He must increase and I must decrease. My job has been to walk you into the throne room, into the presence of God Most High. And now that I've done that, it's time to leave you with Him.

So, on the page or two that's left, write your own prayer. It's not difficult. Just a conversation. Reach up. Cry out. Find your own voice with Him. Let Him know, maybe for the very first time, how much you love Him. How grateful you are to Him in your own words. Praise Him. You can use my words if you need to, but let me encourage you to step off the platform of my language with Him and develop your own. Find your voice with Him. He made you to talk with Him face-to-face. Like Moses, Peter, John, Paul. . . .

So, do it. Start with, "Lord Jesus, Father. . . ." This is where you read back through all your scribbles in the margin, all those questions, those statements, all that conversation along the side and put it in one place.

This is where you begin writing your own story. Where you begin answering for yourself this question: What if it's true?

Because if it is—it changes everything.

When We Stand Face-to-Face

The Mount of Olives fades behind Him. The earth He made grows smaller. A blue dot. Home grows larger before Him. The return trip is quick. The Son of Man enters the gates of heaven wearing a loin cloth. Thunderous, raucous praise erupts from a hundred million voices. Streets of gold are lined twenty and thirty rows deep. Everyone hoping to get a glance. *The King of glory has come in.*

He is returning to His Father.

Angels fling wide the doors to the outer courts. Inside is standing room only. A sea of heavenly bodies. The sea parts, and Jesus walks through. A straight line. Michael and Gabriel bow and pull on the massive door to the throne room. At the far end, twenty-four elders lay prostrate, noses to the floor, having cast down their crowns at His feet. The chorus is ear-splittingly beautiful.

The Father is standing. Eyes singularly focused.

The Son of God enters. He is standing in a river. Or rather, on it. Hovering.

The Father eyes the Son and launches Himself off His throne, closing the distance like lightning. His feet barely touching the ground. When He reaches Him, the Father covers the Son's face in kisses. The Father welcoming home the spotless Son who has done what no one else could. He has ransomed humanity with His very own blood. He alone has prevailed to open the scroll. The Father whispers in His ear, and only the Son knows what He says.

In seconds, they are laughing, dancing, flinging sweat from their brows. Perfect union.

The mansion is larger. Rooms added. Space enough for every last one. The Father leads Him to His throne. Everything is just as He left it. Following the Father's invitation, the Son puts on His robe, straps His sword on His thigh, places His ring on His finger, returns His crown to His head, and takes the scepter in His hand. King and priest.

The celebration begins.

Now, two thousand years later, He is seated at the right hand of God Most High. Interceding for you and me. Praying for us. Commanding His angels concerning us. He has the Father's ear.

Right now, the Alpha and Omega, the Beginning and the End, the Lion of Judah, He who has hair like white wool, eyes like a flame of fire, feet of burnished bronze, He who is literally shining like the sun, who upholds all things by the Word of His power, is seated at God's right hand. And God has made His enemies His footstool. Right now, Jesus, the serpent crusher, is ruling in the midst of His enemies. He is waiting for His Father to send Him back. For His return. To cut the Hound of Heaven loose. Only the Father knows the date.

What's He waiting for? I don't know but I think it has something to do with the needs of the one outweighing the needs of the ninety-nine.

When the Father does send Him, Jesus will return to judge the quick and the dead (2 Tim. 4:1 KJV)—the sons of men. You and me. And on that day, every knee will bow, and every tongue will confess that He is Lord of all (Rom. 14:11).

When my turn comes, and I am brought before the King, my judgment day, I don't know if I will be able to lift my face off the floor, to breathe, or even to think, so let me say now what I will hope to be able to say then:

"I believe these words are true. Every last one."

Author's Note

In this book, I've attempted to stay focused on Jesus. The Word made flesh. I've quoted umpteen Scriptures and only sparingly talked about myself. But maybe this book has piqued your interest in me and what I think, or in my heart or how I might feel about an issue or process—like how do I hope to love my wife or forgive folks who don't deserve it, how do I try to love my children, how do I pray to lay down my life for people? I've wrestled with all of these questions and more, and I've tried to offer my own answers in my thirteen novels. They are how I "work out [my] own salvation with fear and trembling" (Phil. 2:12). At the end of the day, I pray those stories point to Him and not me. I think they do. You decide.

> The LORD bless you and keep you;
> The LORD make His face shine upon you,
> And be gracious to you;
> The LORD lift up His countenance upon you,
> And give you peace.
> So they shall put My name on the children of Israel, and I will
> bless them.
>
> —Num. 6:24–27

The Word Became Flesh

Years ago, I began keeping a document in my computer where I recorded the scriptures where the Word talks about itself. As the document grew, so did the extent to which I began to really value the Word. Somehow seeing all of them in one place impressed upon me the gravity of what they were individually and corporately saying. I would read these scriptures to my boys at breakfast in the morning. (Still do.) The Word tells us that God wrote the Word on our hearts, so I'm hoping to remind their hearts what it says.

I've included those scriptures here. They are in no particular order other than the order in which I discovered them—which tells a story in and of itself. I'd encourage you to read through them. If they are true (and I'm betting my life that they are), then that changes everything.

> Behold I am coming quickly! Blessed is he who keeps
> the words of the prophecy of this book.
>
> —Rev. 22:7

> Heaven and earth will pass away, but My words will by no means pass away.
>
> —Matt. 24:35

> The grass withers, the flower fades, but the word of our God stands forever.
>
> —Isa. 40:8

But it shall come to pass, if you do not obey the voice of the Lord your God, to
observe carefully all His commandments and His statutes which I command
you today, that all these curses will come upon you and overtake you.

—Deut. 28:15

The law of the Lord is perfect, converting the soul;
The testimony of the Lord is sure, making wise the simple;
The statutes of the Lord are right, rejoicing the heart;
The commandment of the Lord is pure, enlightening the eyes;
The fear of the Lord is clean, enduring forever;
The judgments of the Lord are true and righteous altogether.
More to be desired are they than gold,
Yea, than much fine gold;
Sweeter also than honey and the honeycomb.
Moreover by them Your servant is warned,
And in keeping them there is great reward.

—Ps. 19:7–11

Hold fast the pattern of sound words which you have heard
from me, in faith and love which are in Christ Jesus.

—2 Tim. 1:13

All Scripture is given by inspiration of God, and is profitable for doctrine,
for reproof, for correction, for instruction in righteousness, that the man
of God may be complete, thoroughly equipped for every good work.

—2 Tim. 3:16–17

But He answered and said, "It is written, 'Man shall not live by bread
*alone, but by every word that proceeds from the mouth of God.'"**

—Matt. 4:4

Remember that Jesus Christ, of the seed of David, was raised from the
dead according to my gospel, for which I suffer trouble as an evildoer,
even to the point of chains; but the word of God is not chained.

—2 Tim. 2:8–9

---

* That's Jesus quoting Deuteronomy 8:3.

I have treasured the words of His mouth more than my necessary food.

—JOB 23:12

Therefore lay aside all filthiness and overflow of wickedness, and receive
with meekness the implanted word, which is able to save your souls.
But be doers of the word, and not hearers only, deceiving yourselves.

—JAMES 1:21–22

I will put My law in their minds, and write it on their hearts.

—JER. 31:33

In that they show the work of the Law written in their
hearts, their conscience bearing witness and their thoughts
alternately accusing or else defending them.

—ROM. 2:15, NASB

Blessed is the man
who walks not in the counsel of the wicked,
nor stands in the way of sinners,
    nor sits in the seat of scoffers;
but his delight is in the law of the LORD,
    and on his law he meditates day and night.
He is like a tree
    planted by streams of water,
that yields its fruit in its season,
    and its leaf does not wither.
In all that he does, he prospers.

—PS. 1:1–3, RSV

For out of the abundance of the heart the mouth speaks.

—MATT. 12:34

A good man out of the good treasure of his heart brings forth good things,
and an evil man out of the evil treasure brings forth evil things.

—MATT. 12:35

But I say to you that every idle word men may speak, they will
give account of it in the day of judgment. For by your words you
will be justified, and by your words you will be condemned.

—MATT 12:36–37

My son, give attention to my words;
Incline your ear to my sayings.
Do not let them depart from your sight;
Keep them in the midst of your heart.
For they are life to those who find them
And health to all their body.

—PROV. 4:20–22, NASB

But the word of the LORD endures forever.

—I PETER 1:25

As for God, His way is perfect; the word of the LORD is
*proven; He is a shield to all who trust in Him.**

—2 SAM. 22:31

In God, whose word I praise, in God I have put my trust; I shall not be afraid.

—PS. 56:4, NASB

How can a young man keep his way pure?
By keeping it according to Your word.

—PS. 119:9, NASB

Your word I have hidden in my heart, that I might not sin against You.

—PS. 119:11

Your word is a lamp to my feet and a light to my path.

—PS. 119:105

Revive me according to Your word.

—PS. 119:154

---

* A song of David.

*The entirety of Your word is truth, and every one of
Your righteous judgments endures forever.**

—Ps. 119:160

*"Is not My word like a fire?" says the LORD, "and like
a hammer that breaks the rock in pieces?"*

—Jer. 23:29

*For the word of God is living and powerful, and sharper than any two-
edged sword, piercing even to the division of soul and spirit, and of joints
and marrow, and is a discerner of the thoughts and intents of the heart.*

—Heb. 4:12

*Do all things without grumbling or disputing; so that you will prove
yourselves to be blameless and innocent, children of God above reproach in
the midst of a crooked and perverse generation, among whom you appear as
lights in the world, holding fast the word of life, so that in the day of Christ
I will have reason to glory because I did not run in vain nor toil in vain.*

—Phil. 2:14–16, NASB

*Let the word of Christ dwell in you richly in all wisdom, teaching
and admonishing one another in psalms and hymns and spiritual
songs, singing with grace in your hearts to the Lord.*

—Col. 3:16

*My son, if you receive my words,
And treasure my commands within you,
So that you incline your ear to wisdom,
And apply your heart to understanding;
Yes, if you cry out for discernment,
And lift up your voice for understanding,
If you seek her as silver,
And search for her as for hidden treasures;
Then you will understand the fear of the LORD,
And find the knowledge of God.
For the LORD gives wisdom;*

---

* Actually, all of Psalm 119 is about the Word. We tend to forget that because it's so long.

From His mouth come knowledge and understanding;
He stores up sound wisdom for the upright;
He is a shield to those who walk uprightly;
He guards the paths of justice,
And preserves the way of His saints.
Then you will understand righteousness and justice,
Equity and every good path.
When wisdom enters your heart,
And knowledge is pleasant to your soul,
Discretion will preserve you;
Understanding will keep you,
To deliver you from the way of evil,
From the man who speaks perverse things.

—Prov. 2:1–12

Heaven and earth will pass away, but My words will by no means pass away.

—Matt. 24:35

He who says, "I know Him," and does not keep His commandments, is a liar, and the truth is not in him. But whoever keeps His word, truly the love of God is perfected in him. By this we know that we are in Him.

—1 John 2:4–5

If you abide in Me, and My words abide in you, you will
ask what you desire, and it shall be done for you.

—John 15:7

Your words were found, and I ate them, and Your word was to me the joy and rejoicing of my heart; for I am called by Your name, O Lord God of hosts.

—Jer. 15:16

This Book of the Law shall not depart from your mouth, but
you shall meditate in it day and night, that you may observe to
do according to all that is written in it. For then you will make
your way prosperous, and then you will have good success.

—Josh. 1:8

*But what does it say? "The word is near you, in your mouth and in your
heart" . . . that if you confess with your mouth the Lord Jesus and believe
in your heart that God has raised Him from the dead, you will be saved.*

—ROM. 10:8–9

Faith comes by hearing, and hearing by the word of God.

—ROM. 10:17

*And I will give you the keys of the kingdom of heaven, and
whatever you bind on earth will be bound in heaven, and
whatever you loose on earth will be loosed in heaven.*

—MATT. 16:19

*Therefore hear, O Israel, and be careful to observe it, that it may be well
with you, and that you may multiply greatly as the LORD God of your
fathers has promised you—"a land flowing with milk and honey."*

*Hear, O Israel: The LORD our God, the LORD is one! You shall love the LORD
your God with all your heart, with all your soul, and with all your strength.*

*And these words which I command you today shall be in your
heart. You shall teach them diligently to your children, and shall talk
of them when you sit in your house, when you walk by the way, when
you lie down, and when you rise up. You shall bind them as a sign
on your hand, and they shall be as frontlets between your eyes. You
shall write them on the doorposts of your house and on your gates.*

—DEUT. 6:3–9

*For Ezra had prepared his heart to seek the Law of the LORD, and
to do it, and to teach statutes and ordinances in Israel.*

—EZRA 7:10

*Hold fast the pattern of sound words which you have heard
from me, in faith and love which are in Christ Jesus.*

—2 TIM. 1:13

*For whatever things were written before were written for our learning, that
we through the patience and comfort of the Scriptures might have hope.*

—ROM. 15:4

Let us hold fast the confession of our hope without
wavering, for He who promised is faithful.

—HEB. 10:23

By faith we understand that the worlds were framed by the word of God, so
that the things which are seen were not made of things which are visible.

—HEB. 11:3

His Son, whom He appointed heir of all things, through whom also He made
the world. And He is the radiance of His glory and the exact representation
of His nature, and upholds all things by the word of His power.

—HEB. 1:2–3, NASB

But the word of the LORD was to them, "precept upon precept, precept
upon precept, line upon line, line upon line, here a little, there a little."

—ISA. 28:13

He also is wise and will bring disaster, and will not call
back His words, but will rise against the house of evildoers,
and against the help of those who work iniquity.

—ISA. 31:2

The grass withers, and the flower fades, but the
word of our God stands forever.

—ISA. 40:8

So shall My word be that goes forth from My mouth; it shall not return
to Me void, but it shall . . . prosper in the thing for which I sent it.

—ISA. 55:11

But on this one I will look: on him who is poor and of a
contrite spirit, and who trembles at My word.

—ISA. 66:2

I am watching over My word to perform it.

—JER. 1:12, NASB

Blessed are those who hear the word of God and observe it.

—LUKE 11:28, NASB

*[Jesus] might sanctify her [the church], having cleansed
her by the washing of water with the word.*

—EPH. 5:26, NASB

When I read what the Word has to say about itself, I'm often reminded of one of my favorite authors, Louis L'Amour. He wrote, "If you go amongst the Philistines, it is better to go armed." I like this.

Blessing and Curse Scriptures

A s I've read Scripture, I've kept a running list, in no particular order, of passages that speak to or promise the breaking of curses and of being overtaken by blessing. This is by no means a complete list. But it is a good start. Feel free to add your own. I pray these often.

Unless you believe that I am He, you will die in your sins.
—JOHN 8:24, NASB

And through Him everyone who believes is freed from all things,
from which you could not be freed through the Law of Moses.
—ACTS 13:39, NASB

All have sinned and fall short of the glory of God, being justified as
a gift by His grace through the redemption which is in Christ Jesus;
whom God displayed publicly as a propitiation in His blood through
faith. This was to demonstrate His righteousness, because in the
forbearance of God He passed over the sins previously committed; for the
demonstration, I say, of His righteousness at the present time, so that
He would be just and the justifier of the one who has faith in Jesus.
—ROM. 3:23–26, NASB

So then as through one transgression there resulted condemnation to all men,
even so through one act of righteousness there resulted justification of life to all

men. For as through the one man's disobedience the many were made sinners, even so through the obedience of the One the many will be made righteous.

—ROM. 5:18–19, NASB

What shall we say then? Are we to continue in sin so that grace may increase? May it never be! How shall we who died to sin still live in it? Or do you not know that all of us who have been baptized into Christ Jesus have been baptized into His death? Therefore we have been buried with Him through baptism into death, so that as Christ was raised from the dead through the glory of the Father, so we too might walk in newness of life. For if we have become united with Him in the likeness of His death, certainly we shall also be in the likeness of His resurrection, knowing this, that our old self was crucified with Him, in order that our body of sin might be done away with, so that we would no longer be slaves to sin; for he who has died is freed from sin.

Now if we have died with Christ, we believe that we shall also live with Him, knowing that Christ, having been raised from the dead, is never to die again; death no longer is master over Him. For the death that He died, He died to sin once for all; but the life that He lives, He lives to God. Even so consider yourselves to be dead to sin, but alive to God in Christ Jesus.

Therefore do not let sin reign in your mortal body so that you obey its lusts, and do not go on presenting the members of your body to sin as instruments of unrighteousness; but present yourselves to God as those alive from the dead, and your members as instruments of righteousness to God. For sin shall not be master over you, for you are not under law but under grace.

—ROM. 6:1–14, NASB

Therefore, my brethren, you also were made to die to the Law through the body of Christ, so that you might be joined to another, to Him who was raised from the dead, in order that we might bear fruit for God. For while we were in the flesh, the sinful passions, which were aroused by the Law, were at work in the members of our body to bear fruit for death. But now we have been released from the Law, having died to that by which we were bound, so that we serve in newness of the Spirit and not in oldness of the letter.

—ROM. 7:4–6, NASB

Therefore there is now no condemnation for those who are in
Christ Jesus. For the law of the Spirit of life in Christ Jesus
has set you free from the law of sin and of death.

—Rom. 8:1–2, NASB

If by the Spirit you are putting to death the deeds of the body, you will live.

—Rom 8:13, NASB

For Christ is the end of the law for righteousness to everyone who
believes. . . . for "Whoever will call on the name of the Lord will be saved."

—Rom. 10:4, 13, NASB

Therefore you are no longer a slave, but a son;
and if a son, then an heir through God.

—Gal. 4:7, NASB

I have been crucified with Christ; and it is no longer I who live, but
Christ lives in me; and the life which I now live in the flesh I live by
faith in the Son of God, who loved me and gave Himself up for me.

—Gal. 2:20, NASB

Christ redeemed us from the curse of the Law, having become a curse for
us—for it is written, "Cursed is everyone who hangs on a tree"—in order
that in Christ Jesus the blessing of Abraham might come to the Gentiles.

—Gal. 3:13–14, NASB

For all of you who were baptized into Christ have clothed
yourselves with Christ. There is neither Jew nor Greek, there is
neither slave nor free man, there is neither male nor female; for
you are all one in Christ Jesus. And if you belong to Christ, then
you are Abraham's descendants, heirs according to promise.

—Gal. 3:27–29, NASB

If you are led by the Spirit, you are not under the Law.

—Gal. 5:18, NASB

He made Him who knew no sin to be sin on our behalf, so that
we might become the righteousness of God in Him.

—2 COR. 5:21, NASB

For He rescued us from the domain of darkness, and transferred us
to the kingdom of His beloved Son, in whom we have redemption,
the forgiveness of sins. . . . And although you were formerly
alienated and hostile in mind, engaged in evil deeds, yet He has
now reconciled you in His fleshly body through death, in order to
present you before Him holy and blameless and beyond reproach.

—COL. 1:13–14, 21–22, NASB

For you have died and your life is hidden with Christ in God.

—COL. 3:3, NASB

In these last days [He] has spoken to us in His Son, whom He appointed
heir of all things, through whom also He made the world. And He is
the radiance of His glory and the exact representation of His nature,
and upholds all things by the word of His power. When He had made
purification of sins, He sat down at the right hand of the Majesty on high.

—HEB. 1:2–3, NASB

Through death He might render powerless him who had the
power of death, that is, the devil, and might free those who
through fear of death were subject to slavery all their lives.

—HEB. 2:14–15, NASB

For by one offering He has perfected for all time those who are sanctified.

—HEB. 10:14, NASB

But when Christ appeared as a high priest of the good things to come, He
entered through the greater and more perfect tabernacle, not made with
hands, that is to say, not of this creation; and not through the blood of
goats and calves, but through His own blood, He entered the holy place
once for all, having obtained eternal redemption. For if the blood of goats
and bulls and the ashes of a heifer sprinkling those who have been defiled
sanctify for the cleansing of the flesh, how much more will the blood of

*Christ, who through the eternal Spirit offered Himself without blemish to
God, cleanse your conscience from dead works to serve the living God?*

—HEB. 9:11–14, NASB

*And He Himself bore our sins in His body on the cross, so that we might
die to sin and live to righteousness; for by His wounds you were healed.*

—I PET. 2:24, NASB

*For Christ also died for sins once for all, the just for the
unjust, so that He might bring us to God, having been put
to death in the flesh, but made alive in the spirit.*

—I PET. 3:18, NASB

*If we confess our sins, He is faithful and righteous to forgive
us our sins and to cleanse us from all unrighteousness.*

—I JOHN 1:9, NASB

*Jesus Christ, the faithful witness, the firstborn of the dead, and the ruler of the
kings of the earth. To Him who loves us and released us from our sins by His
blood—and He has made us to be a kingdom, priests to His God and Father.*

—REV. 1:5–6, NASB

*Then behold, they brought to Him a paralytic lying on a
bed. When Jesus saw their faith, He said to the paralytic,
"Son, be of good cheer; your sins are forgiven you."*

—MATT. 9:2

*When Jesus saw their faith, He said to the paralytic,
"Son, your sins are forgiven you."*

—MARK 2:5

*"But that you may know that the Son of Man has power on earth to
forgive sins"—He said to the paralytic, "I say to you, arise, take up
your bed, and go to your house." Immediately he arose, took up the
bed, and went out in the presence of them all, so that all were amazed
and glorified God, saying, "We never saw anything like this!"*

—MARK 2:10–12

When He saw their faith, He said to him, "Man, your sins are forgiven you." . . . "But that you may know that the Son of Man has power on earth to forgive sins"—He said to the man who was paralyzed, "I say to you, arise, take up your bed, and go to your house."

Immediately he rose up before them, took up what he had been lying on, and departed to his own house, glorifying God. And they were all amazed, and they glorified God and were filled with fear, saying, "We have seen strange things today!"

—LUKE 5:20, 24–26

Notes

INTRODUCTION

1. Ps. 69:12
2. Ps. 69:21
3. Lev. 17:11

**CHAPTER 1: THE WORD BECOMES
FLESH—AND DWELLS AMONG US**

1. Luke 2:1
2. Deut. 6:4
3. Rev. 4:3–5
4. John 3:16
5. Heb. 1:2–3, NASB
6. Col. 1:16–17, NASB
7. 1 Tim. 6:15–16, NASB
8. John 1:2–5
9. Rev. 1:8
10. Rev. 3:14
11. Rev. 5:5, NASB
12. Eze. 28:12–15
13. Isa. 14:12
14. Isa. 14:12, NASB
15. Heb. 12:2, NASB
16. John 17:14, 26
17. Rev. 5:13
18. Rev. 1:16
19. John 1:1–2, 14
20. Luke 19:40
21. Luke 1:32–33
22. Isa. 53; Ps. 22
23. Mal. 4:2
24. Luke 2:23
25. Luke 2:14
26. Isa. 7:14
27. Isa. 9:2
28. Phil. 2:6–8
29. Isa. 9:6–7
30. Matt. 22:44; Mark 12:36; Luke
    20:42–43
31. Acts 2:34–35
32. For more information on the
    throne room, see Isa. 6:1–4; Dan.
    7:9–10, 13–14; Eph. 1:2–22; Col.
    1:15–18; Heb. 1:1–12; Rev. 4:1–11.
33. 1 Sam. 3:10, NASB

CHAPTER 2: WE'RE ALL BLEEDERS

1. Mark 5
2. Mark 5:23
3. Matt. 9:20–22; Mark 5:25–34; Luke 8:43–48
4. Mal. 4:2

CHAPTER 3: THE CHORUS OF THE UNASHAMED

1. Mark 10:46; Luke 18:35
2. Deut. 34:3
3. Josh. 2:11
4. Josh. 6:25
5. Josh. 6:26; 1 Kings 16:34
6. Mark 10:48
7. Ezek. 37:24
8. Isa. 11:1–2
9. Luke 1:31–33
10. Luke 18:39
11. Isa. 29:18; 35:5, KJV
12. Joel 2:32, KJV
13. Ps. 146:8
14. John 1:29
15. Matt. 9:2
16. Matt. 9:10–11
17. Matt. 9:12–13
18. Matt. 9:25
19. Mark 8:22–25
20. Luke 18:39
21. Luke 18:13
22. Mark 10:50, KJV
23. Ps. 139:15–16
24. Luke 18:42
25. Matt. 9:22; Mark 5:34; Luke 8:48
26. Rom. 14:23
27. Heb. 11:6
28. Matt. 11:5

CHAPTER 4: WHAT ARE YOU TAKING TO THE GRAVE?

1. John 8:7
2. Heb. 4:15
3. Ps. 90:8
4. 2 Sam. 12:5–7
5. Lev. 20:10
6. 1 Sam. 16:7
7. John 8:10–11

CHAPTER 5: TALK TO THE HAND—JCILOA

1. Matt. 16:13
2. Matt. 16:16
3. Matt. 16:17-19
4. Num. 13–14

CHAPTER 6: WHAT'S THAT YOU'RE CARRYING?

1. 2 Sam. 15:23, 30
2. Ps. 3:3
3. Matt. 26:36
4. Matt. 26:38
5. Matt. 21:9
6. Luke 19:40
7. Ps. 22:2
8. Ps. 22:11
9. Matt. 26:46
10. Heb. 1:2–3
11. Matt. 27:35
12. Matt. 27:55

CHAPTER 7: THE TOUGHEST THING YOU AND I WILL EVER DO

1. John 3:14
2. John 20:12, NASB
3. Lev. 16:18–19, 34
4. Mal. 4:2
5. Luke 24:5–6
6. Luke 24:6–7. Jesus' resurrection on the third day satisfied the Old Testament prophecies given in Ps. 2:7, 16:10, 61:7, 68:18, 102:25–27, 110:1; Isa. 25:8, 26:19, 53:10–12; Dan. 12:2; Hos. 6:2, 13:14.
7. Luke 24:11
8. Luke 13:32
9. Hos. 6:2
10. Luke 24:15
11. John 6:51
12. Heb. 2:14
13. 1 John 3:8
14. Col. 2:15
15. Ps. 110:1–2
16. Lev. 17:11
17. Rom. 6:6, 14
18. Eph. 2:13
19. Isa. 45:2
20. Ps. 24:7
21. Heb. 12:2
22. Matt. 25:21

CHAPTER 8: CHOOSE THIS DAY

1. Mark 2:1–5
2. John 8:58
3. John 9:1
4. John 9:2–3
5. Rev. 1:5–6, NASB

CHAPTER 9: YOU WILL BE HATED BY ALL

1. Mark 5:23
2. Matt. 9:33
3. Matt. 10:1, 7–8
4. Matt. 10:16–18, 22, 28
5. Luke 9:6
6. Luke 9:35
7. Luke 9:43
8. Luke 9:54
9. Luke 9:55-56
10. Luke 10:3, 17–20
11. Rom. 4:17
12. Jer. 29:11; Ps. 94:14, 117:2, 139:16–17; Matt. 10:29–31; Rom. 8:28–29, 38-39; 1 Pet. 2:9; Eph. 1:4–5, 2:10; 2 Pet. 1:3–4; Ex. 19:5; Josh. 1:9; Deut. 31:8; Rev. 21:3–4
13. Matt. 5:10–12, 10:17, 22, 13:13, 23:34, 24:9; Luke 6:20–23, 21:16–17; 2 Tim. 1:8, 3:12; Phil. 1:29; Rev. 2:10; Rom. 8:17, 36; Heb. 10:32–34, 11:25–26; 12:7, 11; Acts 4:3, 5:40–41, 9:16, 29, 12:1–3, 14:22, 20:23–24; 1 Cor. 4:9–13; 2 Cor. 1:3–5, 4:10, 11:23–29; Gal. 3:4, 6:17; 1 Thess. 2:2; 1 Peter 1:6–7, 2:19, 3:17, 4:4, 12–16; 1 John 3:13; John 15:19, 15:2, 17:14; 2 Thess. 1:4–5; Ps. 119:67, 125:4–5; Isa. 38:17; Col. 1:24

14. Gen. 22:1
15. Ex. 15:22–25
16. Ex. 19:6
17. Ex. 15:25
18. 1 Sam. 10
19. 1 Sam. 16:14
20. Job 1:5
21. Job 2:10
22. Jer. 20:12
23. Rom. 5:3
24. 2 Cor. 4:8–9
25. 2 Tim. 1:8
26. 2 Tim. 2:3
27. 2 Tim. 3:12
28. Heb. 11:35–38
29. Rom. 8:18
30. 1 Cor. 13:4
31. Phil. 1:29
32. Phil. 3:10
33. Isa. 53:10
34. Heb. 2:9–10, 18
35. Heb. 5:8
36. Matt. 10:22
37. Matt. 16:24; 10:38
38. Prov. 4:22
39. Job 23:12
40. Jer. 15:16
41. Jer. 23:29
42. Ps. 119:11
43. Phil. 4:12
44. Col. 1:24
45. 1 Thess. 3:4
46. Isa. 64:6
47. 2 Tim. 3:12
48. Heb. 11:25–26
49. 1 Cor. 10:13
50. James 5:13
51. 1 Pet. 2:21, 3:14, 17, 4:1, 16, 5:10
52. 2 Cor. 11:24–27, 30
53. Rom. 9:21, NASB
54. Rom. 9:22-23, NASB
55. Ps. 34:4, 6, 17, 19
56. Rom. 8:16–18
57. Rom. 8: 28, 31, 35–39
58. Job 19:25–26
59. Job 42:2, 5–6
60. Deut. 31:6
61. Ps. 34:18, NASB
62. Ps. 34:19, NASB
63. Ps. 1:1–3
64. Gen. 24:27, 48
65. Isa. 40:29, NASB
66. Isa. 40:31
67. Ps. 18:39
68. Ps. 144:1
69. Phil. 4:19
70. Ps. 27:13
71. 2 Cor. 1:4
72. Ps. 23:5
73. Heb. 6:19–20
74. Isa. 12:2
75. Rev. 19:1
76. Ps. 60:3, NASB
77. Prov. 3:5
78. Ps. 91:2
79. Ps. 84:10, NASB
80. James 1:22
81. Heb. 1:3
82. Isa. 46:10
83. Luke 15:20
84. Matt. 1:23
85. 2 Cor. 5:21

86. Heb. 10:14

87. Isa. 40:28

88. John 1:1

89. Isa. 55:9

90. Ps. 103:11–12

91. John 8:32

92. Phil. 2:13

93. 2 Cor. 12:9

94. 2 Cor. 12:9

95. Ps. 18:39; Isa. 40:31; Ps. 18:29

96. Isa. 45:2

97. Prov. 21:31

98. Ps. 81:7

99. 1 Pet. 3:14

100. 1 Pet. 4:12, 14, 16, NASB

101. Ps. 3:3

CHAPTER 10: NO GONE IS TOO FAR GONE

1. Prov. 25:28

2. Luke 15:15

3. Prov. 6:27

4. Isa. 64:6

5. Luke 15:20

6. Isa. 50:7

7. Luke 15:21

8. Luke 15:24

CHAPTER 11: THE DEEPEST WOUND OF THE HUMAN SOUL

1. Ps. 22:14

2. Isa. 52:14

3. 2 Cor. 5:21

4. Isa. 53:4

5. Matt. 27:46

CHAPTER 12: THE PEG ON WHICH EVERYTHING HANGS

1. Phil. 2:5-8

2. Matt. 20:26–28

3. John 13:15–16

4. John 13:1

5. John 13:18; Ps. 41:9, NASB

6. John 13:21

7. John 13:25

8. John 13:26–27

9. John 13:34

10. Matt. 5:38–42

11. Matt. 5:43–48

12. Matt. 22:15–21

13. Matt. 22:29–33

14. Mark 12:28–30

15. Rev. 21:3

16. John 1:14

17. John 13:34–35

18. John 15:11–13

CHAPTER 13: WILL YOU BEAR HIS NAME?

1. Acts 9:1–2

2. Acts 8:3; 22:4–5

3. Acts 7:58; 8:1

4. Gal. 1:13

5. Phil. 3:5–6

6. Acts 22:3

7. Gal. 1:14

8. Acts 22:28

9. Matt. 3:7

10. John 11:50, NASB

11. Mark 15:32, NASB

12. Acts 9:4–5

13. Rom. 2:4 NASB

14. Acts 9:5

15. Ps. 119:75

16. Acts 9:10; 1 Sam. 3:4

17. Acts 9:11–16

18. Acts 9:17–18

19. Gal. 1:15–17

About the Author

CHARLES MARTIN is a *New York Times* and *USA Today* bestselling author of thirteen novels, including *The Mountain Between Us* and *Send Down the Rain*. Charles and his wife, Christy, live in Jacksonville, Florida. Learn more at charlesmartinbooks.com.

DON'T MISS
CHARLES MARTIN'S NOVELS!

"In this relatable tale of recovery from physical and emotional trauma, Martin beautifully captures the essence of Christian principles of sacrifice and forgiveness."

—*Publishers Weekly*, STARRED review